create a trinity lifestyle

dr bo bryson

WestBow Press books may be ordered through booksellers or by contacting:

WestBow Press
A Division of Thomas Nelson
1663 Liberty Drive
Bloomington, IN 47403
www.westbowpress.com
1-(866) 928-1240

Website Design: Nelsen Technologies
For more information, visit: www.trinitylifestyle.com

Book Design & Layout: Veronica Wadas, Krave Designs

Scripture References: Unless otherwise noted, all scripture taken from *The Holy Bible: ESV (English Standard Version)*, Good News Publishers, 2002. Other notated versions have been taken from Bible Gateway (www.biblegateway.com).

Quote References: Brainy Quote (www.brainyquote.com). These includes any and all quotations not taken specifically from the work cited references.

Editor: Anna Keyzer *(office manager at Trinity Chiropractic)*

Devotional Thoughts: All devotional thoughts were written by Dr. Bo Bryson. Each thought was inspired by who Christ is and what He continues to do in Dr. Bryson's life. More devotional thoughts can be found on Dr. Bryson's blog *'Thoughts of a chiropractor.'*

Yoga: Tataya Radtke of Yoga Body & Balance *(Yoga pictures by Keller Photography)*
Tataya's passion for life is evident in everything she does and most profoundly in her devotion to her family and her love for yoga. Tataya has extensive training in Hatha, Ashtanga, Anusara yoga and Inner Power Yoga. She has studied yoga on several continents and has taught yoga internationally since 2003. In April 2008, she and her husband Thomas Radtke opened Yoga Body & Balance (YBB). Tataya's love for humanity; genuine care and concern for her community and commitment to excellence provide her the power and strength to inspire those around her each day.

Raw Food Recipes/Snacks and Grocery Lists: Thomas Radtke of Yoga Body & Balance
Thomas is a Raw Food Nutrition Specialist, Raw Lifestyle Coach and Raw Chef through Ekaya Institute and has a Raw Food Nutritional Science Diploma from GG Enterprises. He has apprenticed at the Ann Wigmore Natural health Institute in Puerto Rico, while also becoming a Living Food Lifestyle Educator. He currently is a licensed Massage therapist, Registered Extended Yoga teacher and a Senior Inner Power Yoga teacher. He is a father of three beautiful children and with his wife, Tataya, owns Yoga Body and Balance in Lincoln, Nebraska. Together, they are committed to awaken people to live a life they love.

ISBN: 978-1-4497-9995-3 (sc)
ISBN: 978-1-4497-9996-0 (hc)
ISBN: 978-1-4497-9994-6 (e)

Library of Congress Control Number: 2013911848

Printed in the United States of America.

WestBow Press rev. date: 7/8/2013

To Jennifer, my wife & best friend.

Without your love, forgiveness
and friendship where would I be?

Thank you for making our home a refuge
for me, our children and countless others.

You have helped me Create a Trinity Lifestyle™.

"The coolest and really the moments that have broken me are the ones where I've realized God knows who I am. I saw Dr. Bo while working on my novel, Havah: The Story of Eve. He asked how I was and I broke down. He gave me a Bible verse, this man who had never met me, and said, "You know, God is really pleased with the work you're doing." Dr. Bo prayed for me and I knew God cared. In his book, Dr. Bo has created a very whole, organic and integrated approach to health. I so appreciate his spiritual approach to life's physical issues."

- *Tosca Lee, NY Times Best Selling Author*

"A masterpiece! Dr. Bo helps people see that prayer, fasting and meditation is not a new age phenomenon but rather a journey into the heart of God."

- *Dr. Dean DePice, Chiropractic Consultant and Speaker, Co-founder & Advisor for TLC*

"There is so much gold here. It is going to bring so much healing to so many people. The topics covered are those conversations you should have had with your parents growing up. Awessssssomenessss."

- *Crystal Munoz, owner of The Flourish Photography*

"This book is chock-full of helpful wisdom and practical advice on the journey to living a healthier lifestyle. Included are easy-to-follow plans that not only 'produce results', but are engaging, fun and beneficial to body, mind and spirit; the trifecta of total health!"

- *Christine Cornwell*

"Physician, heal thyself. This book is so well written in terms of telling friends, patients, and colleagues that Dr. Bo Bryson is a real person who has a real background with thoughts, concerns, fears, failures, successes, and the ability to pick himself up and keep going that I'm inspired to write my own book. Dr. Bryson's background legitimizes him as a man qualified to listen and help more than anything he learned in chiropractic school. Very early in the book, he talks of a patient who had suffered from emotional and physical trauma in the past, and he says, "School didn't teach you how to handle that." And he's right. School didn't. But real life has, and Dr. Bryson has had a real life background that makes him uniquely qualified to help."

- Dr. Gideon Orbach, Chiropractor

"Thanks so much for giving me the privilege to read what God has been putting on your heart. Hallelujah that we each have a purposeful, redemptive story that has been written for us. I was blown away by the message that this book offers! The analogy of working to keep my soil balanced has really given me a new way to look at my lifestyle choices. It has also given me insight to where my priorities lay in relation to Christ and His divine purpose for who He has created me to be."

- Stephanie Wilson

"I love Dr. Bo's approach. He shares his opinion and own journey of health without sounding like a snobby expert."

- Stephanie Mosley

contents

contents

acknowledgements

First and foremost, I thank Christ for His love and the undeserving grace He has lavished upon my life. Without that love, all else seems somehow less. To my wife Jennifer, my best friend, without your devotion I would not be where I am today. To my children, I am honored and humbled to be your Father. Your laughter and love teach me much. To Luis and Crystal Munoz, your love for Christ and others have taught me so much about life and myself. To Thomas and Tataya Radtke, without ya'll, this project would not have been completed. Your passion awakens me to a life I love! To my wonderful staff at Trinity and circle ME, Jennifer and I could not do this journey without you, you truly bless us. To Corey C., Mark K., and Gideon O., your knowledge and passion shape the way I view chiropractic care. To my parents, your continued guidance and friendship blesses me. Our 'Monday talks' mean more than you may ever know. To my sister, there will never be words to express my gratitude for loving me as you do. To my brother-in-law, your journey increased my faith. I miss you! To Mr. and Mrs. B (my parents-in-law), thank you for the trips and making me laugh along the way. To Mr. Ivan, although you no longer are alive, your challenging conversations still help shape and solidify my thoughts and beliefs. To Tom and Grady, your mentorship has helped me in more ways than you can ever know. I thank Christ for Godly men like you! To my many friends & colleagues, thank you for loving and challenging me. Lastly, to the patients, your lives, your stories and your trust have been woven into the fabric of Trinity.

"

Take this journey with Dr. Bryson to a life of balance, to a healthier life, a fuller life, a more meaningful life. You will be blessed and amazed.

- *Mark A King, DC*

"

forward

Many people struggle to find balance in this fast paced world. Often, we get caught up in habits that keep us unbalanced and unhealthy. This can happen with our physical health, mental health, or spiritual health. It is easy to become negative, to eat food that does not nourish our bodies, or to become chronically sedentary, leading to a wide range of problems and challenges.

Create a Trinity Lifestyle leads you back to a life of balance. Early in the book, Dr. Bryson discusses, quite openly, his own struggles with living in balance, especially spiritually. His honesty is refreshing, and it will help you to realize we all have our own path to follow as we learn to live a Trinity Lifestyle. We can have a life where we eat real food that is nourishing to our body, we can exercise in a way that increases our strength, flexibility, and cardiovascular health, we can have open and honest relationships with our family and friends, and we can have a deep connection to God.

There are several key factors and recurring themes whenever groups of people who live long and healthy lives are studied and analyzed. What they have in common is consistent physical activity and exercise along with food that is simple, real, and unprocessed meaning lots of vegetables, fruits, nuts, lean meats and wild fish. The other key elements to longevity are a vibrant social network and a deep, rich spiritual foundation.

While these factors (exercise, food, social connection, and spiritual foundation) may seem like common sense ingredients, they are not, as many people do not know this or have forgotten. These key factors to a long and healthy life have been researched and studied. It is not just genetics or luck, although this plays a limited role. More important are lifestyle choices we routinely and habitually make. This comes back to balance, to a Trinity Lifestyle.

Having a specific plan for success is essential. The outline for success in this book lays out a step by step plan. Take this journey with Dr. Bryson to a life of balance, to a healthier life, a fuller life, a more meaningful life. You will be blessed and amazed.

- Mark A. King, DC

"

I have come to believe over
and over again that what is
most important to me must
be spoken, made verbal
and shared, even at the
risk of having it bruised or
misunderstood.

- *Audre Lorde*

"

preface

The idea of writing a book has been on my mind for some time, at least 2-3 years, maybe longer. But I never knew what to write about. What do people need or want to hear? Will people read what I have to say? Even as I write these words I wonder if I know what I am doing. In all honesty, there is a part of me that is fearful of this project but there is a bigger portion that is excited. And with that excitement I desire to share so much more than an idea about living a healthy lifestyle. Many books offer that. What I offer is my desire to share a story. A story that is about living unhealthy, making unhealthy choices, the consequences of those choices, forgiveness, redemption, restoration and love. I want you to know there is hope - a confident expectation of what is to come. No matter where you may find yourself this moment; allow a glimmer of hope to shine in and be amazed at the outcome.

As you read you will notice a common theme – a thread that ties this book together. It starts on the cover and runs deep within each page and text. It is based on the scripture Mark 4:1-9:

> Again he (Jesus) began to teach beside the sea. And a very large crowd gathered about him, so that he got into a boat and sat in it on the sea, and the whole crowd was beside the sea on the land. And he was teaching them many things in parables, and in his teaching he said to them: "Listen! Behold, a sower went out to sow. And as he sowed, some seed fell along the path, and the birds came and devoured it. Other seed fell on rocky ground, where it did not have much soil, and immediately it sprang up, since it had no depth of soil. And when the sun rose, it was scorched, and since it had no root, it withered away. Other seed fell among thorns, and the thorns grew up and choked it, and it yielded no grain. And other seeds fell into good soil and produced grain, growing up and increasing and yielding thirtyfold and sixtyfold and a hundredfold." And he said, "He who has ears to hear, let him hear."

You see, in essence, your life - your mind, body and spirit - is the soil. What type of soil it is matters. I believe all of us have been through each stage as described in Mark 4. We have all had "ravens" steal our seed, we have all had lack of depth, we have had our seeds choked out by the "thorns" and we have all had certain seeds bear fruit. And just because one part of your soil is bearing fruit does not mean another part of your soil is not being choked out by weeds. All parts of your soil must be producing fruit for optimum health. As you read ask yourself: How can I make my soil more fertile, deeper and richer than I ever thought possible?

Before we venture further, you the reader must know three things. First I do not know everything. I have learned much but have much more to learn. You must also know that you may be at a different stage of life than me or any other reader. That is okay. Ecclesiastes 3:1 reminds, "For everything, there is a season; a time for every activity under heaven…" If this is not your season to start an adventure, relax and know your season is coming and read this book with the intent to learn something about yourself and life. If this is the season for you to start Creating a Trinity Lifestyle, read this book as a guide to help you. Just remember that this book is not the end-all-be-all. Wherever you find yourself, whatever season you are in, the questions to ask yourself are these: What type of soil am I? What seeds have I been given and have they produced fruit?

Second, this is not a book about chiropractic or why you must go to a chiropractor, although being adjusted regularly would help your overall health for many reasons (neurologically, immunologically, mentally and physically). This is not a book about alternative health and ways to heal disease. This is not a book bashing the medical establishment. This is not a book explaining everything that probably needs explaining. This book is not an exhaustive study on one particular topic. Libraries are filled with books intended to be a snap-shot of life. Hopefully, this book will cause you to look at your life from all aspects and angles in order to understand why you do what you do. This book is about creating a lifestyle that is simple, as stress-free as possible, healthy and balanced.

Third, this book is written from a Christian perspective. My faith is who I am and what I do and to separate this book from my faith would be dishonest. Thus, if you are a Christian, my hope is that while you are reading you will be able to see Christ in every part of your life (not just on Sunday). If you are not a Christian, my purpose in writing is not to convince you of Christianity. My goal is not to "save you." My desire is that you would know the depth, width and height of the love I have come to know. For both the Christian and non-Christian, my hope is that by reading, you will be able to get up each morning with purpose and with passion even in the midst of difficulty. My hope is that you will be able to find a lifestyle that is healthy for your mind, body and spirit.

Are you ready? A pre-cautionary warning to the reader: What you learn about yourself may forever change the soil of your life. "For I am about to do something new; see, I have already begun! Do you not see it? I will make a pathway through the wilderness. I will create rivers in the dry wasteland" (Isaiah 43:19).

chapter 1

introduction

Memories, like rain, run through my soil; refreshing and restoring. Memories, like rain, run through my soil; refreshing and restoring each part of who I am. I wonder what to write. I am not a farmer. I did not grow up on a farm. Forget farming, I am not a gardener and I am unsure if I would even like planting a garden. It takes understanding, work and time. So maybe this journey will give me a greater appreciation of the food I eat. My granny had a vegetable garden and a chicken pen. Once as a child, I remember helping granny feed the chickens. I had a band-aid on my big toe and a chicken must have thought it looked like corn because the chicken came over and pecked my toe. Wow, I still remember the pain. Memories, like rain, run through my soil; refreshing and restoring.

As I was reading, praying and journaling one morning this idea was birthed into me; that our soil matters and from that soil, fruit comes forth. I believe our lifestyle can be or maybe should be shockingly simple, yet deeply healing and restorative. However, in our fast-paced, drive-through, instant, click-here culture, simplicity has been lost and replaced by a mentality that in order to be productive we must be busier, bigger and better than the person next to us. The question that keeps coming to my mind is: Really? Does busier, bigger and better create health or even success? After treating many patients and talking with many people it is evident that most,

if not all, people want a "health and/or diet plan" to follow. But upon further investigation what people actually need is a rhythm to their life that is not only healthy but productive. And that is the underlying premise of the Trinity Lifestyle – to create "soil" that is deep and rich, that is able to withstand seasons of drought, disease or pests and able to produce fruit. It is the idea that each person can create a balanced rhythm to their life, a balance of faith, family, recreation and work.

> "Live a balanced life - learn some and think some and draw and paint and sing and dance and play and work every day some."
>
> - R. Fulgham

What is good soil? Well, agriculturally speaking, when I first started writing I had no idea. And honestly I am still unsure if I do. But I will try to explain what the main four soil types are, what constitutes good soil and how to improve soil. Later, I will briefly mention the soil versus the seed and why that matters.

There are four main soil types: (1) Sand, which is the largest particle, but one that does not easily hold nutrients. "Sandy soils drain rapidly and there is ample air for the plant roots. They are easy to cultivate...but they dry out very easily and because of their rapid drainage, nutrients are quickly washed away" (The Garden Book 194). (2) Silt is a medium size particle. It feels smooth and powdery. When wet it does not feel sticky. "Silt can be difficult to cultivate because it is not flocculated (able to form lumps or mass)" (The Garden Book 195). (3) Clay is the smallest of particles in the soil. It is smooth when dry and sticky when wet. It is able to hold the most nutrients yet it "is difficult to cultivate because it is slow draining and has little air penetration" (The Garden Book 194). (4) Loam is a grain mixture of sand, silt, clay, plant nutrients and organic matter. "This is the ideal soil...it is easy to cultivate, retains moisture and nutrients" (The Garden Book 195).

Now that the four main types of soil are identified, what makes soil good or bad? "A good soil will contain all the nutrient elements necessary for the well-being of plants. Earthworms, insects, burrowing animals all contribute to the organic content of the soil. Both water and air are also necessary. In poorly drained soils, the plant's roots are restricted and the lack of air inhibits the plant's up-take of minerals from the soil" (The Garden Book 194-195). At some level, all soil needs to be improved. Even the richest soil can be helped by adding organic material. The benefits of improving soil include: (1) reduced erosion; (2) improved root penetration and access to soil moisture and nutrients; (3) improved emergence of seedlings and (4) greater water infiltration, retention and availability. And in even simpler terms, improving soil makes the nutrients in the soil more accessible, helps reduce diseases, retains moisture, and controls weed growth.

> "Build a healthy soil for healthy plants. Water less, weed less, fight fewer pests and reap a more bountiful harvest."
>
> - Linda Tilgner
> (Tips for the Lazy Gardener, 18)

To help show how this soil information relates to you I have created a chart (see Figure 1). I have equated sand to the mind. Like sand is the largest particle; the mind is the largest driving force behind all our actions and thoughts. Just like sand; your mind can be readily cultivated but if not used it will "dry out and lose nutrients." The silt is compared to your body because just as silt can be difficult to cultivate, the body takes time, energy and resources for any positive results to occur. The clay is like your spirit. For just as clay is able to hold the most nutrients, our spirit, some would call it "the soul," is the very essence of who we are. Both clay and the spirit can be difficult to penetrate. The loam I equated to balance in our lives. Just as loam is the perfect combination of sand, silt and clay; balance in our life occurs when we purposely engage our mind, body and spirit in healthy activities.

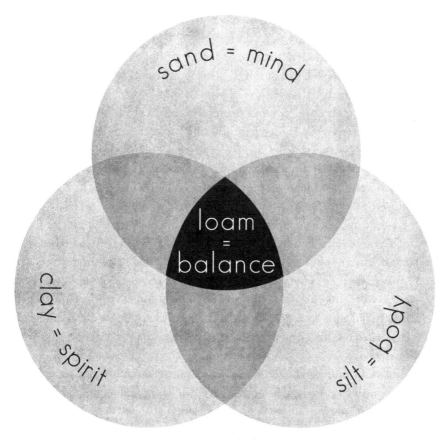

Figure 1: Balance

How does it relate? What is the connection between the soil of the Earth and the soil of my life? Just as the richest of soil needs to be cultivated; our mind, body and spirit also need cultivating. For fun, let's take a moment to look at what it takes to prepare soil. First, you have to examine the soil. To see what type of soil it is. Is it sandy? Does it have too much silt? Is there too much clay? What type of soil matters in regards to the fruit you wish to produce. Once soil type is determined the question to ask is, if this soil in the best location for what I intend to grow? Is there too much shade or too much sun? Then the question becomes, what do I want to plant? All this needs to occur before any actual manual labor takes place. The labor comes from cleaning the soil of un-needed debris, tilling the area (breaking up the ground), weeding the area, planting, watering, harvesting, etc.

Is the same not true of our own soil? We have to decide if our mind, body and spirit are in balance. Is there too much sand as to not allow the proper amount of silt and clay? Once determined, we must decide where to start. What area(s) do we want to work on? Is my own thought process or someone else's casting shadows or creating light? Then what do I actually want to plant in my mind, body and spirit that will cause the type of fruit I am looking for? Matthew 7:16 reads, "By their fruit you will recognize them. Do people pick grapes from thorn bushes or figs from thistles?" Our labor comes from removing un-needed things in our life; some good and some not so good. Our labor becomes an act of love as we break up the ground in areas of our life that may have not been touched for a while. Our labor comes from weeding out the un-necessary and planting, watering and harvesting the necessary.

But still you may be thinking how do I improve my soil? Let's correlate the terms I used above for improving soil structure to improving our mental, physical and spiritual health. The benefits of improving our own soil include: (1) Reduced erosion of the seed that is sown in our life. Consider that our soil could be so eroded that even if the seed is sown, if there is nothing to sustain it, the very seed we need will be stolen by the over-crowding in our life. (2) Improved penetration of truth in our heart and mind. (3) Improved emergence of life-giving words due to reduced hardening of our hearts. Consider that if our hearts are hardened by past hurts, offenses and the like, no matter if the seed goes deep; it cannot emerge and produce life. It will die before it reaches the surface or be choked out quickly once it does. (4) Greater infiltration, retention & availability of faith, hope and love. Consider that as we allow the seed a fertile place to grow it will cause a deeper infiltration than we ever thought possible. This depth of infiltration will allow a greater retention of nutrients. As the nutrients are retained, diseases may be resisted, "weed growth" can be controlled, and other beneficial aspects can be noticed. Plus, once fertile soil is achieved and properly maintained, a 30-60-100 fold increase of fruit will seem like a small harvest.

Before you start rejoicing at the potential of a great harvest I want you to consider one other thought. Song of Solomon 4:12 describes the bride (that is you even if you are a man reading this) as a "garden locked up." Have you ever thought about yourself as a garden locked up? I think many of us are without knowing it. We try to open the gate because at one time we had the key. Where is it now? We peer over the gate to see weeds, dry ground and decaying fruit lying all around. We slowly drop our shoulders and walk away thinking the effort to unlock our garden is not worth the reward. That could not be further from the truth. Your garden needs to be unlocked. Your soil is waiting to be cultivated. It may take work but the rewards will be wonderful. My hope is that you find the key to your locked garden and begin turning that dry and dead soil into fertile ground.

As shown by Figure 1, the ideal soil type is Loam: a perfect combination (balance) of sand, silt and clay with just enough of the right amounts of added material. In nature, soil has to be balanced to be productive. Does this same philosophy hold true in my life or in your life? I would dare to say yes. Your mind, body and spirit must be in balance. Your mind, body and spirit are interrelated in ways you may not understand or even care to know. However, if you truly want to live healthy, you must. Let me share two stories.

Story 1: Ruth (name changed) came to my office about 4-5 years ago. Physically, she complained of right shoulder pain and lower neck pain. She admitted her stress level was rather high due to home and work situations. At home she was divorced and now newly married and admittedly still working through "issues." At work, she sat at a desk all day answering phones, entering data and engaging customers. At that time, I treated Ruth with chiropractic, myofascial therapy and rehab. She improved and her pain was reduced after 3-4 visits so she decided she would call me when she needed to see me again. Fast forward 5 years later and Ruth is back in my office. She now complains of the same symptoms as before but says they have escalated. Ruth now complains of hip, ankle, wrist, neck and mid-back pain. She went on the internet and self-diagnosed herself with multiple illnesses. I examined her. Her muscles were, as expected, extremely tight. Her joint function was limited at best. But what happened next underscores the connection between the mind, body and spirit.

I start asking Ruth questions like, "What has happened in the last few months to a year? Any slips, falls, accidents, etc..?" She tells me nothing has changed except she and her husband almost got a divorce. They had bought a house at the beginning of the year and were unable to sell their other home for some time, her daughters moved back in with her and she was deciding whether or not to take a promotion at work. As she told me all these things Ruth acted like it was normal life. I looked at her and then re-told her what she told me and said, "No wonder you are having pain. You do not have any of those illnesses that you looked up on the internet. You have stress that is affecting every part of you." Ruth started weeping and in the midst of her tears replied, "No one has ever laid it out there for me like that." As I continued to treat and talk with Ruth, she told me she didn't want to be a failure again (she was referring to another divorce). I looked at Ruth and said to her, "You are not a failure. God loves you very much and literally sings and dances over your life." "But will He love me if I get another divorce," came her reply. Ruth's mind was not being cultivated with the truth of hope or love. Her body was feeling the effects of the mind. Her posture spoke of heaviness and despair. Her spirit was barely penetrable. Before she left, I prayed with Ruth. I prayed that her mind would have wisdom, that her body would be healed and that her spirit would know the love of Christ.

Story 2: I had treated Jill (name changed) for neck and back pain three times with good results. There was some pain reduction and increased movement but something was still missing. On her next visit I decided to use the TENS (Transcutaneous electrical nerve stimulation) unit. Although it is more complicated, for simplicity, let me say this machine helps relax muscles and reduce pain. So, I placed the pads on Jill's back, set the timer and left the room. I returned in no less than 3 minutes to check on her and instead of relaxing, Jill was crying uncontrollably. Thinking the machine was hurting or even burning her, I quickly turned it off. I started apologizing for the machine. She stopped me and said these words, "I am sorry. The machine was not hurting me. It had nothing to do with that per say. The tingling sensation reminded me of when my dad would stick me with a cattle prong." I was speechless. I had no words to say to her except sorry, which did not seem to fit, but that was all I had. They do not train you in school for that one. Jill's body response led to a memory that not only affected her mind but her spirit.

I could share hundreds of similar stories. These not only highlight the connection between our mind, body and spirit and also illustrate the principle of what is called the bio-psycho-social aspect of health, disease and lifestyle. Bio-psycho-social is defined as, 'of, relating to, or concerned with the biological, psychological, and social aspects, in contrast to the strictly biomedical aspects, of disease.' To simplify, Bio – means the biology of the problem. Is it a nerve, muscle, joint, digestive issue, heart issue, cancer, etc? It is what is causing the dysfunction in your body. Psycho – means mind. It does not mean you are crazy. Psychosomatic (mind-body) connections are real and valid. How your mind processes information, good or bad, absolutely influences your body's responses. Social – means your sphere of influence. How you handle the biological and psychological aspect of your health not only affects yourself but your family and friends. Your mind, body & spirit (your soil) is synergistically working to create balance and rhythm. Your soil needs to be Loam; balanced and fertile!

chapter 2

> God enters by a private door,
> into every individual.
> *- Ralph Waldo Emerson*

my soil

" I went for a walk today. I spotted a beautiful green field with lots of trees and plenty of sunshine. I saw us running around and acting crazy; wrestling and you tackling me to the ground, laughing and then a big kiss. We could lay there for a while and enjoy the sun. I also kicked a few rocks. One big one kept going to the other side. It wasn't any fun having to chase it by myself. It's been six days, I miss you terribly. I look out the window at every single car I hear go by in hopes that it is you. Each time my heart stops and then it has to start again when I realize it is not you. It is so hard to breathe these days. No laughter. It is a beautiful day here; I hope the sun is shining on you." These are the words of my wife, Jennifer, written on 11-16-03. These words are taped to the inside of the back flap of my Bible. These words move something deep within my spirit that I do not know if I can fully explain but I will try.

I was raised in the South. To give you a reference point, my hometown is approximately 70 miles above the Florida line and is proud to have the entrance to the Okefenokee Swamp Park as one of its main attractions. The soil of the South is culturally different than any other part of the country. Saying, "Yes Ma'am" and "No Sir" is expected. It is not taken as an insult. People for the most part enjoy family, say hello, lend a helping hand and love to fish and hunt. They like sweet tea, boiled peanuts and collard greens. On Sunday, most people in the south attend church. The South is like the buckle of the Bible belt where churches still have Sunday school and multiple other services. People go to church for a number of reasons; many go because it is what you do in the South. Although diminishing, racism still runs deep through the soil. Until 1994, my hometown had two high schools; a county school (98% white) and a city school (98% black). Yes, the South is wonderful and yet, like any culture, like any soil that has too much sand, silt or clay, it has its blemishes and inability to be cultivated.

I was raised in a loving home. I was not beaten. I was fed, clothed and played with. I was not abused verbally nor was I fatherless. In all accounts, I grew up privileged. My mom and dad, like any married couple, had their share of problems but never divorced. I am eternally grateful for that. I am the youngest of two. My sister, Misty, has always been my biggest fan even when I did not deserve it. She covered for me more times than I can count.

I have hundreds of memories from my childhood that I could share with you. The point is not for you to know my entire history but it is important for you to know how my soil has been cultivated. We lived next door to my dad's parents. I called them granny and grand-daddy. My grand-daddy died when I was around three. His name was Bo. The story, as it has been told to me, was that he had a limp and as a youngster I was able to mimic it perfectly. Thus, I got the nickname Bo. But my real name is William Glen Bryson, Jr. My mom's parents lived in Augusta, Georgia. I called them meme and papa. Although I was not physically close to them, I loved them. Papa had a naked hula girl on his bicep that he could make dance by flexing his bicep. I thought that was the coolest thing ever. As I think about my own tattoos, I wonder if that had an influence on me. Hmmm?

During my youngest years my dad worked for K-Mart. We moved around a lot. He worked long hours to provide and was often gone. However, despite that he never missed one of my games or neglected to take time to play with me. Thanks Dad! At some point, while working for K-Mart my dad injured his back. He was off work for some time. This may have been one of the poorest financial times we went through as a family but one of the richest memories I have. Let me explain. Before my dad was injured, as I said before, he worked long hours. During this time, we seemingly could afford whatever we wanted and although family time was wonderful it could seem sparse and infrequent. When my dad got injured he was home, a lot. Did you get that? He was home! But being home meant he was not working. This meant less finances. As a family we picked up cans on the side of the road and turned them in for money. We fished at a local pond and ate what we caught for dinner. We went without; at least we went without what we were used to having. The financial times seemed lean but the family times were richer than ever before. I am sure my mom and dad have a different memory of this because now as a parent I could see how that situation would be stressful but from a kid's perspective, it was a wonderful time. You see, I did not care about the stuff; I cared about and longed for my dad and mom to be home. I wonder how many other children feel this way.

> "Sometimes the poorest man leaves his children the richest inheritance"
>
> - R. Renkel

"Sticks and stones may break my bones but words will never hurt me." That is a lie. Words hurt and their effect lasts for a long, long time. There we sat, Ginny and myself, on a raised flower-bed outside of the middle-school cafeteria. We were in the seventh grade. As we chatted, two of my friends walked up and started poking fun at me by saying these exact words, "Bo, your nose is big for your face." Then they walked off, laughing. Yes I still remember their words. They struck much harder and deeper than a stick or stone could ever go. I tried to laugh it off but it visibly affected me. Ginny looked at me and through a smile said, "No it isn't." She was a dear friend from that day forward. Funny how words go deep within your soul and they do not need much watering to grow. Reminds me of weeds! This weed affected my personal image for many years, and to some extent, probably still does.

At this point in my life, we were living in Waycross, Georgia. My dad no longer worked for K-mart but had begun working for the Jones Company. My mom was working as a tax appraiser. I was in junior high. The middle school years seem to define many things in a young person's life. Like being called names, being bullied, being the cool kid, being the good-looking kid, being the red-neck– whatever your role is in junior high – it starts to define you. My role was the popular, cool kid. I was a jock. I was a straight 'A' student and I played football and basketball. I tried playing baseball but got hit with the ball in the nose (maybe it was too big). I never played in the band as I thought it was, "uncool". Looking back now I was wrong. Oh how I wish I had learned an instrument. During these years I started learning how to be whatever people needed me to be. I could be the "cool kid" or I could be the "pseudo red-neck". I was able to integrate into many social groups.

Interestingly enough, I hung out with the pastor's kid from our church. He, by far, was the best looking and coolest kid and just by being around him, he made me cooler. Funny how that works, huh? I can remember him and me sitting in the back pew of the church. His dad was preaching and he was rolling a joint. What was he thinking? What was I thinking? As a kid, we always went to church. Every time the door was open, we were there. I was raised in a Baptist Church. I am thankful for that now because it grounded me in many truths. But the one thing church was not, was fun. I saw church as a list of "do-nots and I-cannots." You could not drink, smoke, dance, have sex or anything else others outside the church were doing. The problem with that was the others looked like they were having more fun. In reality, they were not and I know that now. My parents went to church with us. Thankfully they did not just drop us off and leave. But, and they will admit this, their relationship with God at that time was superficial at best. They were playing the "game". The "game" goes like this: to be a good Christian you go to church, act right on Sunday and then live how you desire the rest of the week. The "game" was about appearance so what others perceived about you was not what was really true. And I became good at that game. I created a world where I was the good church kid, the popular jock, the straight 'A' student, the obedient son and the loyal friend. I was what everyone needed me to be. Because of that I was unsure who I really was.

"If you do not know Jesus as your personal Savior and you want to meet Him, tonight is your night. Do not leave this building without knowing for sure. If you die tonight, are you sure where you will spend eternity?" This was the invitation from the stage; night after night and year after year. I am unsure when I said a prayer inviting Jesus into my life. But what I do know is that I did it at summer camp every year I attended. And in reality I did it multiple times within the week at camp. I did it because I felt guilty for my actions not because I was in a relationship with God. For all intents and purposes, I was a good Christian. I had the outer shell intact but on the inside I was an insecure, fearful kid and later, an insecure, fearful adult. I am reminded of a verse; Matthew 23:27, "You are like whitewashed tombs, which look beautiful on the outside but on the inside are full of the bones of the dead and everything unclean." That described me.

It was my ninth grade year. Autumn (name changed) was a senior and I was a freshman (remember I was the cool kid). I can remember it clearly because this day defined many that would follow. It was a Saturday. The Georgia/Florida game was on TV and my two friends and I were watching it. My parents were gone and Autumn came over, we went into the back room and I lost my virginity; something I had no business losing at such a young age. We kept dating if you can call it that. A few weeks later as I am feeling like a champion, I got a phone call from Autumn. She said, "I am pregnant." My world came crashing down. What was happening? I went from being a champion to losing everything. The other thing she told me was that she did not know if it was mine. She was also in a relationship with another older male. My mind races, am I still the cool kid? What am I going to do? I immediately told my sister. After much discussion among ourselves it is decided Autumn will have an abortion. I will pay half and the other guy will pay half. My sister's boyfriend at the time loaned me the money and I later worked it off for him cutting down and loading trees. The abortion center was in Jacksonville, Florida. An hour and half drive with Misty's boyfriend and me in the front seat and Autumn and the other guy in the back. An awkward, long drive to say the least. We got to the abortion center, dropped them off and waited. They returned, we got back in the car and drove home. That was the end of it. No more baby, no more relationship. This memory came rushing back to me in July 2007 as I listened to a young man speaking about how the abortion he paid for affected him. How he never thought about it at the time; he took a life and disrespected the woman he encouraged to get the abortion. He then said these words, "Most people think abortion only affects females but that is a lie. If there is a male in the audience or watching via the webcast that has been affected by abortion, God wants you to know He forgives you and loves you." The words struck deep and I fell to my knees weeping at the memory as it flooded my mind. I had never dealt with it or thought much of it but here I was almost 20 years later dealing with an issue that I had allowed myself to forget. Here is what I will tell you. That day the Lord used one word (one seed) to fall deep into the soil of my heart and mind. I was a wreck. However, that day I was forgiven. The shame was gone. The hiding was gone. I was free. And in that freedom, my soil became richer.

A mile from my house was a clay pit surrounded by a great wooded area; it was a wonderful adventure land for a boy. It was my place to ride my bike, build forts and to hide away from the game of life. It was my sanctuary and the place I would choose to end my life. The bullet dropped between my legs. I was still alive. The words seemed to scroll across my mind. Only moments earlier I had the gun in my mouth ready to end my life. I was in 10th grade. I have no logical reason to tell you why I was sitting against that tree. All I can remember is that I was not living up to the standard that I thought I should. No one put this standard on me. I just felt the weight of perfection. I was not good looking enough, I was not the best athlete; I was not the best student; I simply was not. "When life begins to fall through the cracks and embarrassing sin threatens to reveal our less-than-perfect identity, we scramble to put up a good front...we cover and hide until we can rearrange the mask of perfection and look good again" (Manning). And I was tired of rearranging the mask - the easiest fix; kill myself. And even in that I could not do it. I pulled the trigger but the bullet hit the ground. I was too scared to pull it again. I took the gun back home; rearranged my mask and kept playing the game. The game of being the perfect son, perfect student and perfect friend continued.

My senior year I was voted Prom King and Best All-Around Student. I even had a football scholarship. I was at the top of the world. At the last moment I decided to not take the football scholarship. The reason I gave was that I wanted to follow my girlfriend to the college she was attending, Georgia Southern. Truth was I was afraid of even attempting to play football at the college level. Everything in me screamed of failure and I knew it was easier to run than to admit. It is amazing how fear of failure can grip every part of your life.

For the most part my college years were uneventful. I really had no idea what I wanted to do. I chose biology because I thought I wanted to be a doctor. I loved helping people but in reality being a doctor meant you were a success, correct? So with that knowledge I went to classes keeping up an appearance as the perfect student. During my senior year of college I was manager of the student union. That is when I saw her; the beautiful green and blue eyes that captured me. It was Jennifer. It was the end of a seven year relationship and the beginning of another. (I would like to take a moment and apologize to the girl I dated for 7 years. I treated you poorly and disrespected you many times. For that I am sorry. You deserved better, much better.)

On mine and Jennifer's first date we went out with her friends. I got sloppy drunk and passed out on cement steps across the street from the bar. Jennifer was kind enough to take my wallet and watch so I didn't get mugged. I remember puking on her friend's car, her friends picking me up and dropping me at the door (literally they dropped me) and then sleeping on the bathroom floor. That was the beginning of our relationship. Wow, it amazes me that she went back out with me. But Jennifer and I continued to date and as my graduation approached, the fear of the unknown was building. I took the MCAT (the medical school exam) and did fairly well but I never applied to schools. I was afraid that I would not get accepted. I asked Jennifer to marry me out of desperation. She said yes but later broke it off.

I graduated Georgia Southern as Cum Laude with a BS in Biology and a minor in Chemistry in 1996. I moved back home and started working at a grocery store stocking shelves. I was making more money in college than I did when I got out. This was a humbling experience for a prideful 21 year old. However, one thing my parents taught me was a good work ethic. So I worked until I got a "real job" as a lab tech. It was a great job with many benefits; however, I was not wired to sit and titrate all day. But what was I to do? My fear drove every decision I made.

At this point, Jennifer had finished her junior year at Georgia Southern and had been accepted to the Medical College of Georgia in Augusta. Her school and my job were two and a half hours apart. We got married in April of 1998 and moved 30 minutes away from her school. I drove two hours one way every morning and night to work for about 6 months. It is a miracle I was not killed as I fell asleep many times. I finally quit titrating and started working for Orkin in Augusta. My job was termite work. If you are not from the south, let me tell you, we do not have basements, we have crawl spaces. My job was to sell the contracts and dig the trenches underneath the homes. Needless to say, this was not the job for me although it was a great learning experience.

"Why don't you try chiropractic?" These were the words of my wife as we sat in our apartment when I was working for Orkin. My words were, "Okay." Many people ask how and why I became a chiropractor. There it is. No great story of being healed by an adjustment. In fact I had never been adjusted before I went to chiropractic school. I applied to school and on the day Jennifer graduated; we moved to Kansas City for Chiropractic school. New soil.

For those who do not know, chiropractic school is 4 years. For all intents and purposes, the first 2 years are identical to medical school with the last 2 years are focused on chiropractic. I remember the first week we were in Kansas City. This was the first time we had lived outside of Georgia. Jennifer's parents helped us move in. When they left, my wife was crying and crying. We bought a TV and sat there, watching it for hours, wondering what we were doing. Isn't it great and yet not so great how TV can numb the brain? Jennifer started working at a local hospital and I started school with the mentality that I was going to be the best chiropractor Cleveland Chiropractic College had ever seen. Desiring perfection, I arrived early to school and stayed late working on hands-on techniques every day.

During chiropractic school, Jennifer and I attended church fairly regularly when I was not too busy studying or traveling to weekend seminars. Remember the white-washed tomb? That was still me. I can remember sitting at the coffee shop reading my Bible 3-4 times per week. This kept my outside looking beautiful but in reality I had no intention to live the life I was reading about. I was slowly decaying.

In school, I met Corey. He was a couple of semesters behind me. He and I became friends and we traveled to seminars together, learning and then teaching in classes and clubs on campus. My fear of failure was pushing me to succeed. Every-thing in me had to be the best. I was finally going to be a doctor. Now I would be considered a success. Then these words came from a family member, "How long will it take you to be a real doctor?" It was like I was sitting in the middle-school flowerbed again. These words went deep and left a scar.

During my last semester of school, Corey and I decided to open a practice to-gether. I will not speak for Corey but I was too proud to work for someone else be-cause I felt I knew more than anyone else. After visiting Lincoln Nebraska one time, we decided to practice there. Corey was from Nebraska. I told Jennifer that I felt like the Lord was leading us to Nebraska. How could she argue with that? The truth was I just wanted to practice with Corey. He was and is one of the best chiropractors I know. Another truth was I was scared to open on my own. We opened Trinity Chi-ropractic in August of 2003. Moving to Nebraska was again new soil. I did not have time to plant anything of God into my life at this point. This new Nebraska soil did not have room for God because I had to cultivate business. We did visit some church-es in town but I had more important things to worry about than finding a church or cultivating a relationship with God. My goal was to be the biggest clinic in town and to be the best known chiropractor.

"Tell me what you did!" These are the words of Jennifer. It was mid-September 2003, just a month or so after we opened the practice. The entire layout of the story does not matter here but I had to tell my wife I had an affair while I was in Chiro-practic College. Jennifer asked me to leave. I moved out of the house for a couple of weeks. I then had to tell Corey what happened. He seemed understanding. I apologized to Jennifer and she allowed me back in the house. I was trying my hardest to make things right and have a successful practice. I wanted to be a success. But cracks were starting to show in my beautiful white washed walls.

In the beginning of November I was holding it together fairly well. Jennifer had forgiven me for my previous actions. The practice was growing however my internal world was crashing in upon itself. I had cheated on my wife; I was not as smart as the chiropractor I was practicing with and really, I am not a real doctor (or at least those were the words I heard in my head). The crack in my outer shell finally gave way and I fell apart. The fear of not succeeding in my practice and my marriage was too much. I wrote my wife a note and left it on the dining room table. I took money from my personal account and my business account without anyone knowing. The note, in many more words said to Jennifer, "I am done". While Jennifer was at work, I packed my truck with clothes and two guns. I did not call Corey or anyone else. I walked out on my wife and my business partner. I walked out on my life. My plan: to live it up for a week and then commit suicide. What a plan?!? I was gone a week. I had another affair. No one knew where I was. "…It is so hard to breathe these days. No laughter. It is a beautiful day here; I hope the sun is shining on you…" were the words of Jennifer written while I was gone. Even in the midst of her pain she wished the sun was shining on me. Why didn't I kill myself? Was it the people praying for me, God's grace and plan for my life, or the fear of pulling the trigger and only severely injuring myself and then having to live like that? I honestly am unsure the exact reason but I never even took the gun out. Why did I come back? If I did not kill myself, what else was there to do? I could not stay where I was. So I called Jennifer and told her I was coming home.

"I never thought you would do something like this." That is the short (very short) version of what Corey said to me upon my return. Corey and I continued to practice together until 2006. I know those 3 years were really difficult for him. So thanks Corey for staying as long as you did. Jennifer kicked me out of the house; this time for much longer. During the week I was gone Jennifer had changed the house locks and bank accounts. I had no home and no money. Up until this point, I relied on Jennifer's income. The consequence of my actions hit me square in the face. My pride and my life shattered. The inside of the white washed walls were exposed. I had to get an apartment and two more jobs. I delivered papers in the morning from 3 am–6 am, worked at Trinity during the day and then taught Anatomy at a local community college four nights a week. I was tired. I was sad. I was hopeless. In my apartment leaning against the bedroom wall listening to my parents on the phone, I placed a shotgun in my mouth. But instead of a bullet a name, Tom Swihart, hits my mind. Jennifer and I met him and his wife at the very first church we visited in Lincoln. It is now January 2004.

I called Tom and simply asked if he could meet with me. He said, "Yes". We met at Village Inn on a Wednesday morning at 7 am. I verbally vomited all over him. He didn't judge. He did not flinch with disgust. He just listened. Then he said something I will never forget, "What are you going to do now?"

I would meet with Tom for the next 6 years every Wednesday morning. So what did I do next? Upon Tom's encouragement, I started reading the Bible. This time it was not for appearance. It was for my very life. I did not do a Bible study. I just read. I gave up going to all seminars except the ones needed for continuing education. Tom told me, "You forsake all else to save your marriage." Jennifer and I started counseling with Grady and Sandy. We were still living separate but we were dating occasionally. During one of my counseling sessions, Grady said something that impacted me deeply. He said, "Everyday you get up, the enemy has a plan for your life and God has a plan for your life. You get to choose each day. Bo, which will you follow?" I decided that day to follow God's plan having no idea what that fully meant. I just knew I had followed the enemy's plans all too often. I needed a new direction. I needed God in my life more than I ever needed anything. But this time, there was no stage, no invitation, nothing. Could God really forgive me? Could Jennifer forgive me?

"How can I not forgive you when everything you have done to me I have done to Christ?" With those words Jennifer kicked in the gate of my locked garden. I was no longer searching for the key. With those words I saw Christ. With those words my life was forever changed. Before this point I would honestly say I was not a Christian. I do not care how many times I prayed the "sinner's prayer." I was living inconsistently with so much of what Christ teaches. I am not going to debate theology of "once saved always saved." For me, I do not think, I know, I never understood the love and forgiveness that Christ offered until I saw it in my wife. Just so you know these words did not come easily for Jennifer. They came after months of prayer and counseling. Jennifer's revelation of what she said not only spoke to me; it has spoken to many others who know our testimony. Sandy, her counselor, said it is rare for a woman to forgive like Jennifer. Thanks Jennifer for being a rare jewel. And you must also know that forgiveness is not the same as forgetting. Forgiveness is a choice. Forgetting may never occur. According to Jennifer, even now, certain things or certain words may remind her of my actions but then she reminds herself that she has chosen to forgive. Her forgiveness was the water to my dry, cracked soil. To read Jennifer's words on Forgiveness see Appendix F.

> I am forgiven and I am loved.

How did I start cultivating this new soil? I did many things but more than anything I started allowing the love and forgiveness I felt begin to change me. I learned that my actions had consequences and those actions affected many more people than just me. I learned that in order for others to change you must first be willing to change yourself. So I started working on my own soil. I started reading the Bible and praying. Every "good Christian" should do that more right? Well yes but not out of a duty and not to check-it-off a list. That can create guilt and obligation. None of that leads to life. To have an impact, reading God's word needs to be done in response to relationship with Christ. I just started reading the Bible; simply just reading it. Not necessarily doing a bible study. I just wanted and needed the word of God to run deep through me. Since 2004, I have read the bible four times from cover to cover. My plan is simple; start in Genesis and read through to Revelation. I create no time frame and no expectations. I just read and let Christ's tenderness speak to me. I am reminded of a verse: "…Your right hand supported me and your gentleness makes me great" (Psalm 18:35).

I also started praying. Growing up prayer was something you did at bed time, the dinner table and at church. Having no idea what prayer was, I started going to "prayer meetings." These were prayer times at the church during the Sunday school hour. The first time I did, Rodney and Malinda were the only ones in the "prayer class." They were not quiet prayers – they paced, they raised their hands, they quoted scripture – they were vocal! I was sitting there thinking – where am I? This is not how I learned to pray. To be honest, I was a little freaked out. The best part of this prayer meeting was when a mouse ran across the floor and Rodney did not stop praying but tried to stomp it. That was a pivotal point in my prayer life: I thought you can pray and do other things to? What a novel idea.

After that mouse encounter, I felt I was supposed to pray at my office every Tuesday and Friday morning at 5:30 am until the office opened around 7 or 8 am. I can remember the first few times I turned on worship music and started praying for what felt like an hour. I would look at the clock and it would have only been 5-10 minutes. I would run through another prayer list; five more minutes would pass. So then I would just read the bible for an hour. As weeks and months passed prayer actually got more enjoyable. I would walk through each room of my office declaring God's faithfulness and goodness. I would pray for patients by name. I would pray for my employees. I would pray for my wife. I would just ask for His presence to flood me. Prayer was actually becoming part of who I was and what I did. During a time of prayer, God gave me my life verse, Joshua 1:8. It reads, "Do not let this book of law depart from your mouth; meditate on it day and night; be careful to do all that is written in it, then you will be successful and prosperous." Prayer for me now is not about accomplishing anything. It is not about a checklist. It is not about anything but becoming increasingly intimate with Christ. That is my goal. That is my purpose!

The years that followed 2004 until now have been amazing to experience; I look forward to see what Christ has in store in the years to come. How will my soil continue to be improved? What fruit will come? So much more has happened and I wish I could share it all. I am a blessed man. But as amazing as the past 10 years have been, there have also been times of frustration and stress, pride rising back up, fear trying to re-establish itself and times of heartache. Our children have been sick. Friends and family members have gone through rough times. But in the midst of it all, I see the goodness of Christ.

I look back over my life and stand amazed that I am alive. I look back at how many times God sowed seeds into my life – whether through my parents, my awesome sister, pastors, friends, church camp, reading the bible or a host of other ways – and how often they were stolen by ravens. How many times my soil was dry and unable to receive or how often weeds choked out what little growth I had. Then I look at the last 10 years and feel overwhelmed with the seeds of love and forgiveness and how that changed, and continues to change, everything about whom I am. Why do I tell you all of this? Why do I expose the roots that lie beneath my soil? Because it is in exposing these roots that water and nutrients can penetrate much farther. I am not a great man. I am an average guy with a hunger for Christ to move in my life and in the lives of others. I am a man that knows I am forgiven much so I am learning to love much.

The soil of my life was changed and is continuing to change. My soil is finally ready to receive seed that can produce a bountiful harvest. Even still with so much change, there are still areas of my garden that need to be examined, cultivated and improved. My soil is a work in progress. My life is a journey with my family, my friends and Christ. And what an incredible journey it is. So it is with you. Your soil is a work in progress. Today, whatever the condition of your soil; deep and rich, shallow and dry, over-grown with weeds, it can be improved upon. That is the point of my writing. It is to encourage you to cultivate the soil of your life. Beyond what is mentioned above, a key to Creating a Trinity Lifestyle is to take "baby-steps" while also being tenacious. "The spiritual art of tenacity is a learned art. The word 'tenacious' can be defined as 'holding fast, clinging to something.' In a word; stickability: sticking with something or someone to the end" (Briscoe 103). While you might be able to see the soil you would like to have, it will take time and effort to cultivate. It will take putting one foot in front of the other even on the days it seems there is no laughter. It will be a journey. Allow that journey to be fun, challenging, entertaining, creative, caring, loving but most of all filled with grace. There will be days that are difficult. There will be days that you feel like you have failed. That does not mean the journey has ended in failure. It simply means you made a small detour. Forgive yourself. Forgive others. Then start the journey again. As 3 John 1:2, Psalms 20:4, 91:14-16 aptly state, so I pray for you,

> Beloved, I pray that all would go well with you and that you may be in good health, as it goes well with your soul...May He grant your heart's desire and fulfill all your plans.....And because you hold fast to God in love, He will deliver you; He will protect you because you know His name. When you call to Him, He will answer; He will be with you in trouble; He will rescue you and honor you. With long life He will satisfy you and show you His salvation.

chapter 3

is your soil toxic

My office is located on a very busy street so we have lots of traffic but not much foot traffic. Jennifer has wanted to dress up the outside of the building, mainly around the front door, for years. So your question should be, Why hasn't she done it? Well, there are many reasons, but I suppose the biggest reason is me. My toxicity level was too high. Let me explain. Every time she mentioned it I would remind her that she is not at the office everyday so who would take care of the plants and other decorations? Of course it would be me and I did not want to be bothered by it. Thus she would retreat and not do it. However, this past Fall, after the same conversation, we decided to trim bushes, mulch, hang lights, buy mums, pots, hay bales and cornstalk. A Fall scene was created. Jennifer put the mums in the pots and watered them. It was beautiful. Because of my toxic conversation that lingered in her head, she made sure that either she or our staff watered the mums. There was no way this would be any extra work for me. About two weeks go by and the mums start dying. I say nothing then another week passes and one mum specifically looks terrible. I then say the proverbial, "told you so." Yes, my soil still needs to be cultivated. Jennifer says she is sorry but does not understand what happened.

As I was throwing the mums away I notice the pots were full of water and the roots were soaked. She did water them. Jennifer then called her cousin, Deanna, who is a very good gardener and used to own a floral shop. Jennifer tells her the story and Deanna gives her these words of wisdom, "Mums do not like their feet wet." Jennifer, in her concern about killing the plants, over-watered them and killed them. The water – well, actually the excess water – was toxic to this plant. We both had to laugh at this. I wonder if this would've happened if my initial attitude was not toxic? Why do I tell you this story? Well it is to let you know my wife has to put up with much. Even more it shows you that our soil is dependent on what we put into it and how much. Even too much of a good thing can be toxic to our soil. However, let me make one clear statement concerning that. You can never, never, never get enough of God. That is one area where that logic does not and will not work.

You may have never stopped and asked the question, "is my soil toxic?" Maybe it is time to do so. Stop and think about your typical day. Consider the air you breathe, the food you eat, the books you read, the music you listen to, the TV shows you watch, the belief system you have, the work environment, the noise levels, the second-hand smoke, the car packed freeway, the fumes from factories, the clothes you wear, the water you drink, the sleep you get or do not get, the people you encounter and lastly, the mindset and stage of life you find yourself. You see all of this matters and it is all connected. For instance, the food you ate the night before can affect your morning, thus affecting your drive to work, thus affecting your day at work, thus affecting those around you, affecting their drive home and so on and so on. Moreover, "we all see ourselves through a lens of our experience, beliefs and perspectives, we all have our blind spots…our viewpoint can be distorted and the longer we look through a distorted lens, the more likely it is to believe a distorted truth" (Groeschel, 24-25). Simply, our soil and what we put into it matters.

You are probably thinking; wait a second, I can't control all of what goes into my soil so what am I to do? You are correct; you cannot control everything. *Controlling is not the point; being aware is the point.* Being aware is more than what goes into your soil; it is being aware of how we respond to what goes in. For instance, if my soil is just sand, I will be unable to maintain or contain the needed nutrients. This will affect my ability to be healthy. If my soil is silt only; I also have a problem. I cannot hold together the nutrients needed even if they are all available thus I cannot be healthy. If my soil is only clay, this also poses a problem. Although I am able to hold most of the nutrient base, I will still be unable to efficiently and effectively distribute them to produce health. The key is being aware and allowing the sand, silt and clay to mix appropriately thus forming loam. This soil, this perfect balanced soil, as I noted earlier, is the easiest to cultivate. It allows many nutrients to be gathered, contained and distributed for a healthful, fruitful response no matter what goes into your soil.

It is time to peer over that garden gate and look at what lies within. Do you see hard cracked soil with weeds? Do you see small patches of fertile soil? How about in the far corner, can you see the beginning of flowers blooming? Today, be courageous enough to look. And once you look, take the necessary steps to become less toxic.

chapter 4

> One personal choice seems to influence long term health prospects more than any other; what we eat.
>
> – Surgeon General

you are what you eat

The old adage, "you are what you eat" may be more accurate than anyone could have ever imagined. An interdisciplinary effort by scholars in primatology, biological anthropology, archaeology, nutrition, psychology, agricultural economics and cultural anthropology suggests that there is a systematic theory behind why humans eat what they eat" (Food and Evolution 1). This chapter is an overview, very simple and brief, of why we should be concerned with what we eat.

"Granny, can I have more sugar?" I would ask as I sat across from my granny at her dining room table. Sitting in front of me was a bowl of milk with sugar added to it. No cereal, nothing but milk and sugar. After I asked, granny would pass me the sugar and I would pour another spoonful into the bowl. There was nothing better than scooping sugar from the bottom of that bowl and tasting its sweetness. Great memories but what was my granny thinking? "Can you believe you ever ate the way you did while growing up and now you eat like this?" This question was posed by my mom as she visited for the holidays. I thought about that question for some time. You see, growing up, I did not eat organically, I did not eat all the "things you should," nor did I limit my sugar or caloric intake. On the contrary, I ate gallons of ice cream at a time, little Debbie snacks, pop-tarts and the list goes on. Twice in my life, I can remember eating so much that I literally got sick. It is not that my parents did not care what I ate; it is that they did not know what I now know. But even with as much as I know, I still eat sugar. I still overload on carbs. I still do not eat enough fruits and veggies. I give my kids lollipops, an occasional root beer, pizza and chicken fingers and occasionally I still eat too much. Recently I ate 35 chicken wings and then, by the next morning, I remembered why I should not do that anymore. What I have come to realize about food is this, what we eat does matter! What we allow our children to eat does matter! Do I have to eat "perfectly" all the time? No, but eating healthy is a lifestyle choice – a daily choice – a very important choice.

Before I jump into the meat and potatoes of this chapter (no pun intended), let me make three observations. First observation, we need to eat like babies nurse. Let me explain. Have you ever noticed that breastfed babies seem to get hungry more often than formula fed babies? Why is that? It is because human milk is specific for human needs. It takes significantly less energy to digest human milk protein and fats from breast milk than formula. This is why breast-fed babies typically eat every 30-45 minutes if not sooner (Note: I understand that some babies do not follow that pattern). Plus breast milk is constantly changing to meet the demands of the baby and breast milk has natural enzymes which help deliver the nutrients that are needed. Formula has to add, or "fortify", these enzymes and minerals. This fortification does not even approach the quality of breast milk. "No product has ever been as time tested as mother's milk. There is no better safeguard against the onset of allergies and protection from infections" (La Leche League International 6). "So valuable are the nutritional and disease-fighting properties of breast milk that in ancient times it was known as white blood" (Sears, William and Sears 122).

As I have been reading about nursing, the big debate is when to introduce solids to the nursing infants. Some sources say 4 months, some say 6 months and some still say 1 year. However, "scientists all over the world verify that…young babies are better without the early addition of solids to their diet" (La Leche League International 223). The other main point about adding solids was that they help the baby feel fuller thus allowing the baby to sleep longer; a benefit for the parent maybe but most definitely not the child. Remember "both the food choices and the eating patterns you instill into your toddler will help shape his or her young taste buds for lifelong healthy eating" (Sears, William and Sears 115). And please do not misunderstand me, if you chose to not breast-feed or you introduced solids earlier than the experts say; it is okay and your child is okay. Smile, take a deep breath and know you are doing a great job!

Now let me show you how this applies. How often do you eat? It is increasingly known that smaller, more frequent meals are better for your overall health. This can be likened to the nursing baby. As far as the components of food, our food quality in its natural state may be likened to the natural goodness in breast milk. But what do we try to do? We literally eat more, fill ourselves with less nutritional foods with less vitamin and minerals and then call it normal. It may be common but it should not be normal. We need to eat in a way that is healthy; that helps us lose significant weight and maintain higher energy levels throughout the day. How can we do this? By understanding what we eat and how we eat matters! "When you eat foods that don't combine correctly, the digestive system gets mixed signals…weakening the digestive tract and immune system" (Gates and Schatz 11). Foods are primarily fat based, protein based, or carbohydrate/sugar based. Fat, protein, and sugar all digest in different ways throughout the body. For the purpose of Creating a Trinity Lifestyle, the plans presented in later chapters will keep heavy proteins and starches away from each other and eat them with vegetables and healthy fats. This will help you get much out of your food and also allow your digestive tract (really, your whole body) to function at its optimum.

Second observation, we over-complicate eating. Eating should be simple and fun.

Follow these steps to keep it simple:

1. Drink more water.
2. Increase fruit and veggies. This will give color to your meals. Color is good!
3. Decrease simple carbohydrates (this includes whole grains) and processed foods.
4. Avoid low fat foods. They are many times nutritionally void. Fat is needed in your diet and can be healthy and beneficial.
5. Add good sources of protein to your diet; grass fed beef, seafood, poultry and the eggs they produce.
6. Limit your intake of dairy.
7. Be active.

Third observation, we consume too many whole grains. From The Wheat Belly,

> Wheat has become the national icon of health...with "heart healthy" versions of our favorite wheat products chock-full of whole grains. The national trend to reduce fat and cholesterol intake and increase carbohydrate calories has created a peculiar situation...in which products with wheat dominate our diet. The sad truth is the proliferation of wheat products in the American diet parallels the expansion of our waist. (Davis 6)

Simply, wheat (really the over-consumption of wheat) makes us unhealthier. But the question to ask is why? Probably for two reasons: (1) "A wheat belly represents the accumulation of fat that results from years of consuming foods that trigger the insulin response, the hormone of fat storage. This "visceral" fat is unique...it provokes inflammatory responses...it issues abnormal metabolic signals to the rest of the body" (Davis 4). (2) Wheat is the major contributor of gluten in the human diet. Gluten is the protein found in wheat and other related grain products. It is not my intent to fully explain gluten-intolerance and the consequences of it. However, know gluten has been shown to be destructive to our health. It affects our body weight, skin and "there's not an organ that is not affected by wheat (gluten) in some potentially damaging way" (Davis 4).

Next time you are eating at your favorite restaurant, take a moment to look at what is in front of you and others. Do you have water or coke? (Note: for those not from the South, everything is coke.) Is the plate colorful or only brown and white? Is the portion in front of you reasonable? Is it healthy? The answer to these questions can reveal much about your health and your lifestyle.

Whole Foods

Foods found in their natural whole state, just as God has given them to us, assure us sound nutrition for complete health. A bold statement to make yes, but everyday science consistently backs up this statement on a number of levels. Below I have tried to provide you with the information you need to make an informed decision about what you eat and why. However, I challenge and welcome you to search additional information as questions arise and you learn to trust food in its whole and natural state.

To say the body is anything less than a miracle is absurd. What if your body was a car? Would you take better care of it? Many people do actually take better care of their car than their body. Why? Maybe because it is easier to take care of something else besides us or maybe it is because you notice damage to the car before you notice the damage to your own body. Whatever the reasoning, it remains true; the body is an amazing self-regulating, self-healing machine. But even so, our body needs resources. These resources are the food we eat. This simple realization may help when deciding what resources to give our bodies.

> If your body was your car you would take better care of it.

Food in its whole, natural state provides these resources best. I am mainly speaking of raw foods. Why? Two main reasons: First, every part of our nutrition is interconnected to other various parts and pieces. For example, never does our body utilize calcium alone. Calcium once in the blood stream is combined with vitamin C, vitamin D, Magnesium and others to become functional in the body. Like the orchestration of a symphony working together, foods in their natural whole state work synergistically providing all the enzymes and co-nutrients necessary for health and vitality. And what foods do this the best; it is fruits and vegetables because they are more abundant in vitamins, minerals, antioxidants, water and fiber than any other food. Can you hear your mom saying from the kitchen, "Make sure you eat those vegetables?"

Second, eating food in its natural raw whole food state preserves all the nutrient content. "Nowadays, health-conscious people know processed food is devoid of nutrients and try their best to avoid it. Most Americans do not eat the 5-9 recommended servings of fruit and vegetables each and every day. If you really eat 9 servings of fruit and veggies, you will likely not need or want anything else" (Zavasta). Furthermore, cooking actually denatures (aka. damages) proteins and other chemical structures. Cooking, actually it is over-heating, causes the nutrients not to be available to our system because we cannot break them down into the building blocks we need.

This inability to break down nutrients leaves a residue, a higher level of toxicity that our body in turn then must clean up. Remember, a question to ask yourself: Is my body toxic?

Let me stop a moment and interject a thought. Keeping in theme; do we not also do this to the rest of our soil, meaning our mind and spirit? We 'over-heat' our mind by not guarding what goes into it. "Over-heating" (stress, anxiety, etc.) causes thoughts not to be broken down; actually seen for what they really are. This in turn streams into our consciousness affecting not only our mind but the nutrients needed to feed the spirit. This process absolutely leaves a residue that if not dealt with will be toxic to both the mind and spirit and eventually the body. Let me give an example. One of my patients, George (name changed) was told he was not a good father; that he did not know what he was doing. This went into his mind until he believed it. And as he believed it, his spirit was affected. George felt he could never do a good enough job so he stopped trying. This untruth caused an "over-heating" rendering any nutrient needed for health useless. He presented to my office with headaches, neck pain and occasional back pain. 2 Corinthians 10:5 states, "…take every thought captive…" George did not take his thought captive. Even if he did not start off as a great dad, he could have changed. But he allowed the unchallenged thought to "over-heat" his mind affecting his spirit and body. Is there a thought that you have not taken captive that is now "over-heating" your mind?

Back to food - As we learn to eat food in its natural whole food state, should it be organic? I heard it once said, "Organic you are and so should your food be". But what does organic mean? Organic food is food that is grown without the use of synthetic insecticides, pesticides, herbicides, fungicides, hormones, or other synthetic substances. Plus no artificial additives or colors are added to the food. That is the simplest definition of organic food. Now, "natural food" is different. Legally food labeled natural does not have the same strict standards as organic food. While there are no artificial flavors or colors and no chemical preservatives, foods are still processed with hormones and other synthetic substances. Thus ideally yes, everything that you eat would be organic, fresh and local to your region. However, many times we think it is impractical. The question to ask: is it? The bigger picture you may want to consider is this: you will pay for health now preventing disease or you will pay for it later treating disease. Your choice! Have you noticed that when people get sick that is when they start trying to eat healthier and more organic? Why not start earlier? Does eating organically mean you will never get a disease? Of course not! But it may help prevent many of them.

Eating organic food is vital for two reasons. First is this, "today, most of what we eat contains man-made pesticides, fungicides or herbicides" (Scott-Moncrieff 12). These chemicals do not just wash off or disappear, they can add up in the outer skin and in the center of our food. It is astonishing to me the pounds of chemicals put on our food to get it to grow faster and to keep away the bugs. Now if we only ate one watermelon or one pint of strawberries in our lives it would not be a problem. And since we eat a lot over a lifetime, food is the most direct way we build up a toxic level of chemicals in our bodies. Eating organic is important because it limits our exposure to these chemicals.

Second, eating organically is vital because organic food has a higher nutrient density. As foods grow slower there is more time for the plant to utilize the mineral in our soils. This means our soil needs to be healthy so that is has the minerals our plants need. Moreover, plants have their own system to ward off insects and bugs. It may not be as quick or as direct as insecticide but it does work. The only problem is it takes longer and you may lose a plant or two. If you have a small garden losing a plant or two may not be a big deal. However, think of large farms that rely on big crops. Is it any wonder why farmers use chemicals? I am not judging them for doing so; I understand it from an economic perspective. I even had a farmer tell me, if his crops do not produce, he doesn't get paid. If he is gaining by using insecticides what is he losing? The natural process plants use to ward off insects is slow but it actually has health benefits for us as humans. The components that a plant creates to drive off insects are the same components that comprise our nutrition. These components can also affect the flavor of some foods. Insects, plants, the soil and the environment work synergistically for the health of us all. When we take insects out of the equation with insecticides we literally make our food less nutritious thus making the environment and those found in it less healthy.

The following list is the "dirty dozen" or the dozen most chemically applied and polluted foods either externally with insecticides and herbicides or internally with hormones and antibiotics. This list can be found many places with small variations. However, all lists agree that if you choose to not eat organic then try to at least choose these foods organically. So you know, Jennifer and I do not eat completely organic nor do we always eat all the below twelve items organically but we try. However, items #1 and #2 are an "organic –must" for us. The others we do as we can.

1. Meat: beef, pork, poultry
2. Dairy: milk, cheese, butter
3. Strawberries, raspberries, and cherries
4. Apples and pears
5. Tomatoes

6. Potatoes
7. Spinach and other greens including lettuce
8. Coffee
9. Peaches and nectarines
10. Grapes, especially imported
11. Celery
12. Bell Peppers: all varieties

With knowing why and how to eat organically, where do you need to shop? The grocery store of course. May I lend you a suggestion about your grocery store; whether you buy organically or not? Shop the perimeter instead of the middle aisles. The perimeter of the grocery store is where most fruits and vegetables and other fresh items are found. As soon as the middle aisles are entered, processed, packaged and refined foods are found. It is not that you can never enter the middle aisles but next time you are checking out at the grocery store take a moment and look in your grocery cart. The lack of perimeter aisle foods may amaze you. Maybe a good goal would be 75-80% perimeter; 20-25% middle aisle.

> "Today, modern food processors have learned how to trick our bodies and exploit our ancient instincts."
>
> - Jordan Rubin
> (Patient Heal Thyself 122)

What about why you eat? There are many reasons we eat. We eat because it's the beginning of the day, we eat because it is noon and we eat because it's the end of the day. We eat when alone and we eat in good company. We eat to celebrate and we eat to emotionally numb ourselves. Simply put, eating is tied to our culture. A question to ponder; has our culture changed the way we eat and if so, does it matter?

> We as humans are genetically programmed to eat a primitive diet like the one our ancestors ate. The primitive diet consists of simple nutrient-dense foods that are rich in vitamins, minerals, fiber, protein and essential fats. By contrast the modern diet is rich in calories, depleted of nutrients and overburdened with unhealthy kinds of fats. It includes an unprecedented amount of carbohydrates. The modern diet is the proverbial recipe for disaster. It is the foundation of many modern illnesses. (Rubin and Brasco 61)

If we are programmed to eat like our ancestors and it is seemingly healthier, what changed? Many things but it is interesting to note that "primitive people ate a variety of foods consisting mostly of fruits, vegetables, fish and lean meat" (Rubin and Brasco 67). And being hunter-gathers meant that people were not as sedentary as our modern culture. That alone also increased their health. As life became more civilized, as populations increased, as wild game was exploited, as people became less active, a profound shift occurred. Society moved from a hunter-gatherer lifestyle to an agrarian or farming lifestyle. This in and of itself is probably not a huge deal or even "bad". Technology is good. Science is good. Learning is good. But what happens next in the societal shift impacts generations to come.

People moved from farms to cities which meant food had to be shipped. And at the same time, population increased. These two items forced farmers to make more food and figure out a way to ship it long distances. "Farmers now use pesticides… cattle are fed antibiotics and growth hormones…Fruit is gas-ripened…the package food industry serves food with strange combinations of refined flour, hydrogenated oil, corn sweeteners and salt. Refining removes the nutritional value from grain. The machine age has had the effect of forcing upon people…the most gigantic food experiment ever attempted" (Rubin and Brasco 70). Have you ever considered that you were part of an experiment? I had not until I read those words. How has this experiment worked? Are we as a culture increasing in health and vitality or declining? Is the rise of disease in our country an alarm to us or do we think it is normal? To sum up this section, here are five points to consider:

- About 70% of the calories the average person eats come from foods that were not available in primitive times.
- The primitive diet was comprised of 30-40% protein, 20-30% carbohydrates and 30-50% fat. The modern diet in the United States is comprised of roughly 15% protein, 50% carbohydrates, and 35% fat.
- The majority of fats in the primitive diet came from healthy omega-3 fats and saturated fats from grass-fed animals and wild seafood. Most of the fat in the modern diet comes from omega-6 fats, hydrogenated oils loaded with trans-fats and saturated fats from grain-fed animals. (For an excellent resource on omega-3 and omega-6 fats read "Clinical Nutrition for pain, inflammation and tissue healing" by Dr. David Seaman)
- Primitive people obtained their carbohydrates from fruits and vegetables, not refined grains.
- No refined food is found in the primitive diet. That means no canned food, pasteurized milk products, white flour, refined sugar or hydrogenated vegetable oils.

At this point you may be asking yourself: Then how I am supposed to eat? For the purpose of Creating a Trinity Lifestyle, I advise following the plan toward the end of this book. Within this plan, there will be ideas, tips, recipes and other recommendations to help you. But for now, for the average person on any given day, look back – way back and enjoy the wisdom the hunter-gatherers. Do not over-complicate eating and remember the seven simple steps I gave toward the beginning of this chapter. Eat more fruits and veggies. Decrease the amount of simple carbohydrates (this includes whole grains) you consume. Avoid low fat foods. Decrease the amount of dairy. Drink more water. Eat lean, omega-3 rich meat and fish. Be active. There you have it, a simple approach for overall increased health. Why is it so hard? That question will hopefully be answered as you continue to read.

I have tried to show how our modern diet drastically differs from the primitive diet and with that comes the potential for decreased health and increased disease. You are probably thinking to yourself; we no longer live in pre-historic times, we are more educated, more knowledgeable, more technologically advanced and live longer. The questions to ask yourself are: (1) Does education and knowledge increase health? (2) Does technology increase health? (3) Does creating food guidelines increase health? Let me take a moment to shift from the primitive diet versus the modern diet to show you how even the U.S. Department of Agriculture (USDA) has changed within the last 20 years. The food pyramid that most people recognize was created in 1992, even though there were earlier guidelines. Have you stopped to ask yourself, does it represent good eating habits and if so, why? The 1992 food guide pyramid (Figure 2) "is unsafe and pro-inflammatory particularly as it relates to fatty acid imbalances...the pyramid may encourage...deficient diets and lead to an increased incidence of arteriosclerotic disease among other health related problems" (Seaman 101). If you look at this pyramid carefully, grains, although the type is not specified, have the most servings per day followed by veggies, fruits, dairy, meat and then fats. The problem is that this ratio sounds a lot like the modern day diet consisting of mainly carbohydrates and not much else. This also does not take into account the importance of healthy omega-3 fats and a host of other concerns including activity levels.

In 2005, the USDA re-vamped the food pyramid and called it MYPyramid (Figure 3) to make it more personal and appealing. What changed? Not as much as one would think. While activity level, portions, variety and moderation of food are addressed, the consumption of foods remained relatively the same with carbohydrates being the heaviest consumed making up almost 55-60% of the diet. "There is no evidence to support this arbitrary notion... Research suggests that man has historically consumed a diet that contained minimal grain products...and consumption of grain products as

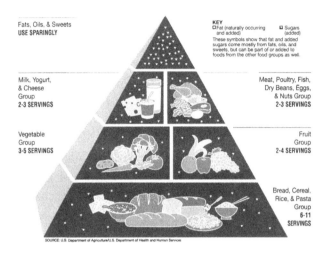

Figure 2: 1992 USDA Food Guide Pyramid

Figure 3: 2005 USDA MYPyramid

Figure 4: 2011 USDA MyPlate

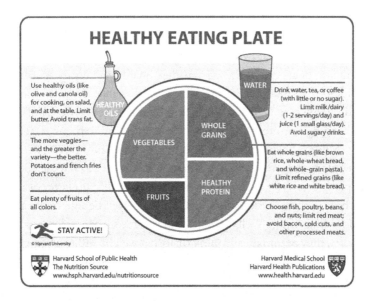

Figure 5: 2011 HSPH Health Eating Plate

the mainstay of the diet brings with it concerns" (Seaman 103). Most recently, in June 2011, the USDA once again changes its food recommendations. They moved from MYPyramid to MyPlate (Figure 4). This time even more has changed. No pyramid because the pictorial of a plate probably resonates with more people plus it is easier to understand. For the first time carbohydrates are not the largest group; vegetables are. Here is something else to consider. No matter what year you look at, 1992, 2005 or 2011, not once is water intake mentioned within the context of healthy eating?

As I was researching this topic, I found that the Harvard School of Public Health (HSPH) released 'The Healthy Eating Plate' (Figure 5) in September 2011. Here's why. "Unfortunately, like the earlier U.S. Department of Agriculture Pyramids, My-Plate mixes science with the influence of powerful agricultural interests, which is not the recipe for healthy eating," said Walter Willett, Professor of Epidemiology and Nutrition and chair of the Department of Nutrition at HSPH. "The Healthy Eating Plate is based on the best available scientific evidence and provides consumers with the information they need to make choices that can profoundly affect health and well being" (Datz). And if you look at the Healthy Eating Plate closely, it resembles the primitive diet more than the modern diet.

Two last thoughts as I close out this chapter. First, people have asked me if this book is about "doing a cleanse or detoxing the body?" It is in the sense that we need to look at our soil (our life), evaluate if it is healthy or unhealthy and then make appropriate changes as needed. However, with a cleanse or detox, the results are often short-term. My hope is that this book will help you make long-term changes that affect your life and the life of your family and friends. "Doctors working in environmental medicine believe that improving diet quality, taking measures to reduce stress and avoiding man-made chemicals whenever possible can help our body's detox system and enhance general health and well-being" (Scott-Moncrieff 12). So in other words, changing our lifestyle to improve our soil can help our system naturally detoxify, thus creating a balance of the mind, body and spirit.

Second, people constantly ask me what diet to follow. They have asked me if this book is a diet plan. Yes, it is a plan to enhance overall health; however, it is not a diet plan. It is much more broad and generous than that. I tell people to eat healthy and happy. What does that mean? Well, I hope I can show you. Most times, when people hear the word diet, they automatically think of losing weight and not being able to eat. That is not what I am proposing. While I am giving recipes and food ideas, I am not limiting the amount you eat; rather I am suggesting a change in the food you do eat. My role is not to limit you; my goal to release you into your full health potential. While weight loss may occur it is not a guarantee. The goal is healthy, deep, rich soil that creates abundant life giving fruit not just a smaller waist line. If you still feel a need to follow a specific diet plan; the question to ask is why and what is my goal? That will help determine what diet to follow. "Embarking on a healthy eating regimen in and of itself can be beneficial. It makes you pause and think about what you eat and how the food you eat affects your health. All diets provide some benefits in the short run, especially for those who previously ate a standard American diet. The problem is that the initial benefits are not sustained" (Rubin and Brasco 142). What I am suggesting is a way to eat, think and be better so that the benefits can and will be recognized for many years to come. You are what you eat…eat well to be well!

chapter 5

> "A crushing hurt comes and the sympathizing, scarred hand of Christ presses the wound; and just for a moment, the pain seems to intensify...but finally the bleeding stops."
>
> - Beth Moore

inflammation:
pain and so much more

t is my oldest son Eilam's first swimming lesson. Jennifer is by herself as I am at a meeting. About an hour into my meeting I get a phone call. Eilam and Jennifer are on their way to Linc-Care (an emergency walk-in type health care clinic). What had happened? Eilam had jumped off the side of the pool while Jennifer was not watching and his chin struck her forehead. He immediately began screaming at a dazed Jennifer and then they saw blood. His chin and to a lesser extent Jennifer's forehead were bleeding. What ensued…the inflammatory process.

While growing up in the South one thing you learn is that people eat a variety of food. From giblets, to hog-jaw, to alligator, all is on the table; literally! One time I tried frog-legs. Yep, you guessed it, they tasted like chicken. We were at a seafood restaurant and I must have been around 10 years old. I had eaten them with no problem. However, that night and into the next morning there occurred a huge problem; I had food poisoning. The frog-legs had been under-cooked. What ensued…the inflammatory process.

During my younger years, I would often travel with friends to sports tournaments or other events. It was great fun; we would all travel on a bus and stay at a fancy hotel. In reality, it was not that fancy but at my age, what did I know? Fancy meant a pool, hot tub and halls to run in. At one of those many events we traveled to; a friend and I were walking down the stairs to load up on the bus. An older adult met us on the stairs. He stopped to talk to us. He then did the un-thinkable. He got really close to me which backed me into the corner of the stair case. He put one hand on my chest and with his other hand "touched my private area." I stood there in shock not knowing what to do. He stopped and then said something. I cannot remember what he said but I said nothing. My friend and I never mentioned it again. It all happened in less than 2 minutes but it seemed like an hour. We walked down the stairs and got on the bus. What ensued…the inflammatory process.

Before I begin, let me give the reader some encouragement. You already know much about inflammation because you deal with it every day. Medically, inflammation is the biological and physiological response to tissue injury. You will recognize it as '*-itis.*' For example, arthritis is inflammation of the joints. Hepatitis is inflammation of the liver. The problem with these names is that they do not address what is causing the inflammation. It is wonderful to know something is inflamed but what is the cause? Practically speaking, inflammation causes heat, swelling, redness and pain. And yes, we have all experienced this. A sprained ankle is a great example.

Inflammation is normally characterized as acute or chronic. However, "we should not limit our understanding of inflammation to the point where we characterize it merely as the body's response to injury. The inflammatory process is actually the healing process. Without inflammation, tissue healing could not take place. It is chronic inflammation that is always destructive…" (Seaman 37). For clarification and practical purposes, it is easier to categorize inflammation into three phases. I will not attempt to explain every phase in detail as entire textbooks are devoted to that topic. Phase 1 can be called the acute inflammatory phase. It begins from initial injury and lasts up to 72 hours (3 days). This phase has a wide array of physiological and neurological responses that start the healing process. "Whatever the trauma [think of the three stories I started this chapter with]…the initial biological response is a generalized non-tissue-specific inflammatory response" (Seaman 38). Phase 2 can be called the repair phase. It can last from 48 hours to 6 weeks. Phase 3, the final phase, can be called the remodeling phase. "The outcome of the acute inflammatory process should be repair and remodeling of the injured tissues. In certain instances, acute inflammation does not resolve and a state of chronic inflammation develops" (Seaman 37). It is this chronic inflammatory state that is the basis of every disease we know excluding congenital defects (birth defects) and even then some would argue that the mother's inflammatory state contributed. Furthermore, besides unresolved acute inflammation, chronic inflammation can be proliferated by a wide array of other causes (see Figure 6).

As you can see from Figure 6, if the normal neurophysiological response does not happen or is impaired chronic inflammation can result. (Note: this can happen for a host of reasons not to be discussed here because it deals with a vascular response and a cellular response). As complicated as that may sound, let me try to give you an example you may understand. When you cut your finger, the acute inflammatory process occurs. The blood clot formation and scab that results is the vascular and cellular response. What if that response did not work, the wound would not heal, infection may occur and it could become chronic and systemic (whole body).

How do we treat inflammation? The old thinking was R.I.C.E. which stands for rest, ice, compression and elevation. The more modern version of this is M.I.C.E. which stands for movement, ice, compression and elevation. Research and patient testimonies have proven that slow, controlled movement is best for healing. Is that all we do to treat inflammation? Of course it isn't. We use ice bags, heat packs, rice

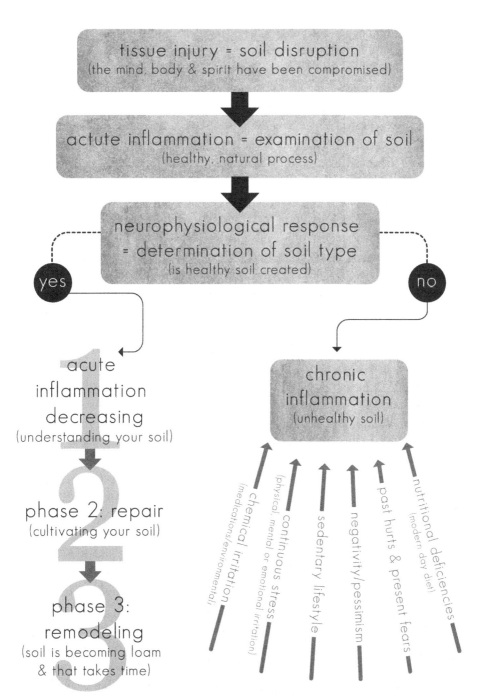

Figure 6: Inflammation

bags, therapeutic patches and many other devices to try to help. (Note: Ice is best used for acute injuries. Moist heat can be used after 48-72 hours). We go to MD's, PT's, DC's, DO's, PhD's and ND's to seek advice. We take over the counter medications like candy – particularly NSAIDs (non-steroidal anti-inflammatory drugs). We down prescriptions of steroids, muscle relaxers and pain inhibitors. We get injections of narcotic-grade drugs and we have surgeries. We take vitamins and natural supplements in hopes that it will help. The point is we do much to stop inflammation, especially chronic inflammation, but do we ever change our lifestyle habits that may be a major contributor to the problem in the first place? As we learned above, the chronic inflammatory state leads to decreasing states of health. Trust me; I am not saying that at times, NSAIDs, prescription medications, injections or even surgeries are not needed. They are necessary at times and I have referred numerous patients for these interventions. I, myself, will pop an Advil to help alleviate a headache even if I know the headache has been brought on by my lack of stretching or lack of hydration. Let's be honest, many times it just seems easier. But easier is not the point when it comes to increasing health and stopping chronic inflammation.

Let me take a moment to discuss briefly the most common medications and natural supplements that we take to stop inflammation. This is by no means an exhaustive list however it may help you to understand what you are taking and why.

1. Aspirin & NSAIDs: NSAIDs include Advil, Motrin, Nuprin, Naprosyn and many more. These are thought to help decrease inflammation by blocking prostaglandin and thromboxane production. (For simplification – prostaglandins and thromboxane are pain producers). Chronic use of NSAIDs creates inflammation by changing GI permeability. Side effects may include the interference of bone repair, stomach and small intestine damage. According to Clinical Nutrition for pain, inflammation and tissue healing by Dr. Seaman, 10,000-20,000 deaths occur each year from NSAID-induced ulcer complications.

2. Acetaminophen: Tylenol. This has both pain relieving and fever reducing abilities. There is debate in the research community whether or not this truly helps pain but it seems to block prostaglandin production to a certain extent. The main side effect of prolonged use is liver damage.

3. Corticosteroids: The most common is prednisone but there are many more. These powerfully limit inflammation however they lower the immunological response (the body's ability to fight off chronic illness). "Corticosteroids have a much greater effect on autoimmune disorders but can be beneficial in chronic pain syndromes. Side effects may include avascular necrosis (tissue

death), alteration of ligaments, vertebral osteoporosis and fractures" (Seaman 63).

4. Muscle Relaxers: Examples are baclofen, diazepam (Valium), Flexoril, Skelaxin and many more. These work by inhibiting the central nervous system thus affecting the skeletal muscle. Side effects include drowsiness, dizziness, weakness and mental confusion.

5. Opiates: The most common are morphine and codeine and there are many more. These work specifically by activating the descending pain modulating system with the central nervous system. (That is a fancy way of saying they stop the pain at the brain). Side effects may include mood swings, nausea, vomiting, respiratory depression, itching and much more.

6. Boswellia: A powerful natural anti-inflammatory. The botanical name is Boswellia Serrata. The resin from this tree/shrub is frankincense. Many studies have shown that the boswellic acid has the same anti-inflammatory properties as NSAIDs without the irritation to the stomach.

7. Ginger/Turmeric: Both ginger and turmeric have been used for centuries in India for their anti-inflammatory properties. Both seem to block prostaglandin production like NSAIDs without the serious side-effects.

8. Bioflavinoids: Also called flavinoids. These are the most important plant pigment for the coloration. They have long been valued for their anti-oxidant properties and also have anti-inflammatory properties by blocking prostaglandin production. Fruits and vegetables are the best source. Minimal side-effects if any.

9. EPA/DHA (Fish Oil): Also called omega-3 or essential fatty acids. Much research has and continues to be carried out on this supplement. It has been shown to help overall health but for the topic of this discussion, it helps decrease inflammation by blocking the production of arachidonic acid (the pre-cursor to pain producing cell mediators) without the side effects of corticosteroids.

I could mention more medications and natural supplements, but the point is no matter which one you take, the goal is to stop inflammation, thus stopping pain. Yes pain. Many times, any or all of the above are taken to prevent pain, not necessarily disease. To live healthy is not to just be out of pain, it is much more than that. See Figure 7 which shows the process of our unhealthy soil (chronic inflammation) becoming healthy soil (decreasing inflammation).

Since most people take anti-inflammatory medications to stop a headache, backache, stomachache, etc...(aka – pain); it would be wise for us to understand a little

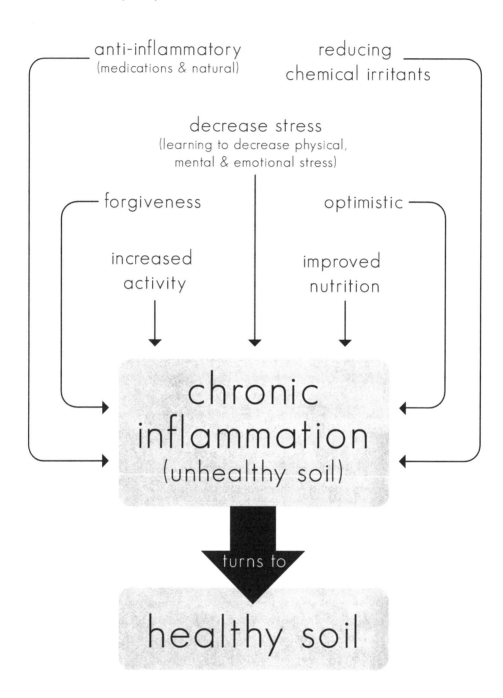

Figure 7: Decreasing Inflammation

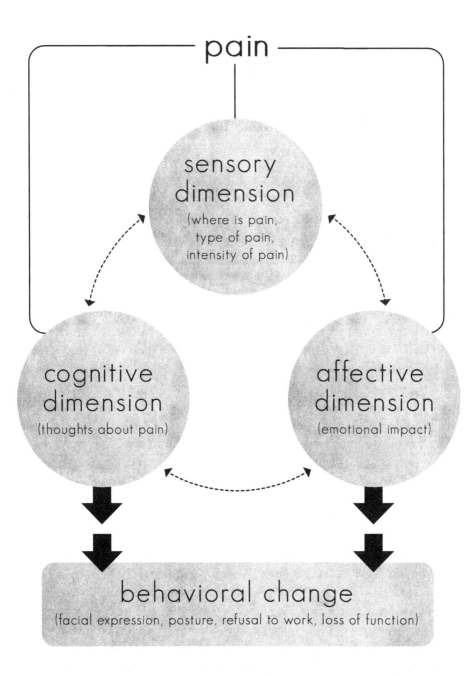

Figure 8: Three Dimensions of Pain
(Pitt-Brooke and Reid 198)

more about pain. The simple and superficial definition of pain is that something hurts. This is the number one reason why people go to the doctor. But looking a little deeper, pain can be divided into three dimensions: (1) Cognitive: thoughts about pain. This dimension is how you perceive the pain to be; good, bad, or indifferent. (2) Sensory: being aware of where the pain is coming from and its intensity. This is the dimension most people are aware of and where treatment is directed. (3) Affective: this is the understanding that for every pain there is an emotional reaction to that pain experience. "Pain (the sensory dimension) to a lesser or great degree alters the way we think (the cognitive dimension) and the way we feel (the affective dimension)" (Pitt-Brooke and Reid 199).

Let's return to how I started this chapter. When Eilam hit his chin (and his mom's head), he immediately knew where the pain was coming from. He had thoughts about the pain and that affected his behavior. Beyond that, his affective dimension also affected Jennifer thus affecting her cognitive dimension. When I got food poisoning, my sensory dimension of pain knew something was wrong. This, in turn, affected my thoughts about that pain and the experience that caused me to have the pain. I have not eaten frog legs since this first experience. When I was molested (never said it that way before, hmmm?), I may not have felt a physical pain however an emotional pain was felt; something was just not right. That affected my cognitive dimension producing shame, thus leading me to tell no one about the experience (affective dimension). Pain (the inflammatory process) affects everyone at some point. How much depends on the painful experience.

Let me give you one more example that may help further. Two people, a construction worker and a concert violinist, get the same paper cut on the same finger. Whom is affected most and why? Both people experience the pain, both people have the same initial inflammatory process however both have different emotional reactions to the painful experience. The construction worker notices the cut, wipes the blood on his pants and continues his day. The pain barely affects him. The concert violinist notices the cut, gently wipes the blood away and his finger (possibly the entire hand) throbs with an aching pain. What is the difference? The cognitive dimension and how that affects the affective dimension. Can you imagine the construction worker telling his foreman he could not work because of a paper cut? Of course not! But a paper cut very well could influence the outcome of a concert violinist's performance. "The crucial message here is that our thoughts and feelings strongly influence biological processes and that has powerful repercussions" (Pitt-Brooke and Reid 200). Figure 8 shows what I have explained above. Pain (resulting from the inflammatory process) is real and how we deal with it matters. Thus, do we just treat the symptoms with interventions or do we try to understand the cause – that is a question we must answer if we are to be truly healthy.

chapter 6

posture:
a snapshot of health

am not a shopper; occasionally I will go to the mall with Jennifer. As she is shopping, I watch people. There are so many people of different shapes, sizes, and colors. The array of color and beauty astonishes me. People are having conversations, kids are crying and all the while, their posture is speaking volumes to me. That person's head is forward; I wonder if they have headaches. That person's shoulders are rounded; I wonder if they have mid-back pain. That person's right arm does not swing as far as the left when they walk; I wonder if they have had a shoulder injury. That person's right foot is turned outward and their back is arched; I wonder if they have hip or low back pain. That person will not make eye contact with anyone; I wonder what has happened. Make no mistake posture speaks; what is it saying? You just sat up a little straighter, didn't you?

"Normal spinal posture helps reduce strain. Unfortunately, our modern lifestyles, in concert with forces of gravity, conspire to ruin our healthy upright posture" (Liebenson 176). What is good and normal posture? Textbooks will tell you normal posture is when you sit or stand up straight, facing forward with the ears slightly in front of your shoulders, shoulders in line with your hips and ankles. Look around, do you see anyone like that? This normal ideal posture rarely translates to real life. To me, good posture is when the spine and muscles work synergistically to provide the best support. However, this does not come from slouching all day nor does it comes from sitting "straight as a board" either. The best posture is a dynamic posture, meaning, movement creates a dynamic tension that helps stabilize. Sit up straight some, slouch a little, cross one leg then the other, stand up some and by all means - move. Do not misunderstand me, I am not stating that slouching is good for your health but when people speak of slouching they are thinking of "bad posture" not a dynamic posture that creates health by movement.

In his book Rehabilitation of the Spine: A Practitioner's Manual, Craig Liebenson, says:

> We are born in the fetal position with our spines rounded forward. As we
> grow, our spine extends both in the lower back and in the neck, which allows
> us to walk upright, look straight ahead and use our hands. Unfortunately,

> modern occupations and lifestyles, by overusing sitting positions in cars, while eating, watching television, and working at computers, have imbalanced our posture. (Liebenson 177)

To say it a different way, we sit too much. What I (and others) call this is a flexion dominant posture. Take a typical day. You and I (and most people actually) sleep on their side curled up in the fetal position (flexion). You then get up and sit at the table or couch eating breakfast, reading the paper or watching the news (flexion). You drive to work (flexion). You sit at a desk (flexion). You drive home (flexion). You sit to eat at dinner and then on the couch to watch TV (flexion). Then, back to bed for some more, you guessed it, flexion. And there you have a typical day for the majority of people – flexed all day = flexion dominant posture. The question to ask yourself is does that matter? The answer is a resounding yes!

Flexion dominant posture (Figure 9) causes a wide-array of health problems from headaches, shoulder pain, back pain, shortness of breath, fatigue and much more. Think about it. Flexion dominant posture causes the head to go forward, shoulders to round, mid-back to round causing potential compression of the diaphragm and lung cavity, low back and pelvis to change position not to mention knee and foot positions. This posture further creates muscle imbalances. Initially described by Vladimir Janda, "muscle imbalance does not remain limited to a certain part of the body but gradually involves the whole" (Liebenson 97). Two imbalances worth mentioning are Upper Crossed Syndrome and Lower Crossed Syndrome. Upper crossed syndrome involves the upper part of the body (head, neck, shoulders). It creates rounded shoulders, forward head, shoulder elevation and shoulder blade winging. This will cause tight chest muscles, tight upper trapezius muscle and levator scapulae muscle (lower neck muscles), tight suboccipals (upper neck muscle) plus weak lower to middle trapezius (middle back muscles). Other muscles are also involved but these are the major players. Lower crossed syndrome involves the lower part of the body (low back, hip and legs). It creates low back arching, a forward titled pelvis, protruding abdomen and a turned out foot. This will cause tight hip flexors (muscle in front of the upper thigh), tight low back muscles (erector spinae), tight external hip rotators plus weak glutes (butt muscles) and abs. These imbalances matter and can create long term health problems.

Posture even effects breathing. Let's try two experiments to learn how. First, slouch over and take a deep breath. Now, sit up straighter and take a deep breath. Did you notice the difference? Second, while sitting, find a good posture, not too slouched and not too straight, where you feel comfortable and relaxed. Place your right hand

. Figure 9: Flexion Dominant Posture

on your chest. Place your left hand on your belly. Take a deep breath. Which hand moved? The hand on your chest should not move or move only minimally. When you take a deep breath, your belly should go out allowing the lungs and diaphragm to expand. This is proper breathing. Because of flexion dominant posture and the resulting muscle imbalances, we tend to be "chest breathers." As you chest breathe, the shoulders elevate and neck muscles become tense. The fact is, posture affects our breathing and as our breathing is affected so is every physiological process in our body. How? Well, breathing brings in vital oxygen that is carried throughout our body to help release or store energy. This is not only important from an external daily activity perspective but also from an internal body processing perspective. Furthermore, this internal and external change affects more than the physical body, much more.

It should be fairly obvious how posture affects our physical body, what about our mind and spirit? Remember when I spoke about the three dimensions of pain, the cognitive and affective dimensions both led to behavioral changes with one of the major changes being posture. Pain affects posture. Sickness affects posture. Mental or physical abuse affects posture. Think about it. When you are sick or not feeling well, does your posture change? Absolutely. When you are mad or upset, does your posture change? Absolutely. Many times a flexion dominant posture ensues. I had a patient recently that would not look me in the eye. She had rounded shoulders; her head was looking down and overall depressive posture. After much probing, I found out this patient had been verbally abused for years. No physical abuse, yet her physical body manifested with a postural change that spoke volumes to anyone willing to listen. The question is, are you (and I) willing to listen to what our body is telling – many times screaming at us?

Posture tells a bigger story than we have been led to believe. Posture gives a clue to what may be going on in the mind, body and spirit. Posture is affecting your health but the questions to ask are: (1) Why do I have the posture I have? (2) What habits at work or home have contributed? (3) What are ways I can make small adjustments in my posture that will make the most impact? Once you have identified the answers to these questions, you are on the way to having a dynamic posture that will build and extend your health for years to come.

chapter 7

> Adopting the right attitude
> can convert a negative stress
> into a positive one.
> *- Hans Selye*

stress influences everything

L ook in the mirror or look at the people around you; what do you see? Do you see a Trinity Lifestyle or do you see a lifestyle of stress? What do I mean by a lifestyle of stress? It is a lifestyle that is constantly running from here to there, grabbing whatever food it can to survive, barely getting any sleep and many times relational problems abound. This may seem far-fetched, sadly it is not. Many people walk around with a lifestyle of stress that is slowly killing them. A patient I recently encountered proved this to be true. Theresa (name changed) is in the military and presented to my office with headaches and neck pain. She said the pain came from sitting all day. I asked her about her stress level and she said it was great; she thrived on it. She loved being busy and the stress of the job and the stress of the deadlines and the stress of being the only female in her office. Upon further questioning, she did not really thrive on the stress. It was just her made-up preconception to help herself cope with the daily pressure. She was trying to keep up and trying to prove herself good enough. After the underlying issue surfaced, I looked at Theresa and simply told her that she no longer had to prove anything and God loved her for her. She looked at me and started crying. All that stress was a cloud hanging over her head. The tears were a release of that cloud. By recognizing that stress was a problem, Theresa is now doing much better, with not only her headaches but life. She is starting to cultivate a Trinity Lifestyle instead of a lifestyle of stress.

We all have stress and we all encounter stressors everyday; from the food we eat to the TV we watch to the drive home. Stress is ever present. So the question is: How do we deal with it? Hans Selye, MD, known as the Father of Stress, wrote, "Mental tensions, frustrations, insecurity, aimlessness are among the most damaging stressors, and psychosomatic studies have shown how often they cause migraine headache, peptic ulcers, heart attacks, hypertension, mental disease, suicide, or just hopeless unhappiness. **It's not stress that kills us; it is our reaction to it**" (Selye). Did you catch that? Stress does not kill; it's how you handle it over time that does. It is our choice to what extent the stressors affect us. For instance, we have learned that certain foods can stress the internal environment of our body. If we know that and still choose to eat that food, it is our choice to introduce that stressor to our system. Likewise, we encounter stressful situations everyday and as we continue to stay in stressful environments or introduce stressors to our body, stress becomes chronic, leading to disease. This chronicity of stress is not supposed to be or cannot be handled by our body. Let me explain a little further. To distinguish, we can break stress down into eustress (good stress) and distress (bad stress). If persistent stress decreases function or mental ability, whatever the cause, this is known as distress and may lead to anxiety or withdrawal (depression) behavior. In contrast, if the stress involved enhances function (physical or mental, such as through strength training or challenging work) it may be considered eustress. However, please know that what may be eustress for one person can be distress for another and vice versa. This is why stress affects each person uniquely and individually. As that stress affects us individually, it most definitely affects our family and community. Moreover, the human body cannot distinguish physiologically the difference between eustress and distress. Our bodies (actually all mammals) are meant to handle stress in short periods not prolonged periods. This neurological handling of stress is called our "fight or flight" mechanism. It was first discovered by Walter B. Cannon. His theory states "that animals react to threats with a general discharge of the sympathetic nervous system, priming the animal for fighting or fleeing," And if those stressors are prolonged for whatever reason, it can start a cascade of destruction that leads to multiple disease processes. Breaking down the nervous system (very simply and brief) a little further, there is the (1) Sympathetic Nervous System (SNS): This regulates the flight or fight response. It is sometimes called the adrenaline rush response and (2) Parasympathetic Nervous System (PNS): This regulates the rest and digestive response. Ideally the SNS responds when we encounter a stressful situation to help and then turns off allowing the PNS to take over. These opposing yet complementary systems are supposed to work in concert with one another allowing the body to handle stressful encounters.

Let me make it a little simpler: A zebra is grazing in the open prairie enjoying the grass, not worrying about anything. Then from the corner of its eye, it spots a lion crouching. The zebra immediately reacts (a general discharge from the SNS) priming itself to either flee or fight. This response leads to increased blood volume being pumped from the heart into the extremities, respiration increases and digestion slows. This promotes survival. If the zebra is not caught and eaten by the lion, once out of harm, immediately the body responses return to normal (PNS takes over). That is how the neurological handling of stress should occur. We have a stressor – our body responds appropriately - then returns to normal after the stressor has subsided. The problem in humans is that many times the stressor never resolves, thus our body is not able to return to normal. We keep thinking the same negative thoughts, we keep eating the same nutrient void food, we keep participating in the same unhealthy activities and we never stop "running from the lion" even if it is not chasing us anymore. Another way to say it is, we live in a hyper-sympathetic state where our fight or flight mechanism is always going. We never allow the PNS to help and we never slow down so we can return to normal. And as we continue to run and run and run; as we continue to fret and worry, our body is becoming increasingly unhealthy.

Moreover, I find it very interesting that 1 Peter 5:8 states, "Be alert and of sober mind. Your enemy the devil prowls around like a roaring lion looking for someone to devour." Hmmm? Was it just a coincidence that God would choose to say the enemy is like a lion? Doubtful since he knows our physiology and how we react to "the lion." Listen, your life is short; it is but a vapor. You have 86,400 seconds per day. Why would you want to spend them in a hyper-sympathetic state running from a "prowling lion" that has already been defeated. Be alert and look at the stressors in your life. Be sober minded and honestly evaluate how to reduce them. Please stop running, fretting, worrying, anxiously living in a sympathetic state. Take a breath. Enjoy the 86,400 seconds you have every day and allow your body to return to normal.

> "It's not stress that kills us; it is our reaction to it."
>
> - Hans Selye

chapter 8

> The love of family and
> the admiration of friends are
> much more important than
> wealth and privilege.
> - *Charles Kuralt*

family and community

A s I start this chapter, I wonder how qualified I am to write about family relationships from parenting and marriage to community relationships. All of these have a huge, possibly the greatest, impact on our soil (aka. lifestyle). I have read numerous books about parenting, fathering and marriage relationships from "experts" in their respective fields. These authors are much more insightful in areas that I have only begun to see. This chapter is in no way trying to be an exhaustive parenting, family and marriage text. Rather, it is an honest discussion how our relationships in these areas affect each of our lives in positive and negative ways. At the time I am writing, I have been married fifteen years, have three children, two businesses, two homes (one is a rental property because I could not sell it) plus we have a couple living with us (our housemates we call them). You see, I have had some experience in marriage, in parenting, in business and other community relationships yet I am still learning much – it would seem daily and even hourly I am learning. As I write this chapter, you, the reader, need to know: (1) I am not advocating one parenting style over another. (2) I do not know your unique circumstance, which may or may not dictate your family/community relationships. (3) I believe family and community matter. How you were raised and what community you grew up within does affect your soil. The question is how and (4) If you are single, do not skip this chapter. Although you may not think it applies to your life right now, it does.

Marriage

"Love is patient, love is kind. It does not envy, it does not boast, it is not proud. It is not rude, it is not self-seeking, it is not easily angered, and it keeps no record of wrongs. Love does not delight in evil but rejoices with the truth. It always protects, always trusts, always hopes, and always perseveres" (1 Corinthians 13:4-7). Does that type of love express your marriage? It should as it is read at most weddings (Christian or not). We allow someone to read these words over our newly married life; do we stop and consider what they mean? I can say, without a doubt, I did not. What if we said this in our marriage vow instead? "My love will often be unkind, boastful, rude, self-serving and I will know when I have been wrong. My love will try to protect myself. My love hopefully can be trusted but if it gets too hard; it may not persevere." That is more of the truth, isn't it? Our love is conditional based on our expectations and presumptions. Love is not conditional; love is a choice. And in that choice, love becomes so much more.

I have been married 15 years and I have only scraped the surface of what it means to be a married man. I do know that marriage is a high calling. In Christian-hood, marriage is held high and rightly so. From the beginning of Genesis to the end of Revelation, God speaks of the marriage with purpose and passion. God even parallels the love of Christ as the love of a bridegroom and the church as a bride. "How beautiful you are my darling! Oh, how beautiful…how handsome you are, my beloved! Oh, how charming…" (Song of Solomon 1:15-16). Words like that and many more express the love of a bridegroom and bride and that of Christ and the church. I love the passion that Christ, the bridegroom, has for the church, his bride. That passion is what ignites a man and woman to seek and pursue each other. It is a passionate love affair for the ages. Better than any Romeo and Juliet; better than any romance novel or movie, is the all-consuming love of a husband and wife. It is powerful. It is life-changing. It is creative and ever evolving. That is love.

What about sex before marriage? Ever heard the saying, "Gotta try it before you buy it." I heard this multiple times growing up from older males. The reference was of course to have sex before marriage so you can see if you "really like" the person. What a complete lie! What else is a complete lie is that God just does not want you to have fun so you cannot have sex. Where does it say that? I heard it said from the pulpit that sex is not permitted outside the marriage but no further explanation why. I believe the reason God in His infinite wisdom desires a monogamous sexual relationship within marriage is because He knows the beauty of intimacy. Both Jennifer and I had sex before marriage and trust me; emotional and spiritual baggage can be associated with that. Whether comparisons happen, false expectations or just a loss of marital intimacy – sex before marriage "steals" something from your future husband and/or wife. However, I believe the church has misled (unknowingly) many young people to think if they wait until they are married; the marriage night is going to be great and awesome. It is wonderful but the sex may not be that great and that can lead to a frustration if you have waited for this "great sexual experience." Often that frustration increases if either party has viewed pornography (in any of its forms) and thinks what they saw is normal. It is not normal. It is a violation of both the men and women. The point of waiting or as some call it – saving yourself, is not that the first sexual encounter is wonderful (although it may be) but rather it is to give yourself fully to your spouse so both of you can grow in emotional, spiritual and sexual intimacy. To me that is the beauty of waiting and the genius of God's plan – a lifetime of learning and lovemaking with your spouse that grows, matures and becomes more intimate and wonderful.

Covenant or contract? Covenant is defined as a confirmation of promise, a binding, intentional agreement with purpose. Contract is defined as an agreement between two parties. If you look at your intent when you got married, was it a covenant or contract? For me, I entered marriage with a contract mentality and the kicker; I did not even know it. Although commitment is technically a synonym for both covenant and contract, when considering the difference, a covenant speaks to something much deeper. A contract seems superficial and easily negotiable when things may not go as we like them. I think this may be why couples that live together before marriage are missing a key ingredient to making the relationship work, the marriage covenant. A mindset that says I am committed no matter what, a mindset that is about the whole versus the individuals. At best these types of arrangements are a contract and at worst a loss of intimacy and friendship. I am not speaking against anyone who lives together before marriage but not living in covenant can make it easy to part ways when things do not work out. So, why do many marriages fall apart? Is it just because the couple perceived a contract? Of course not.

> "A person standing alone can be attacked and defeated, but two can stand back-to-back and conquer. Three are even better, for a triple-braided cord is not easily broken."
>
> - *Ecclesiastes 4:12*

> Some say that marriages fail because of lack of commitment. Some say the problem is that couples today lack a proper spiritual foundation. Others say the root of the problem is that couples are simply not willing to sacrifice. Regardless the reason, the demise or success of a marriage can almost always be traced to the first year of the marriage. (DeVries 17)

Look at it from the viewpoint of soil. In your backyard, you decide to plant a garden in a new area of the yard. Since this soil has never been touched before you have no idea what type it is or how to cultivate it. So, in your hopes to have a successful garden, the soil is left alone. You throw seeds out sporadically, allow weeds to grow and do nothing to tend, prune or cultivate the soil thus the seeds you plant may or may not produce fruit. You sacrifice little for the garden you want. After 3, 5 or 7 years later, you are disgusted at the garden because it is not satisfying or producing fruit. The assumption: that soil was no good and you decide to try the soil somewhere else; thinking other soil has to be better. That seems like a silly illustration because we would never think of doing that to the garden soil but we do it to the "marriage soil" all the time. "The seeds of failure planted in the first year of marriage are seeds that over time grow strong enough to corrode commitment" (DeVries 18). As that commitment corrodes so does the marriage. "Your marriage and your life are going to be a hundred times more satisfying, more resilient and more prosperous if you intentionally develop the right habits the first year" (DeVries 18). Developing and cultivating your soil in the first year is important; what if you are past the first year? What if the seeds of failure have already been sown? Even if they have and even if it has been 10, 20 or 30 years, would you be willing to take a moment and look back at the first year and see how you cultivated your soil and what seeds you planted? Maybe you never understood the soil or maybe you planted the wrong seeds or maybe you never took time to cultivate the soil you had. Figure it out then humbly ask for forgiveness if needed or possibly forgive if wronged. Then, make today the start of another first year. As cliché as it is, today is the first day of the rest of your life. It is your choice. Choose to love. Choose to forgive. Choose covenant.

Let me tell you a story. As a husband, I am about to blow my wife away and score some serious points. Even though we are at the beach with my family, I cannot wait to get back home and surprise Jennifer. For months, I have listened to her talk about colors for each room, how she would like the colors to flow and what type of bathroom tile she likes. For months, I have re-visited each room with her just to see if what I think she says is actually what she said. I have coordinated it all; I have a friend (someone Jennifer trusts) who is leading the painting team, directing them, picking all the paint and tile out. The day arrives and we leave for vacation. We will be gone for 1 week. They have 1 week to paint the entire outside of the house, add columns, build a bunk bed, tile the bathroom floor and paint the inside of the house (excluding 2 rooms and the basement). A big project for 1 week however they assure me it can be done. We pull into the driveway and Luis and Crystal meet us outside with a video camera to catch Jennifer's reaction. She was shocked. The house no longer looked the same. So much had changed, maybe too much. Jennifer seemed happy enough about the surprise. Two days after we got back I asked her a straightforward question, "Are you happy I did that for you? Do you like it?" She then just looked at me and said, "Not really." That was not the answer I was expecting. What do you mean you do not like it? I went to all this trouble for you! All I was thinking about was you! I was mad and hurt. I literally left the house and went for a walk. We did not talk for a few hours after that. Once I was able to chat with her I realized the heart behind the matter. She did like the fact that I would go to all that trouble and even liked most of the work however she felt like I stole her home from her because she had no say in the colors, planning, etc. I told her for months I listened to her and asked her many times what colors. She said that was not the same. If she would have known, how much more excited could she have been. Plus how could I spend that amount of money without considering her? Okay, she had me there. This surprise ended up teaching me a valuable lesson. And it is not to ever surprise my wife, rather what does it mean to love her well. I thought I loved Jennifer well by giving her such a big surprise but when I asked her if that loved her well, she said, no, you love me the way you think I need to be loved. And husbands, that is a big difference. Jennifer said, "In this instance, loving me well would have been to take me to the store and let me shop for colors, for bathroom tile; to look through magazines to see what I like. You just did it to get the job done." Jennifer was not being rude just honest. And in that honesty, I understood. Prior to this surprise, I had often said, "I want to love my wife well." And in thinking I was doing that, many times I was not. Yes I loved her however not specific to the way she needed to be loved. If I were honest, I did not (and still do not) want to go shopping for paint and bathroom tile. By me doing it all, it was easier, faster and the job was completed. But there is one major problem with that; I felt pretty good about myself as a husband for accomplishing a task and loving my wife however my wife felt left out and un-loved. Wow, I have much to learn about how to love my wife. And that learning is part of the marriage journey.

People speak different love languages just as people speak different real languages. Think about how frustrating and ineffective it is to speak English as your primary language if your audience is Chinese. The audience will have no idea what you are attempting to say even if you think you are communicating it really well. "In the area of love, it is similar. Your emotional love language and the language of your spouse may be as different as Chinese from English. No matter how hard you try to express love in English, if your spouse only understands Chinese, you will never know how to love each other" (Chapman 14-15). That is what happened (and still happens) to Jennifer and me. I was speaking love in English and she needed me to speak love in Chinese. And you know what, I do not know Chinese but I can learn it; it will take time and effort and I know it will be worth it.

> Seldom do a husband and wife speak the same primary love emotional language. We tend to speak our primary love language and become confused when our spouse does not understand what we are communicating. We are expressing our love but the message does not come through, because to

them, we are speaking a foreign language. Therein lies the fundamental problem. (Chapman 15-16)

So you have a reference point, the five love languages as defined by Gary Chapman, author of The Five Love Languages, are (1) words of affirmation (2) quality time (3) receiving gifts (4) acts of service and (5) physical touch. These five "languages" are the way people receive love. For instance, all of my "acts of service" for Jennifer did not make her feel loved. What makes Jennifer feel loved is when I spend "quality time" with her. A husband once told me that his wife feels most loved when he gives her gifts — even when it is as small as a hand written note. Most married couples do not have the same love language. Jennifer and I do not have the same love language. If I am to love Jennifer well, I need to learn (and continually learn) her primary love language. If I know her love language, my ability to communicate clearly and effectively will be exponentially greater. And in that, I can begin to love my spouse well. It will also help to understand my primary love language because what happens most often is that we love our spouse in the way that we feel most loved. Another way to say it: We love others in our primary love language, not theirs. Let me mention one other piece of advice about the love languages. Communication clearly crosses the line to every arena of your life. In order to nor be frustrated, learn another person's love language so you can communicate, whether that person is your child or your co-worker.

My last thought about marriage before I leave this section is about a portion of scripture that I think speaks to the heart of every marriage. However, I think it has also been abused and the cause for much debate and honestly why I think many people view Christian marriage as chauvinistic. The scripture is Ephesians 5:22-27:

> Wives, submit to your own husbands, as to the Lord. For the husband is the head of the wife even as Christ is the head of the church, his body, and is himself its Savior. Now as the church submits to Christ, so also wives should submit in everything to their husbands. Husbands, love your wives, as Christ loved the church and gave himself up for her, that he might sanctify her, having cleansed her by the washing of water with the word, so that he might present the church to himself in splendor, without spot or wrinkle or any such thing, that she might be holy and without blemish.

At first glance many say that this makes the man superior to women. Nothing could be further from the truth and that is not even close to the heart of God. A point to consider as you look at scripture or hear someone speak/write about it: One should never build a theology on one scripture or a section of scripture. The Bible must be taken as a whole. And if you look at the entirety of scripture, men are not superior to women. Do men and women have different roles? I think so. Think about it? What do most men want; respect. What do most women want; love. Let me briefly explain the word submit which may make it more digestible for some. A synonym for submit is acknowledge. So, when a wife submits to her husband, she is acknowledging him, but mostly she is showing him respect, which is what he wants/needs most. And know that submitting is not forced. You might be able to force someone to obey out of fear but the beauty of this verse is that the wife chooses to submit and in that choice love wins every time. A husband's call is to love as Christ loved the church. This means that the husband lays down his life for his wife. That nothing else – not work, not hobbies, not friends, nothing – takes precedent over his bride. I Peter 3:7 (NLV) states, "Likewise, husbands must give honor to your wives. Treat your wife with understanding as you live together...she is your equal partner in God's gift of new life." I have to wonder if husbands truly loved their wives like Christ loved the church, would wives have trouble submitting [acknowledging].

To sum this section up: Marriage is a journey with some bumps. Marriage is a covenant. Learn your spouse's primary love language so communication is easier and more effective. Husbands are to love their wives; wives are to respect their husbands. Love is a choice each moment of every day. Choose wisely.

Parenting

"Parenting is a lot like gardening. As a parent, you must find a way to set a fence around your garden with a gate. Then you must choose who comes in and goes out, so that you can protect your quality of life" (Silk 92). I want to guard my family's quality of life. And just like in a real garden that needs tending, cultivating, protecting and sometimes pruning, our "family garden" is no different. It needs attention, soil cultivation, protection and positive discipline. How does that happen? How do we set a boundary that seemingly changes with each season? How do we prune and protect all in the same day? It is called parenting; a topic that I feel inadequate to write about because in reality, I wonder many days if I have any clue as to what I am doing. There is no handbook for such a task although there have been numerous books written telling you the why's and how's and 1, 2, 3's of parenting. While there is much useful information to be gleaned from these books; the Bible gives the three best pieces of advice I can think of: (1) Proverbs 22:6, "Train a child in the way he should go and when he is old, he will not depart from it." I do not desire to debate this verse theologically as too many sides have built a case for themselves using this one verse. Let's keep it simple. Train your children. In order to do that you must first, be present; second, be engaged; third, be consistent. (2) Psalm 127:3-5, "Children are a heritage from the LORD…Like arrows in the hands of a warrior are children…Blessed is the man whose quiver is full of them." Children are a heritage and should be treated as such even as difficult as it is sometimes. A warrior is trained to be present, engaged and consistent. When a warrior points his arrow, he knows the intended target and shoots with conviction. Aim your children, release them with conviction and watch them hit their intended target. (3) Deuteronomy 11:18-20, "Fix these words of mine in your hearts and minds…Teach them to your children, talking about them when you sit at home and when you walk along the road, when you lie down and when you get up… Write them on the doorframes of your houses…" Do more than talk about living; let your children watch you live. Being present, being engaged and being consistent are choices. This choice can seem hard in the moment however if planted correctly, will cultivate soil that will multiply 30-60-100 fold.

The term "we choose to parent" came about per a conversation my wife and I had with our housemates and dear friends, Luis and Crystal Munoz. We chatted with them for some time one night about parenting, about marriage, about a host of things. A couple of days later, Luis told me he could not stop thinking of what Jennifer said in the midst of our conversation. I had no idea what it was so I asked. Luis replied, "Jen stated, that we choose to parent." Luis then explained how he had never thought about it that way; that many times, he and others put more "research hours" into choosing a car or cell phone than they do thinking about giving birth or even parenting. Why would we not think that we have to choose to parent as well? Once Luis told me this, we discussed it further. It really got me thinking about how we have chosen to parent and why.

> "The most urgent domestic challenge facing the United Sates at the close of the twentieth century is the re-creation of fatherhood as a vital role for men."
>
> - Robert Lewis
> (Raising a Modern Day Knight 21)

I will not tell you how you should parent because although I do know you must be present, engaged and consistent. Your marriage is different than mine; your children are different than mine but giving you my experience may help yours. I have 3 children, 2 boys (Eilam & Kale) and 1 girl (Fallon). As I write this sentence, my oldest is 6 years old and ever changing in front of me. My middle is 3 and makes me smile every day. My youngest is my daughter and is now 1 year old. "I have to give her away one day," were my exact words to Jennifer as I changed her first diaper. It is so weird how I never had that thought when changing my boy's diapers. For those reading who have teenagers, I know I do not understand that stage yet but I will. Life is busy in this stage but so is every other stage. I look at my parents beginning the retirement years and their life is no less busy, just different. Each stage has it surprises, challenges, parties, roadblocks and heartaches. I have much to learn. Let me address something before I continue: I do not pretend to know the depth or intensity of commitment a single parent has to undertake. While I think some, maybe most, of what I write will apply; I also know that single parents have a set of struggles and challenges that are beyond my experience. Whereas I applaud all parents for choosing to parent, I truly admire and wish to encourage single parents that choose to parent. Don't give up and don't give in; it is worth it.

I offer a wise thought our mentor couple gave us. They said, "If you have good, foundational principles, many formulas will work." Meaning this, our parenting style (formula if you will) may, and most likely is, different than yours and that is okay. Though there is much pressure to conform to one particular parenting theory or style, the beauty is this; there is freedom of choice to choose one, both, many, neither, none or any combination in-between. But we must ask ourselves as parents: What are our foundational principles? For Jennifer and me, we try to keep things as simple as possible. We settled on these principles: that we as parents must be (1) present (2) engaged and (3) consistent. These three words guide us to be parents that are "attached" to our children in a healthy positive way. "Attachment is always taking place, and all parenting is a central component of the creation of attachment. When a baby is cared for in a wholly sensitive way, a secure relationship will likely develop and form a foundation of health to underpin the child's entire life" (Porter 44-46).

"What were we thinking?" came Jennifer's response as Eilam woke up crying. You see, in our desire to be attached to our child, we vowed not to carry them in the car seat. Thus we bought a car seat that could not be detached from the car. It's called a car seat for a reason, correct? But what we soon learned, if our child is sleeping in the car, a detachable car seat would be beneficial. In our attempt to be attached parents, we allowed our brain to become detached. Oh the things you learn as parents. For instance, another piece of advice our mentor couple gave us was this, "Remember you are raising adults not children." I had to wrap my brain around that one for a while before I understood that. But isn't it true; from the time your children are born until, well, forever, you are teaching, grooming, coaching and even corralling them at times to be responsible adults. And in raising adults, many lessons have to be taught not only to the child but also to me as a parent. One lesson that I find myself constantly battling is the tension between making the child the center of the universe and at the same time teaching them the world does not revolve around them. While being "attached" could seem extreme to some, all parents do it, just with differing styles and tactics. The purpose of attaching myself to my children is to raise confident adults who know they are not the center of the universe even when many days I accidentally or purposely place them in that seat. Furthermore, to raise adults that are not self-centered, self-serving or self-seeking is to let them see you, as a parent, not being self-seeking or self-serving. It is not that you will do it perfectly all the time; that is not the point. The point is to let what you say be followed by what you do and those have to be consistent. If not, your attachment becomes detachment and you wonder what happened.

Ever heard parents say, "I have no idea how all my children turned out so different." Sure you have, maybe you have said it. Think about that statement. Its premise is wrong. Why would you ever have raised your children the same way? Yes the foundational principles are the same but how you carry that out will more than likely will be different for each child. Each child is unique and with that uniqueness, has their own personality and flare. I look at my two boys and how different they are. It blows me away that they both came from the same parents. While they have some tendencies the same, the way they process information, the way they carry themselves, the way they communicate is different. It is wonderful, yet challenging. I find myself trying to communicate with Kale (my youngest boy) in the same manner I do with Eilam (my oldest). It does not work and then I get frustrated, never stopping to realize the little boy in front of me is not Eilam but Kale. And then I have Fallon, my little girl. Wow, she is much different than the boys! All three are unique and wonderful and in that I am challenged and blessed.

As we became parents, if someone asked our children, "What is the Bryson family about?" What were they to say? We wanted them to be able to give an answer that was more than just words; something that Jennifer and I not only believed but also try to model. What we decided to do was create a family crest (see Figure 10) that would represent our family. It is painted on a wall in our home.

Let me briefly explain it. The key represents the "keys we have been given to bind and to loose…" (Matthew 16:19). The three outer loops represent the Father, Son and Holy Spirit, even deeper they represent the words to the right: to build, to restore and to prosper. The larger center circle is our family. The smaller circle is our friends and community. The cross reminds our family that it is the cross of Christ

to build

to restore

to prosper

Figure 10: Bryson Family Crest

that unlocks hearts. What is the Bryson family about? When asked, our prayer is that our children would say: to build…to restore…to prosper! Meaning, we are not only to build each other up as a couple, we are to build our children up with love and respect, and also build up those around us. We are to restore those moments in our lives that have been stolen or destroyed by past hurts and seek restoration in all instances. We are to prosper in all that we do whether or not it looks like success in the world's eyes. We are to help others prosper.

Two last thoughts specific to parenting: (1) Learn to play again. "Playful parenting is a way to enter a child's world, on the child's terms in order to foster closeness, confidence and connection. Play is the way children make sense of their world. Play is not easy for adults because we have forgotten so much" (Cohen 2). As adults we often forget to have fun because we live in a world that is "serious business." We forget to laugh. We forget how fun crawling on the floor can be. I love going for a walk with my children. What would take me 3 minutes, when they are with me, takes 30 minutes. They play along the way. They stop and look at the leaf, the crack in the sidewalk, the dirt path made by ants and they laugh. I am focused on the destination, not the journey. Now, some would say, you cannot always take 30 minutes but what I am learning to ask is: Really? I have lost the art of being fascinated with simply playing. When asked, "Dad, will you play with me?" My resounding answer must be yes. (2) Learn to discipline in a way that connects with your child's heart. "Graceful administration is the core idea behind 'Discipline that Connects.' When children learn to expect grace in discipline, rather than power and control, their heart becomes more open to the redemptive power of the Gospel" (Jackson and Jackson 20). Jennifer is much better at graceful administration than I am. It astonishes me to watch her connect to our children's heart as she handles the messes, whine fests or lying. I tend to exert power and control in my disciplining effort, which often leads to struggle and frustration for both my child and myself. With this form of discipline, I, as the parent, ultimately get what I want however it leaves me to wonder has it communicated to the child I love and respect them. The point of discipline must be to positively affect the child. With that in mind, before I discipline, I am learning to prepare my own heart so I can connect to my child's heart. I am beginning to realize, "it is in discipline that our efforts to disciple our children to love and follow God can become vibrantly real" (Jackson and Jackson 10).

Seven parenting tips that have made an impact:

1. Play and laugh with your children. Tell them you love them. It creates memories.

2. Be a parent, not the coach. Your kids have enough coaches. They need a parent.

3. Guard your child's heart. Protect their innocence.

4. Take every opportunity to be a teaching moment. Discipline has to connect to the heart.

5. Limit the number of potential no's.

6. You cannot build your child's character in the fast lane. Meaning as we rush from this event to that event we lose an important component of family. That is intentionality & time.

7. Your children are watching more than they are listening.

Before I leave this section, I would be remiss not to mention what it means being a child. We are all children. You were born to a mom and dad. You are forever someone's child – you are forever a son or daughter. Think about something. In every area of your life you have a choice, except this one. You do not get to choose whose child you are. You are a gift to them regardless if they receive you as a gift or not. Parents make mistakes. Parents have no idea what they are doing. In some instances parents are abusive. No matter if your parents were great and present or abusive and un-interested; as a child, whether young or now older, you have a choice to love and honor your parents. Ephesians 6:2 reads, "Honor your mother and father – which is the first commandment with a promise…" What's the promise? It can be found in Exodus 20:12, "…then you will live a long, full life in the land the Lord God is giving you." Honoring is a choice. If you have been verbally, physically or sexually abused by a parent, I am deeply saddened and I do not say such words flippantly or haphazardly. I do know that if you choose to forgive (which is honoring); you will live a long, full life. If you choose not to forgive, your life will be full of offenses, hurts and even bitterness that (as you learned earlier) will lead to chronic inflammation and disease. Please know that forgiving someone does not mean you are saying what they did to you is okay. If they hurt you, it is not okay, but you still can forgive. You must forgive if you are to be whole. Parents should ask for forgiveness too. And for those whose parents have never asked for forgiveness, Christ stops all of eternity to stand in their place and say to you "I am sorry for hurting you. I am sorry for abandoning you. I am sorry for not being there when you needed me most. I am sorry for being selfish. I am sorry for not saying I love you more. I am sorry for all the times I worked late and was not home. I am sorry. Will you please forgive me?"

Family Systems:

Besides beginning to understand and communicate with your spouse effectively and having foundational principles that guide (not dictate) parenting, another important area to consider is: Family Systems. The Family System theory states you cannot and should not separate the individual from the whole because the family is made up of interrelated objectives, exhibit similar behaviors, have regular interactions and are interdependent on one another. Trying to understand our marriage, parenting style and other interactions in life through the Family System lens can give insight into why we do what we do. As Jennifer and I started to realize we were parented in similar ways in some areas, we also had to come to grips with the fact that other areas were in sharp contrast. Our family systems were and are different and now we are trying to create our own family system. What are we to do? In order to figure that out, we had to evaluate whether we duplicate, react or differentiate from our individual family systems. The questions that Jennifer and I have asked and I am sure we will continue to ask are: (1) Do we duplicate (good and/or bad) patterns that we were raised with? (2) Is this marriage/parenting moment a reaction to how we were raised or something that affected me in my childhood? (3) Are we learning to differentiate between how we saw our parent's marriage and how we were raised from how we would like to be married and raise our children? Are we able to look at our upbringing and truly discern what was "good and bad" and from that knowledge, apply it to our marriage/ parenting?

Let me give you one brief example of how this applies to Jennifer and I. Growing up, Jennifer's dad took care of everything outside the home: cars, yard, landscaping, etc. Whereas her mom did everything on the inside: cleaned house, washed dishes and clothes, etc. Jennifer's dad is very handy and can fix almost anything. I grew up with my mom and dad doing both. My dad did less on the inside but my mom did quite a bit in the yard. My dad, unlike Jennifer's dad, is not very handy. It is not that he cannot fix things but he blesses others by allowing them to do it for him. One day when Jennifer went outside to ride the bikes with the kids, the tires were not blown up because the bikes had not been ridden in a while. Immediately Jennifer got slightly irritated that I did not take care of that (like her dad would have). She was reacting to our family system based on hers. As she sat there and processed the situation (differentiation), she realized that I would have taken care of it if she had asked me to do it before I went to work. Plus, she realized that she could blow up the tires just as simply as I could. Similar situations come up all the time from how we deal with marriage conflict, how we discipline the children and even how we clean (or not clean) the house. Our family systems have affected us. The question is: will we duplicate, react or differentiate as we start our own family system. As Jennifer and I continue to dive into our family system, we know this will not only help our marriage/parenting; it will also help every other relationship that revolves around our family.

Community

Community can be defined as a group of people living in the same locale sharing common interests, goals, and values and participating in similar activities. Community is your sphere of influence. This is your family and friends however it reaches much further than that. Your community is also your neighborhood, workplace and city. Jeremiah 29:7 reads, "Seek the peace and prosperity of the city in which you live and pray to the Lord on its' behalf, because if it prospers, you too will prosper." This is an important aspect of Creating a Trinity Lifestyle – being aware that your influence, positive or negative, does affect the community in which you live. For instance, instead of complaining about your neighbors grass, why not influence them by helping them mow. Instead of grumbling about the local school system, why not influence it by praying for the school board or become involved as a volunteer. Instead of gossiping about your co-worker, why not influence them by showing them kindness, love and respect regardless of how they treat you. As you Create a Trinity Lifestyle, you will profoundly understand that your journey absolutely affects those around you. Your role is, in the words of Gandhi, "Be the change you wish to see in the world."

Jennifer and I have learned much about ourselves by having another family (aka. Family System) living with us. As I mentioned at the start of this chapter, we have housemates, Luis and Crystal Munoz. They have been living with us for almost two years and by the time this book is complete they will have moved out. When they moved in with us, Jennifer and I thought we were helping them out financially until they decided what they would be doing and where they would be going. I believe we did that but Luis and Crystal's intent of moving in was not motivated by finances; they wanted to experience community. It has been such a blessing to have them with us but at the same time challenging. I know all of us have learned much about

"See that your chief study be about your heart, that there God's image may be planted, and His interest advanced...that love...succeed."

- R. Baxter

ourselves. Living with another family unit (whether related or not) reveals much about one's own perceptions, nuisances, biases, judgments and fears. It helps define healthy and unhealthy boundaries. It is one thing to have someone stay with you for a week-long vacation but quite another having someone share life with you. But when we bought our new home; having others live with us was a direct purpose we had in mind. We wanted our children to know that our house is not our own; that because of God's blessing, we are able to bless others. Our family (including Luis and Crystal) is a community. Your community is part of your lifestyle and how you interact with your community matters. Below I will briefly mention three areas of community life.

Neighbors: I can remember growing up in a neighborhood where I knew the children and adults in the seven houses around mine. We would talk in the street as we walked by, we would ask each other for help if needed and we would look out for each other's homes when vacationing. Now, I live in a neighborhood that has all garage doors that open for a moment to drive in and then close for the rest of the night. It seems much harder to talk to my neighbors. I am not saying it is them at all because it is really easy for me to close the garage door and stay inside. Our neighbors, and thus our neighborhood, matter. They matter because they are people with real stories and real lives. I would like to share three different ideas Jennifer and I had to engage our neighbors. (1) We have twenty-two houses on our street. When we moved into our home we wanted a way to meet the neighbors. We had a local coffee/pastry company make twenty-two gift bags; we placed a small letter in each bag introducing our family and early one morning I dropped off a bag to each home. (2) We have a 3-story tree house in our backyard. We built it for our children (and me of course) to enjoy, even more, we built it for the neighborhood kids. We wanted a purpose to have them in our backyard. We had a neighborhood event where we turned the tree house into a stage. We handed out invitations to our immediate neighbors. We provided food and entertainment for one night in our neighborhood. (3) As I told you before, our heart as a family is to build, to restore and to prosper. With that in mind, during holidays one year, we decided to send a letter to our neighborhood (143 homes). The letter briefly introduced who we were then it simply asked if we could pray for them knowing that the holidays were a stressful time for many. I share this with you not to say you have to do anything like Jennifer or I do; however, the question I would like to ask you is this, what have you done to purposely engage your neighbors in the last week, month or year? If you have done nothing, purpose today to start simple; help your neighbor mow the lawn, take over a homemade meal or place a hand-written note in their mailbox. Your neighbors are part of your lifestyle whether or not you want to acknowledge them. Why not engage and be purposeful while creating a lifestyle you desire.

Work Place: Our work place by all accounts can be our second home. We spend 8-12 hours per day talking to and engaging other people. If honest, sometimes we enjoy going to work more than we enjoy going home. I think it is because we seem to be valued and honored at work where we, many times, do not feel valued at home. Regardless of that, our work place is an important part of our overall lifestyle. Where we work, how we work and the people we work with matter. Often we forget that and are only concerned with ourselves, our own projects, deadlines and paychecks. Plus many Christians feel they should be an effective witness for Christ at the workplace; many times they the complete opposite. Os Hillman lays out what he calls the Four Attributes of an Effective Workplace Witness. They are (1) a quality of excellence (2) a foundation of ethics and integrity (3) extravagant love and service (4) signs and wonders. He writes that "to be effective we must possess a work ethic that is of high quality, be ethical and integriteous, show extravagant love and service and then watch God move in the workplace (signs and wonders) by tangibly and practically meeting your co-workers where they are at in their time of need" (49). I have been blessed enough to help patients not only with chiropractic but tangible needs such as groceries or Christmas presents for children. I have seen multiple people come to know Christ in my office and for that I am eternally grateful. Let me share three other examples of what I have done in the workplace. Again, this is not to say you have to do this; I am simply sharing my journey. First, I have set aside two dedicated prayer times each week where the public is welcome to come and pray. Plus, my staff and I meet before the morning and afternoon patients and pray for them. Second, my front office staff picks three to five random businesses or people each week and writes a hand-written note of encouragement to them. We purposely do not include a business card. This note is a practical step to encourage and give hope. Third, I have my office manager write off three patient account balances each month. She includes a note of encouragement with the bill that reads: Your account is now $0. The people in your workplace matter. How can you show them that today?

Church: When I speak of the church in this context, I am speaking not of the global church (although that is important); rather I speak of the local church. This church is a vital part of many people's lifestyle or it is at least one day per week. "By this all men will know you are my disciples; that you love one another" (John 13:35). This is Christ speaking to his disciples and to us. The non-church world (the non-Christian) should be able to look at the conduct of a Christian's life and see the fruit of love pouring out on believer and non-believer. Beyond the Bible, the Christian is Christ's letter to the world! 2 Corinthians 3:2-3 reads, "You yourselves are our letter, written on our hearts, known and read by everyone. You show that you are a letter from Christ, the result of our ministry, written not with ink but with the Spirit of the living God, not on tablets of stone but on tablets of human hearts." But many times, a non-believer sees Christians fighting, gossiping and doing everything else except loving one another. I believe that Christians (different denominations – Baptists, Methodists, Assembly of God, etc....) end up fighting over the traditions of men versus the actual doctrine of Christianity. This forces us to take our eyes off of Christ and look at what the church down the street is doing or not doing. What does it matter if someone goes to a mega-church, a small church, a house church, a coffee shop church, a missional church or a non-denominational church? It doesn't as long as it is teaching foundational Christian beliefs but we fight tooth and nail like it does. And the non-believer looks on wondering where the love is that we profess to have. Is it any wonder why many non-believers never enter the church doors (no matter how that church operates)? The church is a vital part of our lifestyle. However, please recognize church is more than a Sunday experience, it is more than a building, and it is more than something we do. Church is who we are. We are the church of Christ. It is not about doing. It is about being. And in that being, we gather as a body of believers to encourage and exhort then we take the church every place we go.

As I close out this chapter, I pray for you and your family – that your marriage would abound in love with all knowledge and discernment - that you would understand what your foundational parenting principles are - that you could look at your family system and know if you are duplicating, reacting or differentiating. I pray that you would look at your community and see how you can make a practical difference in the lives of those around you - that your home would be filled with love and that your children would not be only taught this love but that this love would be demonstrated in and out of your home.

chapter

the principle of rest

E xodus 20:8-11 reads,

> Remember the Sabbath day, to keep it holy. Six days you shall labor, and do all your work, but the seventh day is a Sabbath to the Lord your God. On it you shall not do any work, you, or your son, or your daughter, your male servant, or your female servant, or your livestock, or the sojourner who is within your gates. For in six days the Lord made heaven and earth, the sea, and all that is in them, and rested on the seventh day. Therefore the Lord blessed the Sabbath day and made it holy.

I am not going to try to convince you that the Lord made heaven and earth or if it was six literal days or over a longer period. Nor am I going to debate whether the Sabbath is Saturday or Sunday or some other day of the week. What I do want you to understand is this: never observing a Sabbath (however you choose to define that word) can be detrimental to your health. Before we venture farther into this topic, I would like you to ask yourself a few questions: Is it hard for you to simply sit and rest? When you try to rest, does your mind wander to what you should or should not be doing? Does taking a day to rest and renew create stress for you? Is the "noise" in your life too loud? If your answer is yes to those questions then you need a Sabbath more than you know.

I am not going to try to convince you that the Lord made heaven and earth or if it was six literal days or over a longer period. Nor am I going to debate whether the Sabbath is Saturday or Sunday or some other day of the week. What I do want you to understand is this: never observing a Sabbath (however you choose to define that word) can be detrimental to your health. Before we venture farther into this topic, I would like you to ask yourself a few questions: Is it hard for you to simply sit and rest? When you try to rest, does your mind wander to what you should or should not be doing? Does taking a day to rest and renew create stress for you? Is the "noise" in your life too loud? If your answer is yes to those questions then you need a Sabbath more than you know.

What I am speaking of here is much more than observing a Sabbath one day a week. It is much more than going to church on Sunday, then taking a nap and think- ing that the Sabbath is satisfied. It is about creating a Sabbatical rhythm to your life.

What do I mean by this? Creating a Sabbatical rhythm to your life means daily recognizing the need for refreshment. It means being able to shut out the noise of the day. It means finding daily inner peace. It means "being still so you can know God…" (Psalm 46:1). But you must know it is more than just the amount of sleep you get; although proper sleep (babies need 12-16 hours/day; children need 9-12 hours/day, teenagers need 7-9 hours/day, adults need 6-8 hours/day) plays a vital role in promoting physical health, longevity, and emotional well-being. It is more than just saying a five-minute prayer at dinner or bedtime. It is more than taking a walk at lunch once per week. A Sabbatical rhythm is purposely and intentionally creating daily Sabbath moments that revives and refreshes the mind, body and spirit. Let me use myself as an example. Here is my typical week of Sabbath moments. On Monday and Wednesday mornings I meet with other men in an accountability type setting for one hour. An accountability setting for me is one in which I can openly and honestly share my life. On Monday and Wednesday I have set aside dedicated times of prayer. Other days of the week, mostly mornings, I spend 20 minutes or so reading and occasionally journaling. During my drives to and from the office I listen to worship music and allow my mind and spirit to be refreshed. I often shut my office door for two to five minutes just to pray and refocus. All the above creates a sabbatical rhythm to my life that helps refresh and renew. What will your daily Sabbath moments look like?

Do you remember how the natural soil can be compared to your own soil? Do you remember how the best soil is balanced and fertile? Do you remember how each area of your life affects your soil? The principle of rest is no different. The natural soil needs a Sabbath. Exodus 23:10-12 reads:

> Six years you shall sow your land and gather in its produce, but the seventh year you shall let it rest and lie fallow, that the poor of your people may eat; and what they leave, the beasts of the field may eat. In like manner you shall do with your vineyard and your olive grove. Six days you shall do your work, and on the seventh day you shall rest, that your ox and your donkey may rest, and the son of your female servant and the stranger may be refreshed.

Did you catch that? The reason the land needs a Sabbath is so the soil and you can be refreshed. That is the principle of rest: to be refreshed! While we do not see many, if any, farmers, resting the soil every seven years, we do see farmers practicing what is known as crop rotation. Crop rotation is the successive planting of different crops on the same land and "the foundational reason for organic management is the creation of a healthy farm system that builds soil fertility and prevents proliferation of weeds and disease. To be sure, creating a crop rotation can be challenging. It involves hard thinking and compromises between your immediate financial goals and long term goals of the farm" (Kroeck 2). Looking past immediate monetary gain; creating healthier soil with decreased incidence of weeds and disease; that is creating a Sabbath for the soil.

If the natural soil needs a Sabbath, how much more does your own soil? The foundational reason for a Sabbath is the creation of healthy body systems that prevents proliferation of ravens, thorns and scorching disease (remember Mark 4:1-9). To be sure, creating a Trinity Lifestyle can be challenging. It involves hard thinking and compromises between your immediate needs and long-term goals of health and vitality. However, the reward is a healthier you, with benefits ranging from your own soil's health to your overall life and those around you. Let me give you an example. While working on this book I would stay up late and still get up early. This routine finally caught up with me. I arose one morning not feeling well and by the end of the day I was nauseated and had a fever. When I arrived at home Jennifer quarantined me. Literally, she told me to go to the guest bedroom and not come out. I submitted so I would not get the rest of the house sick. She brought me soup and the kids said goodnight through a closed door. What did I do in the room? I slept for 12 hours, which is something I never do. The next morning I awoke refreshed and revived. My body was screaming for rest; I did not listen until it crashed. Resting and creating sabbatical moments matter and are vital to a healthy life. Jesus states in Mark 2:27, "Sabbath was made for man, not man for the Sabbath."

chapter 10

> Life is like riding a bicycle.
> To keep your balance you
> must keep moving.
> - *Albert Einstein*

finding balance

et me tell you a story: I was running one day on a trail by a river. As I rounded a corner, I stopped to take a breather and allowed my eyes to scan the horizon of the riverbank. The beautiful green trees and the life that flowed all around struck me. Yet, in the midst of all that, stood one brown, life-less tree. It was just as close to the water, with the same availability to nutrients as the other trees yet it was dead. As I stood there, I felt in my spirit a profound truth. It is this: Many people stand so close to desperately needed nutrients for their minds, bodies and spirits, yet they are dead. They are choosing sometimes, knowingly or many times unknowingly, a life that is not lived to the fullest. Oh how I desire that each of you reading this book would be like a "tree planted by streams of water that yields its fruit in its season, and (whose) leaf does not wither. In all that you do, you would prosper!" (Psalms 1:3).

An unknown author declared: "Watch your thoughts; they become words. Watch your words; they become actions. Watch your actions; they become habits. Watch your habits; they become character. Watch your character; it becomes your destiny." But before you can grab a hold of that destiny, you have to know your identity. You have to know who you are and understand your foundational values. Do you know who you are? Recently, I heard of the Dove Beauty Sketches. (Note: Please search online to view; it is impactful to watch). To keep it simple, a sketch artist has a lady describe herself. The sketch artist never sees her. Then the sketch artist has another person describe the same lady. The sketch artist never sees that person either. After both sketches are complete, the lady is presented with both sketches. The one that is a self-described portrait looks less happy, older, uglier and often tired. The other sketch looks brighter, happier and younger; more like the actual person. In every instance, women described themselves in a more negative way than how people actually view them. The point: You are more beautiful than you think! You are more than what the world says you are, you are more than what your family expects you to become, and you are a friend of God. Let me explain. Jesus said in John 15:15, "No longer do I call you servants...but I call you friends." But

> "I long to accomplish a great and noble task, but it is my chief duty to accomplish small tasks as if they were great and noble."
>
> - Helen Keller

even more than friends you are His beloved children. "I will be your Father and you will be my sons and daughters, says the Lord almighty" (2 Corinthians 6:17-18). As we capture who we are and as we are transformed from slaves into sons and daughters certain shifts take place in our heart.

> First what we know changes as we gain access to the heart of the Father. Second, our experience changes because encounters with God as a friend or beloved child are quite different than as a slave. Third, our function in life radically changes. Instead of working for Him, we work with Him. Fourth, our identity is transformed. Our identity sets the tone for all we do and become. Christians who live out of who they really are cannot be crippled by the opinion of others nor will they fit into other's expectations or realities. Rather, they will burn with the realization of who the Father says they are. (Johnson 25)

Making the above shift, to me, is the key to a life lived in balance. If you never know who you are, you will try to live up to what others think you are until eventually you burn out or give up or both. As I said before, you can never have enough of God. So grab a hold of Him and learn who you are. Then from that vantage point, walk out a balanced life - walk out your destiny!

The goal of Creating a Trinity Lifestyle is to create rhythm and balance within your daily life. You might be asking, "How can I do that?" Let's explore the word balance. Webster's Dictionary defines balance as, "Keep or put (something) in a steady position so that it does not fall." Is that not what we want to do with our life, put each area in a steady position so we do not fall; how do we do that?

An acronym I came up with may help us understand the bigger picture of what the word could mean. **BALANCE** is: **B**eing **A**vailable **L**earning **A**lways **N**ever **C**ompromising **E**ternity **M**inded.

- Being Available is being sensitive to the leading of the Holy Spirit. It means being there for your spouse, children and others. It means learning to say no to more and yes to less. It means viewing interruptions as opportunities.

- Learning Always is gaining perspective from reading God's word. It means realizing we can learn from others and understanding we do not know it all. It means looking at life through the eyes of a child.

- Never Compromising is to live a congruent life where values and actions coincide. It means you teach more by what you do than you say.

- Eternity Minded means "fixing our thoughts on things above." It means understanding this life is but a vapor and it is not all about us. Others are affected by our choices.

As I know who I am, my ability to be available increases because I am not trying to please everyone around me. As I know who I am, I am able to learn from others instead of trying to elevate myself over them. As I know who I am, I will not compromise my position on truth and what I know to be moral. As I know who I am, my mind will be set not on the temporal; it will set on the eternal. As I know who I am, living a life of balance becomes a little easier.

At this point, if you have not already, you may be asking the question: What exactly are we balancing? Is it my work, home and church life? No because our life should not be segmented into nice little compartments. Our life is one of free-flowing acts, thoughts and encounters with other people. All areas of our life are important and all stem from knowing who we are and balancing the mind, body and spirit.

- To balance the mind: You must create an atmosphere that fosters constant learning from reading, playing, laughing, working, and from other sources including family and friends. Turn off the TV and read. Further renew your mind by practicing random acts of kindness.

- To balance the body: You must continue to be active and not sedentary. Practice yoga (Appendix D) or walking daily (multiple times per week). For this purpose, you can use the Yoga poses (Appendix C) or the daily stretches found on the website. However, you may want to try an occasional activity that challenges your inner strength (biking, cross-fit, swimming, hiking, etc...). Nutritionally, continue to eat colorfully, adding seasonal fruits and vegetables, decrease processed items and consume ample amounts of water.

- To balance the spirit: You must daily spend time being intimate with God: reading, journaling, worshiping and praying (not out of duty or a check-off list; it must be from the vantage point of a vibrant relationship). You would never expect to build a vibrant relationship with your spouse or a friend without investing time so why do we expect anything different in our relationship with God?

To create a balance in your life that is not only healthy but productive and restorative you will have to: Be Determined...Be Disciplined...Be Devoted.

- Be Determined: An anonymous quote reads, "Every accomplishment starts with the decision to try." Your willingness to read this far means you are ready to start. Recruit an accountability partner that can take this journey with you. Choose this person wisely. Choose someone that encourages you and also someone who is not afraid to speak truth. Be determined to live a healthier, happier life not only for you but also for your family and friends. Be determined to make a difference. Be determined to change the course of your history.

- Be Disciplined: Jim Rohn, a motivational speaker, states, "We must all suffer from one of two pains: the pain of discipline or the pain of regret. The difference is discipline weighs ounces while regret weighs tons." Do not live a life of regret always wishing to be healthier – always wanting to live a balanced life. Proverbs 28:18 reads, "Without vision, the people perish." To be disciplined is to have focus – to have focus gives us the ability to see – the ability to see casts a vision – the vision casted can create a life that is balanced.

- Be Devoted: Henry Miller, an American author, wrote these words, "True strength lies in submission which permits one to dedicate his life, through devotion, to something beyond himself." The question here is: Where does your devotion lie? Are you devoted only to yourself or are you devoted to something beyond yourself? Because to have a balanced, purposeful life you must realize it is not all about you. Your health – the way you eat, the way you speak, the way you think – the way you carry yourself - does affect others. Your devotion influences the world around you. What influence are you having?

How have I created balance in my life? First, I know who Christ is; He is my life and restoration. He is the reason I can love at all. Second, I know who I am. I am Bo: "Royalty is my identity. Servant-hood is my assignment. Intimacy with God is my life source. So, before God, I am an intimate. Before people, I am a servant. Before the powers of hell, I am a ruler, with no tolerance for their influence. And wisdom knows which role to fulfill at the proper time" (Johnson 88). Third, I balance my mind by reading, listening and talking with others who are wiser than me. I do not have cable TV however I do enjoy occasional TV and I love watching movies. I love to learn from watching my children. Fourth, I balance my body by being active. I go for walks with my wife and play at the park with my kids. Occasionally, I will sign up to do a half-marathon, go for a long bike ride or something more challenging. In reality I just try to stay active. I try to make eating healthy and fun. I also eat pizza, chicken wings and ice cream however I do not do it every day. I love coffee. I drink water and limit the amount of processed foods I eat. I take daily an immune-enhancing vitamin, Vitamin D and Omega-3. Fifth, I balance my spirit by daily spending time with God. Most days, I get up at 5am and meditate on His promises for my life. Most nights I pray with my wife and kids. Weekly I spend time with other men who encourage and challenge me. Sixth, I have come to know my wife as my best friend. She is more than my lover or mother to our children. She is my complement. She influences me and thoughts of her shape my day. Seventh, I desire to give and to bless others. I've heard it said, "If you have one more breath, it is so you can give it away." Lastly, I realize my actions have temporal and eternal consequences.

Before I wrap up this section of the book, I would be remiss not to mention finances as a part of living a balanced life. 1 Corinthians 10:26 tells us "the Earth is the Lord's and everything in it." That means finances too. I am not going to tell you what to do with your money however I will tell you that what you do with your money says much about what you believe to be true. Personally, I have embraced the principle of tithing and giving. From my understanding, tithing is 10% and giving is anything beyond that. I tithe to my local church and I give to others in need. I try to live with an open hand realizing that all I have comes from above. Even in that I must acknowledge none of us are exempt from the temptation of materialism and from the pursuit of the American dream. It bombards us every day on billboards, TV, radio and internet. It is everywhere. Chasing the American dream does not produce happiness. "Money holds the hope of prestige, possession and pleasure but riches lie. The materialistic person, driven by money's promise of fulfillment, will accumulate one thing after another, until one day, to his horror; he will discover his soul is desolate" (Gallagher 170). 1 Timothy 6:10 reads, "For the love of money is a root of all kinds of evils. It is through this craving that some have wandered away from the faith and pierced themselves with many troubles." Notice it is not money that is evil; money is an arbitrary thing that we use to live from day to day. It is the love of money and the constant pursuit of money that God calls evil. This is why Jesus says in Matthew 6:24, "No one can serve two masters, for either he will hate the one and love the other, or he will be devoted to the one and despise the other. You cannot serve God and money." Listen, God is not after your pocketbook, He is after your heart. Make no mistake, your finances will reflect what you believe and display how well you live a balanced life.

Is it easy to create balance on a daily basis? I would be lying to you if I said yes. However, anything worth having is worth the work put forth to obtain it. As I write this book, I have many things that compete for my time. My wife, my children, my extended family, my friends and my two businesses all require time from me. As I have been writing, I have had to balance the desire to write with the balance of realizing what is most important - my relationship with Christ, my wife and my children. Just the other night I had to choose to play monopoly, which I dislike very much, with my son over writing. Was it easy? No. Was it worth it? Yes! As I have been writing, my wife and I decided to update both of our business websites and do work on our house. While I have been writing, my in-laws have decided to move to Nebraska to be closer to their grandchildren (without even knowing it, they are Creating a Trinity Lifestyle). While I have been writing, I have seen my parents challenged in certain areas of life that refined them. While I have been writing, my grandfather and aunt died. Plus, I watched pancreatic cancer take my brother-in-law's life and watched the effects of his death on my sister's life. Toward the end of the editing process of this book, my wife had to have emergency left eye surgery. Her retina and macula detached (which by the way is a big deal). What I have learned: (1) I cannot do this journey alone; actually, no one can. Psalm 28:7 states, "The LORD is my strength and my shield; in him my heart trusts..." and Nehemiah 8:10 declares, "...the joy of the Lord is my strength." (2) If I believe that the character of God is good and kind and faithful, then I have to believe that no matter what situation I find myself. Malachi 3:6 and Hebrews 13:8 promises "I, the Lord, do not change...Jesus is the same yesterday, today and forever." (3) I have come to know more fully the reality of Colossians 1:27, "God has chosen to make known the glorious riches of this mystery, which is Christ in you, the hope of glory." And it is that joy and hope that gives me the ability to live a balanced life, not a perfect life.

I end this section as I started it, with the words of my wife: **"It is a beautiful day here; I hope the sun is shining on you."**

chapter 11

"
It is what we know
already that often prevents
us from learning.
- Claude Bernard
"

soil or seed: which is it

s it the soil that matters most or is it the seed that matters most? That is the question we must answer as we dive into this next section. In the previous section, I laid a foundation for what makes up your soil and why it is important. This section will explain what happens to the seed when your soil is hardened, shallow, thorn-infested or fertile. Before we get into that, let's answer the question: Is it the soil or the seed? To answer this question, we will focus our attention mainly on Claude Bernard and Louis Pasteur and briefly (very briefly) mention Franz Alexander. You may remember these names from your high school science class. Claude Bernard is known for many things including coining the word homeostasis and the soil theory. Louis Pasteur is known for many things including the pasteurization process and the germ theory. Franz Alexander coined the term, 'organ neurosis,' later known as psychosomatic (mind-body).

Bernard's thought was that "when considering the health of the body as a whole, including the mind, it must first be understood that the body is made up of many billions of living cells…every cell must be healthy…and if every cell is healthy…then it follows that the entire body will be healthy too. The principle of total body health has become known as the soil theory" (Horne Chapter 2). Bernard's theory is simply this: You must take care of the soil (the body). In Bernard's theory, the seed is a (bad) germ. I know it may seem counter-intuitive but just like you plant a seed in the garden to grow; this seed – a (bad) germ - needs an environment to grow in – that environment is the body. Thus, Bernard suggested that if the body is taken care of by good living practices (aka: Creating a Trinity Lifestyle), the seed (the {bad} germ) would not have a favorable environment to grow. If the body is not taken care of, the (bad) germ would be able to grow. Thus, if the body is stressed, it can cause sickness and disease to flourish. Conversely, Louis Pasteur argued, "the state of health and disease was not a measure of the soil but rather the seed" (Seward 63). In other words, it does not matter if the body is taken care of by good living practices; it is the strength of the (bad) germ that matters. Think about it this way; Bernard was trying to say that it mattered how we lived and how we took care of our bodies. Pasteur, on the other hand, suggested that our living practices did not have that much impact on our health. Sadly, Pasteur's theory was more widely accepted and has led to the proliferation of the pharmaceutical industry as we know it today. I wonder if this is because taking a medication to get rid of a "germ" is easier than maintaining health living practices. I am thankful for the advancement of medicine when it is truly needed but how much healthier would we be if we concentrated on the soil (body) and not the seed (germ).

Back to the original question. Which matters most: the soil or the seed? Although it cannot be proven, it is highly speculated that on his deathbed, Louis Pasteur spoke these words, "Bernard was right; it is not the seed, it's the soil." Either way, one thing is certain, your health and vitality is determined by good living practices and the impact that has on your soil (body)! Does it mean you will never get sick or possibly contract a disease? Of course not! However, why not give your body a fighting chance to live a longer, healthier and productive life?

In the next four chapters, we will explore the condition of your soil as found in Mark 4:14-20. These verses are the explanation of Mark 4:1-9 (the verses that began this book). It reads,

> The sower sows the word. And these are the ones along the path, where the word is sown: when they hear, Satan immediately comes and takes away the word that is sown in them. And these are the ones sown on rocky ground: the ones who, when they hear the word, immediately receive it with joy. And they have no root in themselves, but endure for a while; then, when tribulation or persecution arises on account of the word, immediately they fall away. And others are the ones sown among thorns. They are those who hear the word, but the cares of the world and the deceitfulness of riches and the desires for other things enter in and choke the word, and it proves unfruitful. But those that were sown on the good soil are the ones who hear the word and accept it and bear fruit, thirtyfold and sixtyfold and a hundredfold. (Mark 4:14-20)

Reworded from The Message, it reads,

> The farmer plants the Word. Some people are like the seed that falls on the hardened soil of the road. No sooner do they hear the Word than Satan snatches away what has been planted in them. And some are like the seed that lands in the gravel. When they first hear the Word, they respond with great enthusiasm. But there is such shallow soil of character that when the emotions wear off and some difficulty arrives, there is nothing to show for it. The seed cast in the weeds represents the ones who hear the kingdom news but are overwhelmed with worries about all the things they have to do and all the things they want to get. The stress strangles what they heard, and nothing comes of it. But the seed planted in the good earth represents those who hear the Word, embrace it, and produce a harvest beyond their

wildest dreams. (*The Message*, Mark 4:14-20)

I present Mark 4:14-20 above in two versions to hopefully help the reader understand the meaning more clearly. Furthermore, at the beginning of each of the next four chapters, I will present the parable from Mark 4:1-9 and then the explanation from Mark 4: 14-20. Following that, I will briefly present how this relates to our mind, body, spirit and food.

One other thought about seeds before I end this chapter. This specific parable was speaking of the word of God (the seed) and how individuals (the soil) receive that word. We all receive words each day that either build us up or try to tear us down. We cannot control those seeds; we can control our soil. Consider the difference you can make, good or bad, in others by the seeds you cast. Do the words or "the seed" you choose to use each day build up or tear down? You cannot choose the type of soil that your seed falls upon; you can control what type of seed you cast. Keep in mind the seed that lands on the hardened path may get blown by the wind to good soil before the birds come and devour it. That means when you speak a word to one person someone else may be listening that will be impacted much greater than the person with whom you were actually speaking. Thus, "let no corrupting talk come out of your mouths, but only such as is good for building up, as fits the occasion, that it may give grace to those who hear" (Ephesians 4:29).

chapter 12

> Listen! Behold, a sower went out to sow and as he sowed, some seed fell along the path, and the birds came and devoured it...The sower sows the word. And these are the ones along the path, where the word is sown: when they hear, Satan immediately comes and takes away the word that is sown in them.
>
> *- Mark 4: 3-4, 14-15*

stolen

T hink about a path. It is a way to get from one destination to another. A path allows thousands of travelers' access to the same place. Along the path, people stop and look, they chat with one another and some just walk. The path can be considered soil that has been trampled and walked upon. Any seed that is cast upon the path does not and cannot penetrate the hardened soil. Thus, the seed is left to be continually trampled upon. Even more so, since the seed cannot penetrate the hardened path, birds of the air come and devour the seed. It is snatched away before it has a chance to take root. How does this relate to our mind, body, spirit and food?

Mind: I think the mind can become hardened because we are prideful.

> Pride manifests itself in so many subtle, but lethal ways... In a hidden desire for the praise and admiration of men, an insistence on being "right," the desire to be noticed and appreciated, fear of rejection, or just pre-occupation with myself, my feelings, my needs, my circumstances, my burdens, my desires, my successes, my failures. These are all fruits of that deadly root of pride. (DeMoss)

As our mind becomes prideful seeds that are cast are never allowed to take root and are stolen.

Body: The body can become sclerotic, a medical term for hardening, because of our sedentary lifestyle. Our sedentary lifestyle allows joints to become stiff, our muscles inflexible, our cardiovascular system diminished and our nervous system less able to adapt. As we continue to become sclerotic, our body becomes diseased and unable to receive any healthful seeds that may be cast upon it.

Spirit: Our spirit becomes hardened due to resentment and unforgiveness. "Forgiveness brings great joy, not only to the forgiven, but especially to the forgiver. The Greek term for "forgiveness" (aphiemi) comes from a word that means "to let go." Forgiveness is a release, a letting go of self-destructive feelings such as anger, bitterness and revenge. Those attitudes poison intimacy with God and harmony with human beings."(As We Forgive Our Debtors - When You Pray, 142) Unforgiveness leads to a hardened heart that cannot and will not be penetrated no matter what seed is cast into it.

Food: I think our food becomes hardened for two reasons, increased processing and increased shelf life. Our food is meant to be eaten as whole and as real as possible. Our food is ever increasing in the amount of its processing and the boxes now stay on the grocery store shelf for months. All this leads to hardening of food making it nutritionally void. As it becomes nutritionally void our health is stolen.

chapter 13

shallow

ying next to that hardened path is rocky ground. Not quite trampled as much as the path, the rocky ground is hard yet a little more penetrable. The rocky ground has some soil but very little so it lacks depth and that is what causes the problem. How does this relate to your mind, body, spirit and food?

Mind: I think our mind becomes shallow when we forget to set our mind on things above. When we just think about our own temporal concerns our mind loses the ability to think on things that are deeper and more profound. When we choose to entertain our minds with unhealthy TV shows, internet or other forms of negative media we make our minds shallow. That shallowness creates a lack of focus and vision. We need to "no longer be conformed to this world, but rather be transformed by the renewal of our mind(s)" (Romans 12:2).

Body: Our body becomes shallow when we expect others to take responsibility for the choices we make or do not make concerning our health. We put the blame on the gym for not being open late enough, we put the blame on the doctor because they do not understand the "real problem" and we put the blame on our friend for not going for a run with us. In truth we put the blame on everyone else except ourselves. Simply, we do not take responsibility for our own health. We want to be healthy in one workout, one chiropractic adjustment or by taking a magic pill. The shallowness of this thought process creates a lack of perseverance and that leads to our health falling away.

Spirit: I think our spirit becomes shallow when we are constantly comparing ourselves to other people. We look at classmates/co-workers/neighbors and we think we do not look as good as them, do not drive a nice car like they do and on and on. Or even worse maybe we look at others and puff ourselves up because we have more than they have, we think we know more than they know and on and on. Either way, this comparing ourselves to others is a slippery slope leading to our self-esteem, self-confidence and self-worth being scorched and withering away. Instead of comparing ourselves, "each one should test his own actions…without comparing himself to somebody else…" (Ephesians 6:4).

Food: Our food becomes shallow when we limit our choices based on the latest and greatest diet fad. We run to this diet and that diet hoping it will change our lives forever only to find out in the end it is shallow and hopeless because no deep lifestyle change has been made. This shallowness creates a cycle of momentary joy however many people fall away right back to their same old habits. Our food choices should not be limited but expanded and enjoyed!

chapter 14

> Other seed fell among thorns, and
> the thorns grew up and choked it, and it
> yielded no grain...And others are the ones
> sown among thorns. They are those who
> hear the word, but the cares of the world
> and the deceitfulness of riches and the
> desires for other things enter in and choke
> the word, and it proves unfruitful.
>
> - Mark 4: 7, 18-19

crowded

Beyond the hardened path and rocky ground lies yet another type of soil, the soil that has depth however is not cultivated for growth. In this soil weeds and thorns dominate and they readily choke out the small seedling once it has sprouted. How does this relate to your mind, body, spirit and food?

Mind: Our mind becomes choked by "thorns and weeds" when we are double-minded. Webster defines double-minded as, "insincere, wavering and marked by hypocrisy." If we are not steadfast, focused and purposeful in our mind we waver and then try to please people by tickling their ears with what we think they want to hear. Our life and words are not meant to tickle the ears of those who hear but rather touch the heart. James 1:8 reminds us, "...a double-minded man is unstable in all his ways."

Body: I think our body becomes entangled with "thorns and weeds" when we give into the idea that pain, sickness and disease are normal. 1 Corinthians 6:19 reads, "Do you not know that your body is a temple of the Holy Spirit within you, whom you have from God?" Your temple, your body, is destroyed as you choose to give up trying to become healthier. Nobody is "healthy enough," everyone could become healthier and every effort is worth it. Give your body a fighting chance and do not give into the lie that you are defined by any condition or disease process you may have.

Spirit: Our spirit becomes choked by "thorns and weeds" when anxiety, worry and fear rule our hearts. CH Spurgeon wrote, "Anxiety does not empty tomorrow of its sorrows, but only empties today of its strength." As our strength is emptied, anxiety and fear cast shadows of doubt over our life. If a shadow of doubt covers our life it will inhibit any fruitful growth. Be reminded and encouraged by the words of 2 Timothy 1:7, "...for God gave us a spirit not of fear but of power and love and self-control."

Food: Food becomes choked by "thorns and weeds" when it is over-laden with pesticides, fungicides, preservatives and growth hormones. These unnatural chemicals choke out the vital nutrients that our food is supposed to contain and deliver. As our food becomes unfruitful we in turn, become increasingly unhealthy.

chapter 15

> And other seeds fell into good soil and produced grain, growing up and increasing and yielding thirtyfold and sixtyfold and a hundredfold. And he said, He who has ears to hear, let him hear...But those that were sown on the good soil are the ones who hear the word and accept it and bear fruit, thirtyfold and sixtyfold and a hundredfold.
>
> - Mark 4: 8-9, 20

fruitful

f you take the time to stop and look, to truly see, you may be willing to look away from where all the rest of the travelers are heading and in the distance you may catch a glimpse of dark, rich, cultivated soil. Once you stop and look, it will cause an interruption not only in your own life, but also in the lives of others that are traveling on the hardened path who are unwilling to look. Picture stepping off the hardened path, looking closer and finding soil that is softer, yet still shallow and rocky. Do not look back at the hardened path as a place of safety, rather look in the distance and take another step. This soil is softer still and seems more fruitful as little buds are sprouting; you also notice weeds. You stoop down and pull some weeds but notice the abundance of them and become frustrated. Feeling defeated, will you turn back toward the rocky ground? As you look again at the fruitful soil, will you deny the yearnings within? No one said it would be easy getting off the hardened path, making your way over the rocky terrain and traversing weeds but you persisted. Standing at the edge of the dark, rich soil, you slip off your shoes and take a daring step. Your feet sink in and at first it is uncomfortable but then it becomes enjoyable. This makes you smile and laugh. The effort was worth it! How does this relate to your mind, body, spirit and food?

Mind: Our mind is a battlefield of thoughts. "We must destroy arguments and every lofty opinion that raises itself up against the knowledge of God, and take every thought captive…" (2 Corinthians 10:5). If we do not capture our thought life, un-truth and lies will lead us back to the hardened path and we become unfruitful. Remember, fruitfulness is the goal. We need to set our mind on things above and "press on toward the goal for the prize of the upward call of God in Christ Jesus" (Philippians 3:14). And as we do that we become fruitful, multiplying peace, hope and joy in the lives of people around us.

Body: I tell my patients every day that it is the little consistent things they do over time that either cause health or disease. The food we eat – the amount of rest - the amount we exercise and the amount of water we consume daily has a cumulative effect on our bodies. Persist in harmful activities and disease is the outcome. Persist in the healthful activities and health occurs. You need persistence to move from the hardened path to the fruitful soil. It is sometimes difficult but it is worth every effort. Remember health is not a gift; it is a choice made each day. Make fruitful choices and enjoy a bountiful harvest!

Spirit: "Count it all joy, my brothers, when you meet trials of various kinds [hardened, shallow or thorny paths] for you know that the testing of your faith produces steadfastness. And let steadfastness have its full effect, that you may be perfect and complete, lacking in nothing" (James 1:2-4). Having a fruitful spirit takes work. It takes "seeking first the kingdom of God" (Mathew 6:33). As you seek and remain steadfast, your spirit will produce fruit that is love, joy, peace, patience, kindness, goodness and faithfulness…" (Galatians 5:22).

Food: How does our food become fruitful? It becomes fruitful when it is eaten it in its whole, natural unprocessed state. Decreasing the amount of hormones and pesticides that are sprayed and injected in and on our food will increase its fruitfulness. So does fruitful food that leads to a fruitful mind, body and spirit have to be organic? Ideally, the best food would be organic, however, for practical purposes, it doesn't have to be. Having fruitful food means making better daily food choices. It means increasing fruits and veggies; decreasing sugar and processed packaged foods; increasing your water consumption and adding vitamins and minerals when and where they are needed. Having fruitful food begins by making small changes in your diet that lead to success and not failure. It is simple, eat healthy and be happy!

chapter 16

> To accomplish great things,
> we must not only act,
> but also dream; not only
> plan, but also believe.
>
> - Anatole France

the plan: how it works

We have covered much territory up to this point and now it is time to present the plan that will help you Create a Trinity Lifestyle. This plan is meant to be a guide to help. It is not meant to be burdensome and it should be easy to follow. This is not to say the process won't be hard and challenging at times however your health is worth the effort. Prior to starting, please consult your healthcare provider if taking medications or if you have a medical condition.

What should you do before you start?

First, you should take inventory of your life. Ask yourself some questions and be honest. Are there habits and attitudes that you need or want to change? How reasonable is it to change one or all of them? What is the most important one to change first? Is it the right time to start? What is your goal when creating a balanced rhythm to your life?

Second, my goal for you is to succeed, not fail. With this in mind, it is suggested that a preparatory 1-2 week period be followed. What does that mean? It means, after you have taken inventory of your life, start weaning yourself from habits you want to see changed. For example, if you drink 2-3 soft drinks per day or 6 cups of coffee per day, you may want to reduce this amount slowly over the 1-2 weeks before going "cold turkey."

Third, during the 1-2 week prep period, look through the 21-day plan(s) and get an idea of what vegetables, fruits and other items that will be needed. One way to fail before you start is to not be prepared. It will be best to buy only what you need for 1 week at a time to ensure freshness and quality.

Fourth, during the 1-2 week prep period, start increasing the amount of fruits and vegetables you eat. Start drinking more water. Reduce the amount of carbohydrates, processed foods and "sugary items" you consume. This will help you transition into the 21-day plan.

Fifth, purchase and/or borrow a blender. Not all recipes will use a blender however it is strongly recommended that you have a blender

> "Health is not a gift but something each person is responsible for through his or her own daily effort."
>
> - R. Nakayam

that is high quality. The blender I recommend is Blendtec. Optionally, you may want a juicer.

Specifics of the Plan

A foundation for the Trinity Lifestyle has been laid; we can now focus on specifics. What I will present now is not an "end-all-be-all" plan. Rather, my intent is to create rhythm and bring balance to your life. The benefit of the Trinity lifestyle is not necessarily to lose weight, although that will most likely be a positive side effect. It is to understand what a balanced life can offer. This means a balance of the mind, body and spirit. This plan will engage all three. Below in a bulleted-style format, I have laid out the specifics of the plan. After the bulleted items is further explanation.

- There are four plans: (a) Raw Food Plan (b) Non-Raw Food Plan (c) Specific Fast (d) Walking (Read-Pray-Walk). Each plan is 21 days in length. Each plan has a beginner, intermediate and advanced version found at the beginning of the plan.
- Each plan has a Spring, Summer, Fall and Winter Version. Depending on what time of the year you decide to Create a Trinity Lifestyle will determine what plan you will follow. Within each specific season, there will be three daily meal ideas plus snacks that will be repeated seven times. This design helps to keep each specific seasonal food plan simple and inexpensive.
- Each plan is to be followed twice per year. For example you could choose to pick Spring and Winter beginner version from the Raw Food Plan the first year. The second year, you may want to choose Spring advanced version Non-Raw Food Plan and then in the Fall try the beginner Prayer Walking Plan. The possibilities are endless. Just remember to have fun.
- Within each of the 21 day periods, you will have:
  - A daily meal idea (excluding the specific fast plan and walking plan). You will notice that each meal is repeated seven times. This is to make the plan as simple and straightforward as possible. Serving size is two adults; however, you can adapt, change and add for your specific tastes and needs. Again, the goal is to not limit or frustrate but to help you succeed. Additional recipes and snack ideas may be found on the website.
  - A daily renewing thought. It is recommended that you have a journal to write down your own thoughts, concerns, dreams and visions. It was suggested by a friend and mentor that I tell the reader that many of the thoughts come from my own experience while reading the Bible, praying and living life. Other thoughts are quotes from authors I have read. I

took my friend's advice seriously and tell you in advance; while I think all the renewing thoughts will apply to your life; some will point directly to Christ while others just ask thought provoking questions. If the thoughts do not seem to resonate with you and I am sure some will not; do not negate the benefit of the nutritional advice or renewing activity. Additional renewing thoughts may be found on Dr. Bo's blog via the website.

- A daily renewing activity. <u>Note</u>: With the help of Tataya Radtke, yoga will be used for a large portion of this purpose (excluding the walking plan). Seven specific yoga poses with detailed instructions have been created for Creating a Trinity Lifestyle. This can be found in Appendix C. Additionally, an introductory yoga video and instructional video of these seven poses can be found on the website.

<u>Note</u>: To help with recipe and mental preparation, before beginning a 21 day plan look ahead at the recipes and grocery list plus at the end of each day you may want to look forward one day. This will help alleviate the possible stress of the unknown. Being un-prepared will cause stress and failure. Let's avoid that if we can! In Appendixes A & B you will find raw/non-raw food recipes plus a grocery list. The grocery list is all-inclusive but not specific. This allows freedom to get as much or as little as you can afford and/or desire.

Why 21 days and why twice per year

Twenty-one days is a reasonable amount of time that most people can achieve. Creating a Trinity Lifestyle is about helping people succeed, not fail. Succeeding in life is about setting realistic goals, and creating rhythm and balance. Another reason for 21 days is to change poor habits into healthy alternatives. Research shows it takes 21-30 days of consistent input and action to create or break a habit. It is not magic! I liken the twice per year idea to what most people do naturally to their home and never think about for themselves. Many people de-clutter or deep clean in their home two times per year (Spring and Fall). Why would we not want to do the same with our bodies?

Precautions

If you have a medical condition or are taking medications that would be counter-indicative to following the "Trinity Lifestyle," please consult your healthcare provider prior to starting. This book is not meant to replace your healthcare provider, so please consult your healthcare provider if you have further questions. However, I have tried to make the plans simple enough that anyone can follow them. If for some reason, you are unable to fully participate: please note that you can still obtain many of the health benefits by creating the rhythm in your life that is described in this book. For instance, you may not be able to fully engage in the 21 raw food plan (any version) but you can increase your vegetables while doing the renewing activity and thought. Start small, be purposeful and watch your health grow!

Can I Create a Trinity Lifestyle while Pregnant or Nursing

Yes, you can Create a Trinity Lifestyle even while pregnant and/or nursing. However, I would suggest adding 2 eggs (range free omega-3 enriched) and 3-5 protein servings per day. Protein is very important for a healthy pregnancy and for healthy nursing; however, please consider the source of protein. If using protein powder, for the purposes of this 21-day food plan, vegan-dairy-free would be the most beneficial. However, if needed, you could use whey protein. Protein powder may be added to the shake recipes. Besides water, you may consider drinking 2-4 cups of Raspberry Leaf tea, as this is very good for uterine health. If you have complicating health factors or questions during your pregnancy, please consult your OBGYN and/or midwife prior to starting.

Can my children Create a Trinity Lifestyle

Absolutely! Will the kids miss some sugar and TV? Sure they will but remember you are not only investing in your health, you are investing in the health of your entire family. My suggestion is that once you choose a plan to follow, allow the entire family to be involved. If 21 days seems unrealistic to you for your children, try 3, 5 or 7 days to begin and then increase over time. Again, the goal is to challenge and succeed! Note: If your child has a medical condition, please consult your healthcare provider before you begin.

What vitamins should I take

I hear this question so much. I believe the reason is that people know they need increased nutrition in the form of vitamins but information surrounding vitamin supplementation is often extensive and many times, just plain confusing. For my patients and myself, I try to keep it simple as possible. Here is what I recommend (and what I take daily): (1) Omega-3 (3,000-5,000 mg/day) (2) Vitamin D (5,000 IU/day) (3) Multi-vitamin with ample amounts of anti-oxidants (Vitamins A, C, E, selenium).

For my multi-vitamin, I use Immuplex from Standard Process. These are the three I recommend for everyone. A pro-biotic would also be useful; however, it is my experience that most people do not want to take more than three pills. The reason: most Americans are already taking prescribed medications so adding vitamins constitutes another pill they have to swallow. Please understand, by no means I am saying this is all everyone needs but it is a great start if you are taking no vitamins at all. I also recommend more specific vitamins/nutrients as the situation dictates.

Final Instructions

Have fun, be positive and know you are doing a great job. Just the fact that you are reading this means you care about your health. That is a great start! Creating a Trinity Lifestyle should not create stress. It should help alleviate it. For instance, if you start and only make it 12 out of the 21 days, re-evaluate, smile and at a later date – go for it again. Let me say it again: have fun. Be willing to try something new and learn as much as you can along the way. Just like you, I am also on this journey. Let's be healthier together! Lastly, "Dear friends, I pray that you may enjoy good health and that all may go well with you, even as your soul is getting along well" (3 John 2).

chapter

raw food plan

- **Beginner Version:** Follow the plan without changing anything else in your life.
- **Intermediate Version:** Follow the plan plus drink only water for the 21 days.
- **Advanced Version:** Follow the plan; drink only water and do not watch TV for 21 days.

Below you will find an outline for what meals will be included in these 21 days. The recipes and grocery lists can be found in Appendix A.

Day 1, 4, 7, 10, 13, 16, 19

Breakfast: Cherry Pineapple Celery Juice
Lunch: Foccacia and Arugula Pea Salad
Dinner: Tabouli

Day 2, 5, 8, 11, 14, 17, 20

Breakfast: Blueberries and Honey
Lunch: Banana Raspberry Celery Smoothie
Dinner: Asparagus Salad

Day 3, 6, 9, 12, 15, 18, 21

Breakfast: Pomegranate or Cherry Cereal
Lunch: Spring Garden Salad with Sunshine Dressing
Dinner: Celery Soup

Snacks

Dry Nuts (almonds, cashews or pecans)
Bananas
Sliced cucumbers

SPRING

Day 1

Renewing Activity: Yoga

I can build pig pens but not a house.

As I talked to a patient the other day about his health and life, He said these words, "I can build pig pens but not a house." He was talking about the expertise that his son-in-law and brother-in-law have in construction. His words made me think, isn't that the point? Some of us are called to build wonderful, elaborate homes but some are called to build pig pens. Both are important. I guarantee the pig farmer is very much appreciative for a well built pig pen just as much as his wife is appreciative of their nicely built home. Neither is more important per say because both builders are called to do a great job. Do you realize you are called?

Day 2

Renewing Activity: Yoga

Choose this day

One of my favorite accounts in the Bible is that of Elijah on Mount Carmel. As I was reading it this morning, I was again struck by the courage and zeal of Elijah. He tells Ahab, "Bring your 450 prophets of Baal to the top of the mount" (1 Kings 18). Elijah says of himself, I am the only servant of the Lord left. Then he declares to the people (and it is a word for us even today) – "Choose this day whom you will serve, if it is the Lord, serve Him. If it is Baal, serve Him. But quit wavering between them!" (1 Kings 18:21). Then he initiates a test that will determine whose God is real. The prophets of Baal will build an altar to their god and Elijah will build one to His God. Which-ever God consumes the altar with fire; He is the true God. The 450 Baal prophets sacrifice a bull, they dance around and they even begin to cut themselves but still their god doesn't answer, the altar sits untouched. Then, and I love this, Elijah mocks the 450 prophets. He laughs at them! It is Elijah's turn, He rebuilds the altar of the Lord, he digs a trench around it and he sacrifices the bull. Just in case any of the prophets or people thought Elijah's wood was too dry (remember it had not rained for some time) he pours 3 jars of water on top. Next Elijah simply prays, "Answer me O Lord that the people may know…" (1 Kings 18:37). Fire comes from heaven consumes the stone, the sacrifice, the water and dust. The people fall on their faces and declare the Lord is God. As I read this account, I pictured Elijah standing in the strength of the Lord – being a hero to the nation. Can you picture a young boy or girl sitting in the crowd watching all this? I am sure they were blown away at what they witnessed. In

SPRING

their minds, they had to think, I want to be like Elijah. He was a hero that day! We all need heroes in our life. Are you ready to climb to the top of Mount Carmel and be someone's hero?

Day 3

Renewing Activity: Walk for 20-30 minutes

Our attitudes, words, actions and often even our unspoken thoughts, tend to have an effect on those around us.

Today, what actions or what thoughts are you carrying that have a positive or even a negative effect on those around you? Are the words on your lips and the attitudes of your heart bringing life to your home or workplace? Or are your words and attitudes bringing strife, grief, bitterness, etc? We must be in our behavior what we are in our state of being. We must be authentic. People are looking for authenticity in a world they consider shallow and full of deception. Do they see authenticity in you?

Day 4

Renewing Activity: Paint, Draw or Journal for 15-20 minutes

Ministry is not some great, profound, extraordinary thing; it is the ordinary done in extraordinary ways.

Helen Keller said it this way, "I long to accomplish a great and noble task, but it is my chief duty to accomplish small tasks as if they were great and noble." I think many people think ministry is done primarily by paid clergy on Sunday. Some people even think ministry is just some big event that takes place like a convention, a Sunday morning service or a revival, etc. While ministry does take place at these venues, it also happens at the grocery store, at home and at work. If we are honest, all of us want to accomplish some great notable task but what if the greatest task you are called to is to love well? Your ministry might not look like you think it would or should and it probably goes unnoticed many times. Is that enough for you or must it be posted on the front page of the paper? Must our biography be filled with letters and accomplishments or would it be enough if our epitaph read, "Well done, he/she loved well."

SPRING

Day 5

Renewing Activity: **Yoga**

"In everyone's life, at some time, our inner fire goes out. It is then burst into flame by an encounter with another human being. We should all be thankful for those people who rekindle the inner spirit." –Albert Schweitzer

As I was thinking about this quote – I thought about the many people who have come alongside me to rekindle my spirit. Those people who have spoken words of life, encouragement and at times, correction over me. I praise God for the people He brings in my path even when they are people that I would not normally cross paths with intentionally. I heard someone say the other day, 'God brings people in your life not so they can be changed but so you can be changed.' That statement is so true. M Williamson said:

> Our deepest fear is not that we are inadequate. Our deepest fear is that we are powerful beyond measure. It is our light, not our darkness, that most frightens us. We ask ourselves, 'Who am I to be brilliant, gorgeous, talented and fabulous?' Actually, who are you not to be? You are a child of God. Your playing small doesn't serve the world. There's nothing enlightened about shrinking so that other people won't feel insecure around you. We were born to manifest the glory of God that is within us. It's not just in some of us; it's in everyone. And as we let our own light shine, we consciously give other people permission to do the same. As we are liberated from our own fear, our presence automatically liberates others.

Day 6

Renewing Activity: **Yoga**

He surprised me

"He surprised me when He ran to me." These are the words of a song I heard while I was driving. The song was about the prodigal son when he came home and his father went running to meet Him. The Father did not wait for his lost son to make his way to the door but ran out to Him. It must have shocked the son to see such a sight. That is what God does with us – He runs to us with arms wide open and declares – my child I love you – welcome home! And that surprises us because we too are shocked by a God that loves so deeply. We are shocked by a God that is moved with so much

SPRING

compassion that He runs down the road to hug us. I think that He surprised us, He still surprises us and He will forever surprise us because He loves to surprise us! Are you surprised by His love or do you take it for granted?

Day 7

Renewing Activity: Walk for 20-30 minutes

I wonder if they'll say that when I'm are dead?

I read a story where a man was told that he was spending too much time serving and giving too much away. His gentle but honest response was, "I wonder if they'll say that about me when I'm dead?" The point being this: our life is short, a vapor, and most of the time we live selfishly thinking only of ourselves and what we need or want. So, right now, what are you focused upon, is it eternal or temporal? In the words of 2 Corinthians 4:18, "So we fix our eyes on not what is seen but what is unseen. For the things that are seen are transient but the unseen is eternal."

Day 8

Renewing Activity: Write an encouraging letter to a friend or family member

Your identity is your most valuable possession

Identity is defined as (1) the characteristics that make something or someone recognizable or known, (2) the distinct personality and (3) what makes an entity definable. In the movie *The Incredibles*, the mom hands her kids "masks" and says to them, "Your identity is your most valuable possession…" I had never heard that line before. She was simply telling them, you may be wearing a mask to help "save the world" but that is not who you are. Your real identity, the one under the mask, needs to be protected and it needs to be guarded. In the same way, our true identity, who we really are, needs to be protected because so many other things will try to rob us of who we are. If our identity is stolen long enough or if we are wounded deeply enough, we will put on masks at work, at home and at church to either try to be something we are not or to hide. Are you wearing a mask today?

SPRING

Day 9

Renewing Activity: Yoga

Do not sacrifice the ultimate for the immediate.

I heard the above words in a sermon a few months ago. The pastor was speaking on Genesis 25:29-34. He spoke about Esau giving up his birthright for the temporal pleasure of a bowl of lentil soup. Esau was the firstborn so all his father had was his but when faced with the immediate pains of hunger he chose to trade what his birthright would have allowed him for one meal. The pastor said that Esau could have called his servants to get him food or asked his dad, but he did not. Instead Esau chose to sacrifice the ultimate provision for his immediate need. How often do we do this? How often do we allow ourselves to forget about the ultimate – whether it be spiritual, physical or emotional goals – how often do we just take the immediate pleasures instead of the ultimate provision? Another way it could be worded – how often do we settle for the 'good' of God instead of going for the 'best?' I dare to say more often than we care to think.

Day 10

Renewing Activity: Yoga

We are the plan of God and there is no plan B.

Ever walked by a homeless guy on the street? Ever drove by a stranded car with someone needing help? Ever saw a mom in a grocery line stressed out? Ever seen anyone in need and wondered if you should help but then rationalized why you should not, could not or would not? Sure, we all have done it but what if that was God's plan for us that day – to help the homeless, to help the stranded, to speak words of kindness – what if we are God's plan and there is no plan B?

Day 11

Renewing Activity: Interval Walking (10 minutes forward then 2 minutes backward) – repeat 2-3 times

Jesus you're beautiful

"…your eyes are like flames of fire…your hair is white as wool…your voice is like mighty waters…Jesus you're beautiful…" (Revelation 1:14-15) This is a revelation of Jesus Christ. What is the revelation you are having of Jesus at this moment in your

SPRING

life? Do you see Him as distant, something just added to your life, another thing you have to do – or today, right now – do you see Jesus as beautiful?

Day 12

Renewing Activity: Take a homemade meal (or a plate of homemade cookies) to a neighbor

I will love fully knowing that I am fully accepted.

It has been mentioned that many people struggle with the 'spirit of rejection.' What does this mean? I guess the best way to describe a spirit of rejection is that it is a spirit that deceives you into thinking you are less than or that no one likes you. Because of this you are constantly seeking approval, constantly worried about what others think and constantly worried whether you are accepted, loved and respected. Many of us have been rejected in our lives; does this mean everyone struggles with this spirit? Probably not but it is human nature to want to be loved and accepted. The problem lies in the fact that people have wounds from the past that are used to filter every present and future event. F. Ourlser states it this way, "Many of us crucify ourselves between two thieves - regret for the past and fear of the future." These 'thieves' – these rejection wounds serve as an entry point for a lifetime of seeking approval – trying to control our circumstances to not be rejected – seeking love and acceptance in a variety of unhealthy ways. What wounds, if any, have occurred in your life? Did they make you feel rejected? Are you seeking approval in your life right now?

Day 13

Renewing Activity: Yoga

And it shall be a tassel for you to look at and remember.

Numbers 15:37-40 reads, "The Lord spoke to Moses, 'speak to the people of Israel and tell them to make tassels on the corner of their garments...and it shall be a tassel for you to look at and remember...so shall you remember and do all my commandments and be holy to your God...I am the Lord your God..." As I read, these words struck me as odd yet stirred me at the same time. God is so intricately involved in our lives – that even in the tapestry of our cloths – he wants to be remembered. I do not think that He was "laying down another burden" I think He was yet again reminding the people that He desires to be involved in our daily thoughts. He desires a relationship with us and as we look at the 'tassel on our garment' are we remembering Him? Remember... (a wise word from Mufassa to Simba – remember when he was in the cloud?)

SPRING

Day 14

Renewing Activity: Yoga

Our voluntary thoughts not only reveal what we are, they predict what we will become.

Voluntary thoughts are not fleeting thoughts. Nor are they the thoughts we entertain for work or entertainment purposes. Voluntary thoughts are those thoughts we mull over in our head for long periods of time. These thoughts enamor our frontal lobe taking up time, space and resources. About these thoughts, JC Ryle wrote, "…guard your thoughts and there will be little fear of your actions." Today, what thoughts invade your space? What do these thoughts reveal about you? What actions are at the end of these thoughts?

Day 15

Renewing Activity: Yoga

*Parenting – not politics, not the classroom, not the laboratory,
not even the pulpit – is the place of greatest influence.*

J. Jackson said, "Your children need your presence more than your presents." I believe by becoming parents, we get a small glimpse of God's heart for us. Paul writes in Romans 8:15-17, "…you received the Spirit of son-ship. And by him we cry, 'Abba, Father.' The Spirit himself testifies with our spirit that we are God's children…We are His children, thus we are His heirs…" God tells us that His desire is for us to have a spirit of son-ship, we are not left alone and we are not orphans. We must become engaged, intentional, attached parents guiding, loving and influencing our children for something great. K Hughes writes, "Above all, we [as parents] must make sure that the open book of our lives – our example – demonstrates the reality of our instruction, for in watching us they will learn the most." Your children and my children are watching, processing, creating mental images and attitudes based on what they see at a greater rate than they are listening to what we say.

Therefore Dad, it does matter how you love your wife. Dad, it does matter if you are at home. Dad, it does matter if you hold that new baby. Dad, it does matter if you are engaged and intentional. J. Joubert says about being a Father, "Love or fear. Everything the father of a family says must inspire one or the other." Dad, which do you inspire?

Therefore Mom, it does matter if you respect your husband. Mom, it does matter if you are at home. Mom, it does matter that you sacrifice yourself. Mom, it does matter in the little-un-noticed mundane moments. Mom, it is ok if you go to work – your heart is

SPRING

still for your children. About moms, JR Miller adds, "God sends many beautiful things to this world, many noble gifts; but no blessing is richer than that which He bestows in a mother who has learned love's lessons well, and has realized something of the meaning of her sacred calling." Mom, do you realize the depth of your calling?

Day 16

Renewing Activity: Go to a gas station and pay to fill up someone else's car

Therefore choose life

Choose life! What comes to mind when you read those words. Is it a pro-life slogan and ending abortion? Is it to have a natural life-style? What is it? For me, when I read the words – choose life – I think of my daily choice to choose life-giving thoughts, actions, intentions and relationships. If I don't choose those I may end up choosing life-taking thoughts, actions, intentions and relationships. J Bridges, mentioned choosing our thought-life carefully and intentionally and wrote, "What we allow to enter our minds is critically important. The television programs we watch, the movies we may attend, the books and magazines we read, the music we listen to, and the conversations we have all affect our minds. We need to evaluate the effects of these avenues honestly, using Philippians 4:8 as a standard. Are the thoughts stimulated by these various avenues true? Are they pure? Are they lovely, admirable, excellent, or praiseworthy?" Simply, are they helping? With this knowledge will you choose life or death? To be sure you are choosing one or the other so, which is it?

Day 17

Renewing Activity: Walk for 33 minutes

In God we trust.

Really, do we? K Sande writes, "Trusting God does not mean believing that He will do all that you want, but rather believing that He will do everything He knows is good." When was the last time you or I trusted in God and waited for Him? I am convicted that while I profess to trust in God I wonder at times how much? I wonder where we see this saying daily, "in God we trust" but think nothing of it. Figured it out yet? Look in your wallet, yep, it is on our money. Isn't that interesting? I find it is especially interesting since so much talk focuses on our economy and the United State's debt ceiling. Didn't Christ say, "You cannot serve two Gods'. You will love the one and hate the other. You cannot serve [put your trust in] both God and money." So our money, the very thing that many put their trust in, conveys the truth to point us to how we should be living our lives. Hmmmm?

SPRING

Day 18

Renewing Activity: Go to a park and play – Slide down a slide – Swing on the swing (Repeat many times)

I want to be like?

A story I recently read recalled, 'When the wife of missionary Adoniram Judson told him that a newspaper article likened him to some of the apostles, Judson replied, "I do not want to be like a Paul or any mere man. I want to be like Christ. I want to follow Him only, copy His teachings, drink in His Spirit, and place my feet in His footprints. Oh, to be more like Christ!" Is that my desire? We may think it wonderful to be compared to Paul but is it? That is not our calling. Our call is to be molded into the image of Christ. 2 Corinthians 3:18 calls to us, "...beholding the glory of the Lord, [we] are being transformed into the same image..." Into what image are you being transformed? Is it what you see on the television or in magazines? Or is your desire for something greater? Make sure you know who you are trying to match and mimic because friends, enemies, your spouse and children are watching.

Day 19

Renewing Activity: Yoga

Prayer is not a monologue but a dialogue.
Prayer is not about changing God but about changing us.
To be too busy to pray is to prove how lazy you really are, Prayer is the work.

"One day Jesus was praying in a certain place. When he had finished, one of the disciples came and asked, 'Lord, <u>teach us TO pray</u>...Jesus said, '<u>WHEN you pray</u>, pray like this; Father how great is your name, let your kingdom come....<u>Ask (and keep asking)</u> and it will be given, <u>Seek (and keep seeking)</u> and you shall find, <u>Knock (and keep knocking)</u> and the door will be open..." Luke 11:1-13 (emphasis added) Did you catch that? WHEN you pray not IF you pray...which is it for you?

SPRING

Day 20

Renewing Activity: Yoga

> *The Bible is both prognosis and therapy; a mirror and a window.*

Stanly Tam, in *God Owns My Business*, wrote "I do not understand why so many Christians read a Bible abounding in promises to make them something beyond themselves and yet settle for a spiritual vitality so mediocre as to seem virtually non-existent." Is it because the only day we pick up the Bible is Sunday? I would have to say, yes it is – we love so many things except the one thing that can set us free – Christ Jesus and His precious word.

Day 21

Renewing Activity: Plant a flower (a perennial) so you can be reminded of what you have accomplished

LIFE – Living Intentionally Focusing Eternally

I had a patient say the other day in my office that they were doing well but then life got in the way. I had a friend say to me that he was trying to navigate through "the cloud of life". As I thought about those two statements, I thought about the word LIFE and what it means. As I thought about it the words, 'Living Intentionally Focusing Eternally' came to mind. I thought I was rather clever coming up with that motivational saying, then I Googled it and sadly I am not the first to come up with it. Needless to say life is meant to be lived intentionally within the context of our daily tasks and relationships. We should be fixing our thoughts on the kingdom of God having an eternal perspective while we are walking through this life. So the question to ask yourself: is this what kind of life is getting in your way? Life (Living incidentally focused errantly) or LIFE *(Living Intentionally Focusing Eternally)*? Either one of these will dramatically affect the outcome of your day.

S U M M E R

- **Beginner Version:** Follow the plan without changing anything else in your life.

- **Intermediate Version:** Follow the plan plus drink only water for the 21 days.

- **Advanced Version:** Follow the plan; drink only water and do not watch TV for 21 days.

Below you will find an outline for what meals will be included in these 21 days. The recipes and grocery list can be found in Appendix A.

Day 1, 4, 7, 10, 13, 16, 19

Breakfast: Watermelon
Lunch: Grapes and Avocado Tomato Basil Salad
Dinner: Squash Soup

Day 2, 5, 8, 11, 14, 17, 20

Breakfast: Cantaloupe Blend
Lunch: Peaches, Nectarines, Plums or Grapes
Dinner: Mango, Cucumber, Tomato, Avocado Salad

Day 3, 6, 9, 12, 15, 18, 21

Breakfast: Apricot, Pineapple Banana Smoothie
Lunch: Romaine Avocado Tacos
Dinner: Raw Corn on the Cob with Lemon and Coconut Oil

Snacks

A simple vegetable like a cucumber, okra, or tomato
A piece of your favorite fruit.

Day 1

<u>Renewing Activity</u>: Yoga

> *It was good that I was afflicted that I might learn your statutes.*

As I was praying, the above words, seemingly from nowhere, came out of my mouth. Of course, they are not my words but rather words found in Psalm 119:71. But as I kept praying I realized just how true this was in my life. Without the circumstances, many times difficult circumstances, that we face we would not learn anything about

SUMMER

ourselves. More importantly, we would not learn anything about Christ. What affliction have you been through or what are you currently going through? And what have you learned from it?

Day 2

Renewing Activity: Yoga

What is the cost of intimacy?

I was listening to a Jason Upton song titled 'Cost of Intimacy.' He sang these words, 'I need you more than music…I need you more than good times…I need more than friendships…I need you more than this life…I am not giving up…" As I listened to the words of that song, my spirit screamed, "Yes! – I need you Lord and I am not giving up – not losing heart for intimacy with You." The cost of intimacy for God was no less than the spilt blood of His son. What is the cost of intimacy for you?

Day 3

Renewing Activity: Yoga

Be my center.

If you sing about God being your center, your main focus and you say "Lord all I want is you - you are enough!" Does your lifestyle reveal this to be truth? Does your verbal accolade go along with what you live out?

Day 4

Renewing Activity: Write an encouraging email or text to a friend

It is our greatest weapon and our greatest strength…With this weapon we can curse or we can bless…With this weapon we can build up or tear down…With this weapon we can proclaim freedom or build a prison…

What is this weapon? It is our tongue, our words or our mouth! Proverbs 18:21 declares, "Death and Life are in the power of the tongue and those who love it will eat its fruits." Proverbs 12:18 expounds, "There is one whose rash words are like sword thrusts but the tongue of the wise brings healing." Jeremiah 20:9 goes on to say that the word of the Lord, "is like a fire in my bones and I cannot contain it." Do you have this same passion for the word - is it burning inside of you so much so that it cannot be contained? But when you let it out - does it produce life or death? Does it kill and divide or does it bring healing and unity? How are you using this weapon?

SUMMER

Day 5

Renewing Activity: **Walk for 20-30 minutes**

...you are near in their mouth but far from their heart... (Jer. 12:2)

As I was reading, God highlighted the above verse to me. And some questions came to mind: Is this where I am? Do I praise God with my mouth but in my heart am I far away? Do I like to spout off praise with my mouth but in my heart harbor resentment, anger, pride, etc? Where am I at spiritually? Do my heart motives and my word usage align?

Day 6

Renewing Activity: **Yoga**

The more we pray, the more we sense our need to pray.
And the more we sense a need to pray, the more we want to pray.

Prayer is the life-source of the Christian! Do not say I ought to pray - let God drive you to pray. Let Him fill you so much with His Heart that prayers just overflow. Let your life be filled with prayer - be the fragrance of Christ - that constant burning - the constant aching for deepness with Him. Let nothing else satisfy. The question begs to be asked, "How is your prayer life?" If we are not praying what are we doing? There is nothing simpler yet more profound than praying and reading God's word. This practice is so deep it takes a life-time to pursue.

Day 7

Renewing Activity: **Yoga**

Set up a standard.

What is the standard by which we live? Is it Godliness or worldliness? A few months back I read a book titled, Intoxicated by Babylon. It said that often we are infused with the sights, smells and tastes of Babylon so much so that we are drunk on our own demise. It went on to say that we have rejected Christ and the simplicity of the gospel because of this intoxication with the pleasures of Babylon. Because of this intoxication what we once had set as a standard, Godliness, has been removed; things we once stood for don't seem important any more. The author's claim was that the

SUMMER

world has a bigger impact on the church than the church does on the world. He stated that because of this fascination with Babylon we claim that church is boring, too old fashioned, not enlightened enough and that Christ and the Bible do not fit into our culture today! Think about it - have you or someone you know made a comment like that? What are you intoxicated with?

Day 8

Renewing Activity: Yoga

Our attitudes, words, actions and often, even our unspoken thoughts, tend to have an effect on those around us.

We must be in our behavior what we are in our state of being. We must be authentic. People are looking for authenticity in a world they consider shallow and full of deception. Today, what actions – what thoughts are you carrying that either have a positive or negative effect on those around you? Are the words on your lips or the attitude of your heart bringing life to your home or workplace or is it bringing strife, grief, bitterness, etc...?

Day 9

Renewing Activity: Go for a slow walk and enjoy the outdoors

Before Jesus called the disciples to ministry He called them to intimacy.

Before Jesus ever had the disciples "go out" and "do ministry" – he called them unto himself. He said follow Me not follow my ministry or miracles. What are you following?

Day 10

Renewing Activity: Yoga

"What is that to you? You follow me!"- John 21:21-22

These are the words of Christ spoken to Peter when he asked what God's will was for another disciple. Peter had just heard Jesus tell him what his death would be like; then he saw the other disciple following them and said, "what about this man?" Christ's answer was simple, what about Him? Why do you want to know? Quit worrying about what I am calling Him to do – You follow me! Are you more concerned with God's will for others or His will for you?

SUMMER

Day 11

Renewing Activity: Yoga

The pull of religion can be far stronger than the freedom of relationship.

Jacobsen calls it "daisy-petal Christianity" referring to the childhood game, "He loves me, He loves me not." The adult version goes something like this, I got the promotion at work –*He loves me*…I did not get a raise – *He loves me not*…I gave money to someone in need – *He loves me*…My child is seriously ill – *He loves me not*…I got a note of encouragement – *He loves me*…My car's transmission went out – *He loves me not*… and on and on. This game wears us out keeping us stressed out as we constantly try to discern if God loves us or not. Jacobsen writes, "So it is time to toss the daisies and discover that it is not the fear of losing God's love that will keep you on His path but the simple joy of living in it every day." So are you willing to toss the daisy?

Day 12

Renewing Activity: Go to a local pool or splash park – smile and have fun

I wonder if they'll say that when I'm are dead?

I read a story where a man was told that he was spending too much time serving and giving too much away. His gentle but honest response was, "I wonder if they'll say that about me when I'm dead?" The point being this: our life is short, a vapor, and most of the time we live selfishly thinking only of ourselves and what we need or want. So, right now, what are you focused upon: is it eternal or temporal? In the words of 2 Corinthians 4:18, "So we fix our eyes on not what is seen but what is unseen. For the things that are seen are transient but the unseen is eternal."

Day 13

Renewing Activity: Yoga

The aim of our charge is love

An anonymous quote reads, "Laugh as often as you breathe and love as long as you live." I think of a small child and how much laughter they have, how the simplest thing brings them enormous pleasure. Small children love so well with their hugs and their smiles can warm our hearts. Their whole existence is wrapped in laughter and love and that is all they know (or hopefully it is). Why do we lose the simplicity of laughter and love as we grow? Is it that we have learned too much, have we become

SUMMER

too educated? Is it that we have been wounded and never want to let that happen again? What is it about adulthood that causes us to forget that our charge is to love?

Day 14

Renewing Activity: Yoga

I'm after your heart

These are words from a song I heard and they linger in my mind. To think that God is after our heart but at the same time we are after His. What is it about the heart that is so intense and so alive? An anonymous quote reads, "The greatest treasures are those invisible to the eye but found by the heart." Do you see it? A great treasure lies within our heart. It is the pearl of great price!

Day 15

Renewing Activity: Yoga

Why is the grass greener?

"The grass is always greener on the other side." How many times have I heard that saying throughout my life? But the questions I have to ask: (1) why do we think it is greener? (2) If it is really greener, why? I thought about my own neighborhood and looking around at the lawns – some are greener than others. Why is that? The overwhelming conclusion is the water. The lawns that are the greenest have been watered more than the lawns that are dry and brown. Spiritually – the same can be true. You may look at someone's life and think that their 'grass is greener.' But is it really? Take a close look and if it is, could it be that they are walking out John 4:14, "...whoever drinks the water I give him will never thirst. Indeed, the water I give him will become in him a spring of water welling up to eternal life." Maybe the better question to ask is: "When does the grass become greenest?" The answer: when we are partaking of living water. Are you partaking to make your grass the greenest it can become?

SUMMER

Day 16

Renewing Activity: Yoga

Preach the Gospel at all times and when necessary use words.

As a patient and I were talking, he referenced the above quote by St. Francis of Assisi. We were talking about being authentic in our life and what that authenticity looks like lived out day by day. I have seen the reality of the above quote within my practice but reworded slightly, "People do not care how much you know until they know how much you care." Is that not a true statement? We may seek out wisdom from people but what we really want to know is if that person really cares about us. Can they be trusted or are they just 'preaching' at us?

Day 17

Renewing Activity: Call someone just to tell them how important they are to you

Nebraska...the good life

What does "the good life mean"? If someone asked you, how would you define "a good life"? What would your response be? Would it be based on how big your home is, how successful your business is, how many children you have or how much money you have in a savings account? Or would it be based on something deeper, something greater and something that stirs passion within you? What is your definition of 'the good life?'

Day 18

Renewing Activity: Walk for 27 minutes

Though I sleep, my heart is awake.

I heard these words in a song and as I listened I thought, yes even though I sleep (literally at night or day dream during the mundane moments of life) – my heart is awake! My heart is awakened to His love in my life and my heart is awakened to His purposes. My heart is awakened to the needs of my wife and my children. My heart is awakened to those I encounter and my heart is awakened and quickened at the beauty I see around me. My heart is awakened to something deeper, something greater and something that calls me and pulls me toward a fascinating love affair. An anonymous quote states "The greatest treasures are those invisible to the eye but found by the heart." What treasure needs to be awakened today that lies deep within your heart?

SUMMER

Day 19

Renewing Activity: Yoga

Who do you call God?

When you pray how do you address God? When you think of the creator what word or name comes to mind? Your answer to this question may reveal your heart in reference to God. David writes in Psalms 9:10 "Those who know your name will trust in you." It is like David is saying you can't trust God unless you know His name. But it is more than just knowing a name it is knowing HIM. You can know my name is William (aka Bo) but if that is all you know you won't automatically trust me. You must know me to trust me. So do you know God? What do you call Him?

Day 20

Renewing Activity: Yoga

Roll away your stone

Jennifer and I enjoy the band Mumford and Sons. Recently, I was stopped by the words to this song, "Roll away your stone and I'll roll away mine. Together we can see what we can find. Don't leave me alone at this time. For I'm afraid of what I will discover inside." As I listened to these words I thought, do I have a stone? I am fairly sure we all do. Am I scared to roll it away to find out what is inside? If there is a stone, am I willing to allow someone to help roll it away or do I think I can do it on my own?

Day 21

Renewing Activity: Journal, paint or draw a picture capturing the last 21 days of your life

I'm bigger on the inside than I am on the outside.

These words came from a young girl when her daddy asked her, "How can you eat all of that cotton candy?" Is that true of you? Are you different on the outside than you are on the inside? Are you a well-polished, seemingly successful person on the outside but a hurt, angry and resentful person on the inside? Jesus said in Matthew 23:27 "… you are like whitewashed tombs, which look beautiful on the outside but on the inside are full of dead men's bones and everything unclean." Christ was addressing character. Your character is who and what you are when no one is looking, when you aren't worried about your reputation. J Wooden aptly reminds, "Be more concerned with your character than with your reputation because your character is what you really are while your reputation is merely what others think you are." So which is more important for you, your character or your reputation?

FALL

- **Beginner Version:** Follow the plan without changing anything else in your life.
- **Intermediate Version:** Follow the plan plus drink only water for the 21 days.
- **Advanced Version:** Follow the plan; drink only water and do not watch TV 21 days.

Below you will find an outline for what meals will be included in these 21 days. The recipes and grocery list can be found in Appendix A.

Day 1, 4, 7, 10, 13, 16, 19

Breakfast: Apple, Beet, Ginger and Lemon Juice
Lunch: Gazpacho
Dinner: Tabouli

Day 2, 5, 8, 11, 14, 17, 20

Breakfast: Pears or Asian Pears
Lunch: Rosemary Broccoli Salad
Dinner: Corn Salad

Day 3, 6, 9, 12, 15, 18, 21

Breakfast: Mulled Apple Sauce
Lunch: Kale Salad
Dinner: Peaches

Snacks

Apple Punch
Ants on a log

Day 1

Renewing Activity: Yoga

This is our warfare...this is our intercession...Jesus reigns over the nations.

Do I realize there is a battle that rages? Do I intercede for that battle? Ephesians 6:12 says, "For our struggle is not against flesh and blood, but against the rulers, against the authorities, against the powers of this dark world and against the spiritual forces of evil in the heavenly realms." Second Corinthians 10:3-4 says, "For though we walk

FALL

in the flesh, we are not waging war according to the flesh. For the weapons of our warfare are not of the flesh but have divine power to destroy strongholds." What battle are you facing right now and how are you warring against it? Are you using man's wisdom or God's? S. Ferguson says, "As in all warfare, the two essential elements in victory is to know your enemy and know your resources". Know your enemy – anticipate the battle – intercede and know your resource. Exodus 14:14 declares, "The LORD will fight for you; you need only to be still." Jesus is not passively interceding for you – His love is active – purposely and passionately warring for you. He loves you and fights for your heart. That is His warfare and that is His intercession.

Day 2

Renewing Activity: Yoga

You came along and told me why I exist.

Think back to your childhood (or maybe even to last week)– what words were spoken over you? What words do you remember the most? Do these words cause you to lift your head up or turn away in shame? Have you recognized the words you speak over yourself, your spouse, your children and your friends? A song I heard stated, "I was aimless, wandering without purpose, I was shipwrecked, I was abandoned and then You came along and told me why I exist." Christ has come alongside me to tell me who I am and why I exist. I no longer have to wander aimlessly because I am not abandoned. He tells us why we exist and He does it through the talents He gives us. He does it through our intimate times with Him. He does it through our school, work and home life. He does it through our successes and failures. He does it through our friends and family. The question: do you receive the words He speaks over you?

Day 3

Renewing Activity: Yoga

I am free in Christ.

Ever wonder what that truly means? I am sure it has multiple – deep – profound meanings but in its simplest, purest form, what does "I am free in Christ" mean? Does it mean that because of the freedom we have in Christ, we can do whatever we want? Surely no but that is the way many act. I know I have acted like that many time using "my freedom" in Christ to justify certain actions. S. Storm writes, "Christian liberty is itself a good thing. But when wrongly used, it can bring disgrace on the gospel." How are you using your freedom?

FALL

Day 4

Renewing Activity: **Go to your favorite local store and buy something for a total stranger**

What do you want to see God do in your life in the next year?

What is your answer to that question? Ever thought about it? I was talking to a pastor last week who has started asking his congregation and others he meets these three questions, (1) What do you want to see God do in your life in the next year? (2) What are you doing to pursue that? (2) How can I help or come alongside to make it a reality? He was telling me that when he asks, most people do not have an answer or if they do, they are doing nothing about it. Then they are shocked that someone wants to help. The answer to those questions shows the reality of your testimony in Christ. So, what are you asking God for?

Day 5

Renewing Activity: Walk for 20-30 minutes

It is a good thing to do one's thinking in relation to real people.

Relationship is a good thing but it is not always easy. To do my thinking, processing and living in the midst of relationship is even harder. J. Piper in 'Don't Waste your life' writes about meeting his wife, "It is a good thing to do one's thinking in relation to real people. From that moment on, every thought has been in relationship. Nothing is merely an idea but an idea that bears on my wife and children…" Every thought or idea does have bearing on others. As it shapes, molds, and changes the person having the thought it also affects those nearest to that person through their actions. When we do our thinking in the midst of relationship – our thoughts can be exposed for what they are – good, bad or indifferent. In exposing them – we grow – we mature – we learn. In learning our relationships also grow - some for a season, some for a lifetime. And without growth, nothing lives very long.

Day 6

Renewing Activity: Yoga

Where do you go to church?

Ever had someone ask you this question? I'm sure you have and you have probably asked it yourself hundreds of times. What do we mean with that question? Aren't

FALL

we trying to categorize people when we ask? For example, if someone states, 'First Baptist', do you not mentally think of what a Baptist is or what they might believe. You may be thinking, no I don't do that. Yes you do and so do I. It helps our brains to categorize and organize but the problem with that is our categorization may be false. People are not fully defined by where they go to church nor do we know what they believe by what church they attend. Maybe the better question is, what has Christ done in your life in the last week, month or year? There is no categorization with that question, just the reality of your own testimony.

Day 7

Renewing Activity: Yoga

Be the two not the ten.

You look at your day and it seems overwhelming – the piles of emails, the stacks of papers - the bills are due – the kids are screaming – the day you had planned takes a dramatic turn and does not work out the way you think it should. What do we do in these circumstances? Do we panic and forget all that we are about? Do we boil over in anger at those around us? Do we only have good days (joyful days) when our circumstances dictate that outcome? RW Emerson noted, "The first thing a great person does is make us realize the insignificance of circumstance." Numbers 13-14 paints a picture of circumstance and twelve people's responses to it. God's people are heading to the Promised Land and Moses sends out twelve men (one for each tribe) to look over the land. Ten report back, "We cannot take the land." But two men report, "Let us go up and occupy the land." Ten looked in fear but two looked at a promise. As you look at you day are you the ten or the two?

Day 8

Renewing Activity: Rake leaves into a big pile – Jump in them and throw them into the air (or create some other fun outdoor activity)

Here...there...everywhere...

I so appreciate Dr. Seuss books. He can turn an ordinary object or thought into a book of delight and laughter. His use of simple language can unlock joy inexpressible. As you look at those three words, Are you the same: here…there…everywhere? Or even a deeper question – do I believe God is the same – here...there...everywhere?

FALL

Day 9

Renewing Activity: Yoga

Jesus, I love you. What's in it for you?

These words were written on a chalkboard. Notice it does not say what's in it for me? His love, His dying, un-ending passionate love and Himself that is my reward and that is what is in it for me! So what is it in for Jesus? What is in it for the Lamb of God – the King of all Kings – the One uncreated – the One who was before all things yet is in all things – what is in it for Him? Ever wondered that or are you too busy thinking of yourself?

Day 10

Renewing Activity: Yoga

The way you invest your love; you invest your life

An investment is defined first as the act of investing effort or resources and second as a commitment, as of support or time. Thus to invest your love is to put forth a commitment, an effort, to give time and support to that one thing. So what is that one thing? What are you investing in today? And is what you are investing in worth what you are investing? If you are investing hundreds of hours at a job you love at the expense of your family, is that the life you want? If you are investing your love toward a hobby, is that what you want your life to be remembered for? If you were to ask your family, friends or even coworkers where you invest your love (thus your life) – what do you think they would say?

Day 11

Renewing Activity: Yoga

The pull of religion can be far stronger than the freedom of relationship.

Jacobsen calls it "daisy-petal Christianity" referring to the childhood game, "He loves me, He loves me not." The adult version goes something like this, I got the promotion at work –*He loves me*…I did not get a raise – *He loves me not*…I gave money to someone in need – *He loves me*…My child is seriously ill – *He loves me not*…I got a note of encouragement – *He loves me*…My car's transmission went out – *He loves me not*… and on and on. This game wears us out keeping us stressed out as we constantly try to discern if God loves us or not. Jacobsen writes, "So it is time to toss the daisies and discover that it is not the fear of losing God's love that will keep you on His path but the simple joy of living in it every day." So are you willing to toss the daisy?

FALL

Day 12

Renewing Activity: Find something in your house you no longer need and give it away.

Come again to us and teach us.

On M*A*S*H, Colonel Potter said, "Having babies is fun, but babies grow up into people!" Knowing the truth of that statement, how many of us as parents start asking for wisdom and grace either before we conceive a child or while the child is in the womb? If we are honest many of us do not ask for wisdom as we parent our children. We just assume that since we have a child we must know how to be parents. But my question is, do we? Did our parents and our grand-parents give us a perfect blueprint to raise our child? Do we actually have the wisdom to steward a soul? It is not just a little body you are taking care of, there is a soul contained in that little, precious body. And that soul is destined for eternity...how are you preparing your child for that eternity?

Day 13

Renewing Activity: Yoga

Sticks and stones will break my bones but words will never hurt me.

R. Kipling writes, "Words are the most powerful drug used by mankind." As a friend and I were playing golf recently he mentioned that he did not like getting made fun of if he hit the ball poorly. Who does? But I had to admit to him when he hit the tree – I could not help but laugh. As we discussed and continued to play the above phrase was mentioned but immediately the realization struck me. Those words are untrue! Ok, sticks and stones may break bones but words do hurt and they leave lasting wounds far after our bones are healed. In Oxygen for the Soul, D. Bingham writes, "A suicide's body was found floating in a river and a note was written on her person. The note had only two words written on it: 'They said.' Do we realize what a word from our tongues can do? It can wreck a local church, mar a child for life, disrupt the harmony of a business office and destroy a marriage." What have you said? Are you 'they'?

FALL

Day 14

Renewing Activity: Yoga

Obligated owner or Committed steward

Do you feel obligated to go to church or are you committed to what God is calling you to do? Do you feel obligated or committed to your spouse? Do you view your marriage as a contract (an obligation that must be fulfilled and easily discarded if it is not on your terms) or do you view it as a covenant (a commitment that was fulfilled when you said I do)? Do you feel obligated to work 'that job' or are you committed to your work as unto the Lord? If single, are you obligated to purity because "the church has told you so" or are you committed to purity because of Christ? Are you trusting and waiting for Him to bring you that special spouse you can give yourself to? Have you asked God to be the 'co-pilot' in your life, only conversing with Him when you need him or is he the pilot? Do you view everything in your life as a gift to be thankful for; are you honored to be a steward of what He has given you?

Day 15

Renewing Activity: Paint, Draw or Journal for 15-20 minutes

What is your response?

Many times my responses are based on what people think rather than what God thinks. My responses are often most noticeable in the little moments of life. Those mundane everyday moments in life are actually where we show our true character. When I am driving in the car and someone cuts me off. When my child asks, for the 400th time, to do this or that and when that same child poops on the floor after we just took them to the bathroom, how do I respond? When my spouse doesn't notice the surprise I left for her. When Starbucks makes my no sugar, one drip, two pump latte wrong, what is your response to God when everyone is watching? Are you courageousness enough to obey? What is your response to God in the moments of life when no one is watching? Are you courageous enough to care even then?

Day 16

Renewing Activity: Yoga

The way, the truth and the life

Jesus states in John 14:6, "I am the way, the truth and the life. No one comes to the

FALL

Father except through Me." Do you believe those words? Do you actually believe Jesus is the way? Jesus is the truth? And Jesus is the life? Or do you remove an 'F' and make the statement read: "The way, the truth and the lie. You see if you remove the 'F' out the word life – you get lie. I believe people are watching you and me. They are watching how we respond to our spouse when conflict arises. They watch how we react or not react to our kid's direct disobedience. They are watching to see how we respond to the person who cuts us off in traffic. Watching to see if we will be honest and give back the extra change that was given to us at the cash register. People are looking to see if we think Jesus is life or if Jesus is a lie. Which do you portray? But deeper yet what do you believe – not necessarily just by words but by your very actions?

Day 17

Renewing Activity: **Yoga**

Life is not about waiting for the storm to pass...it is learning to dance in the rain.

An anonymous quote reads, "Sometimes the Lord calms the storm; Sometimes He lets the storm rage and calms His child." Many storms may come throughout your life and you can run from them. You can hide from them or you can pray they never happen but more than likely a storm will come. What will our attitude be when it comes?

Day 18

Renewing Activity: **Walk for 27 minutes**

I will follow you into the homes that are broken – I will follow you into the world.

Where does Christ want you to go? Does he call you into the places where you don't think He would go? Or does he call you into places you know HE would go into but that you are too afraid to enter? Maybe it is following Him into the tavern. Maybe it is following Him into a single parents home to help them instead of judging them. Maybe it is following Him to a business to patronize it as a blessing when you do not even like their product. Perhaps you need to follow Him into your parents home to apologize for not honoring them (whether or not they honored you). Is it following Him into places you were rude and apologizing? Do you need to follow Him into your own home where your words have caused pain and brokenness? **Where is He asking you to follow Him?** It may not be as far as you think.

FALL

Day 19

Renewing Activity: Yoga

> *It's not that we consciously put God out of our minds.*
> *We just ignore Him. He is seldom in our thoughts.*

If we are honest, how often does God enter your mind throughout the day? Do you have a conscious awareness of the presence of God all day? Do you practice the presence of God like Brother Lawrence spoke about in his book, 'Practicing the Presence of God?' Or do you think about God only in the midst of a need, a prayer at lunch or on Sunday? Where and what is your mind set upon?

Day 20

Renewing Activity: Yoga

> *What good is faith, if it's not tried?*
> *Will I believe and love only when life is well and good?*

A Russian missionary wrote: 'A year back or so, a good Russian friend lost her husband to a brain aneurysm. On one of my trips back, I made it a point to see her. With the two young children in her lap I asked her. "Natasha, how is your faith holding up through all this?" Her eyes flashed with light and a steadiness that shocked me. A quiet reply came, 'I don't understand, but Bill, what good is faith, if it's not tried? Will I believe and love the Savior only when life is well and good'?" If someone asks you how you are doing a myriad of answers may come to mind. You could say fine or good or that you are feeling stressed. But if someone asks you 'what is God up to in your life?' The answers might not come as quickly. What would be your reply? Would you be silent because you do not perceive Him or take time to notice Him? Or could you like the young Russian widow declare with conviction: 'His love surrounds me even if I do not understand it – I am tried and I am tired but my faith is being strengthened all the more.'

FALL

Day 21

Renewing Activity: Take a long bath and reflect on the last 21 days

The tongue is the only instrument that reveals what is in the heart

Eph. 4:29, Luke 6:44-45 and James 3:10 state "Watch what comes out of your mouth. Let nothing hateful come out of it. Speak only what is helpful, each word is a gift. It's who you are, not what you say and do, that counts. Your true being brims over into true words and deeds. What not ought to be is this: blessing and cursing coming from the same tongue; with it we praise God but in the next breath we curse our brother." Each word you get to speak is a gift – once it is given it cannot be taken back. Before you ever say a word, it is harbored in your heart. Proverbs 16:23 states, "For the mouth speaks that which fills the heart. And be sure of this – something is filling your heart – what it is depends on you!

WINTER

- **Beginner Version:** Follow the plan without changing anything else in your life.
- **Intermediate Version:** Follow the plan plus drink only water for the 21 days.
- **Advanced Version:** Follow the plan; drink only water and do not watch TV for 21 days.

Below you will find an outline for what meals will be included in these 21 days. The recipes and grocery lists can be found in Appendix A.

Day 1, 4, 7, 10, 13, 16, 19

Breakfast: Orange Juice
Lunch: Crunchy Walnut Cabbage
Dinner: Cauliflower Paella

Day 2, 5, 8, 11, 14, 17, 20

Breakfast: Banana Spinach Smoothie
Lunch: Citrus of your choosing
Dinner: Yam Apple Soup

Day 3, 6, 9, 12, 15, 18, 21

Breakfast: Grapefruit Juice
Lunch: Apple Pie with Pecan Date Crust
Dinner: The Winter Chopped Salad

Snacks

Date Pecan Nuggets
Glass of Nut Milk or Orange Juice
Sliced Avocado

Day 1

<u>Renewing Activity</u>: Yoga

Cursed be anyone who dishonors their mother and father

I was reading Deuteronomy and I thought to myself, do I honor my mom and dad? What does it mean to dishonor them? I am sure there are many ways to dishonor

WINTER

someone but at the heart of dishonor is disrespect which can be defined as 'not appreciating or having a lack of regard.' Then these questions came to mind, do I seek their welfare? Do I consider them? Do I pray for them to be blessed in their latter years? Am I thankful for them even as imperfect as they are? Even if I can remember things they did not do or things they did do? Then I thought, now as a parent how much am I like or unlike my parents?

Day 2

Renewing Activity: Yoga

Selective Hearing: Christian Style

The urban dictionary defines selective hearing as: to possess the quality to hear only what you want to hear or the act of listening to only what you would like to hear. All people have selective hearing in some form and it is ever-increasing. 2 Timothy 4:3 says, "For a time is coming when people will no longer listen to sound and wholesome teaching. They will follow their own desires and will look for teachers who will tell them whatever their itching ears want to hear." My friends that time is now! You see I have selective hearing Christian style, choosing bits and pieces of God's words and purposes that make me feel better but many times neglecting the whole. God says this should not be. If you and I desire to hear the very heartbeat of heaven – the very heartbeat of Jesus two things must happen. First we cannot be selective in hearing God meaning we must hear His whole word. Secondly to hear a heartbeat we have to be intimately close to the person whose heartbeat we are trying to hear. Do you desire to be that close?

Day 3

Renewing Activity: Yoga

He has called you by name. He knows every hair on your head. He is passionately in love with you! Give His passion permission. His heart is only good towards you. You are not alone for He has adopted you. You can call Him daddy! He is not going anywhere. He loves you too much, believes in you too much and has too much invested in you. His eyes are turned towards you and He is head-over heels for you. Don't run; His heart is good. He dreams over you as you sleep and delights over you as you awake. He's much bigger than you've ever imagined. Open your eyes to the unseen and watch Him do the impossible. Watch Him throw your mountain into the sea. He's in it for the long haul because He is in love and He just can't help Himself.

These words were found on a chalkboard wall in our kitchen. Let them minister to you as they have ministered to us.

WINTER

Day 4

Renewing Activity: Go to your favorite coffee shop and buy someone a cup of warmth

I'm alive to live for you.

I was listening to the words of this song and wondered to myself, "What am I alive for and what do I live for?" Now that may seem like too deep a question to answer but is it? Is not the true, simple yet profoundly complex answer – "I'm alive to live for Christ?" Each morning when I awake, His mercies are new. His joy is my salvation. His peace is imparted. His love is guaranteed. His kindness is bestowed. His favor is released. His justice is called forth. His goodness is shown. What else am I to live for besides Him?

Day 5

Renewing Activity: Walk for 33 minutes. If snow is available where you live - Go sledding…Build a snowman or make a snow angel.

He ate always at the king's table

My friends, we are Mephaboseth, we are crippled without Christ, undeserving of the King's merciful and bountiful love. (2 Samuel 9) And yet despite that He has invited us to His banqueting table. Let's try to picture it. You walk through a big arch way with a banner hanging over it; the inscription says "love". As you walk into the massive hall you see a table set with the richest of fare and all your favorites are there because the King knows your heart. You question, who am I to deserve this? And while you wait for a servant to greet you no one ever comes. Instead the King himself walks up to you and greets you with a smile, the biggest and most welcoming smile you have ever seen. He leads you to your seat, not a seat in the back but to the seat next to His. As you both sit down He turns to you and says, "You have no need to fear any longer, I long to show you kindness and restore to you all that has been lost. You are not my slave; you are my beloved friend and from this day forward you will always eat at my table." That is our king – that is His love. The question is have you accepted the invitation to the table?

WINTER

Day 6

Renewing Activity: Yoga

You're Everything

"How can I stand here with you and not be moved by you?" A question that was brought to my mind this past Saturday as I listened to a song called 'Everything.' How can I say I know Christ and stand with Him but not be moved by His heart or by His very presence? How can I know the creator of the universe – the one that John 1:1-5 declares "was before all things and all things were made through him, the one that casts out all darkness" – and not be moved toward compassion. How can I know the redemption and restoration Paul speaks of in Colossians 1 and not be moved toward love? How can I not be moved by the one I was made for? And if He does not move you, what does?

Day 7

Renewing Activity: Yoga

...the next to me place...

I went for a walk and just asked Jesus, 'What do you want to tell me?' I continued walking hearing nothing but then as sweet and soft as you can imagine, I heard and literally felt these words, "You do not have to fast to prove your love to me. I love you regardless. I love you because I made you." Jesus, in that moment came to "my next to me place." You see, I was thinking of doing a three day fast to "get back to Him – to show my love for Him." I honestly was not thinking of it that way but He revealed my motive to my own heart. It is not that God said do not fast, because sometimes we should, but God's sweet revelation opened my heart to a greater reality of His love for me. Jesus came to 'my next to me place' and you know what, He loves it there. Have you invited Jesus into "your next to me place?"

WINTER

Day 8

Renewing Activity: Call a friend or family member and tell them what they mean to you

I see Your face in every sunrise...The colors of the morning are inside Your eyes...
The world awakens in the light of the day...I look up to the sky and say...
You're beautiful...I see Your face, You're beautiful, You're beautiful, You're beautiful...

Is this how you awaken each morning knowing that Christ calls you His beautiful, beloved one?

Day 9

Renewing Activity: Yoga

"My life has been revolutionized by the understanding I do not have to wait for a future day to be fully yielded to God. I can love Him with my all even today. Equally, I do not have to wait for heightened spiritual events to abandon myself unto God. Rather, I can love Him fervently through the ordinary and mundane parts of life. Love amidst the common is actually exactly what He asks of me." (Entirety, D. Chandler)

How this resonated in my heart. We do not have to wait – His kingdom can come upon the earth – it can manifest right now. To love God with all that we are we do not need an event, a concert or any great super-spiritual experience we can love God fully in the midst of cleaning the house, taking care of the children, treating patients, working at the computer, or going to one more meeting. It is in the ordinary that He calls us to be extraordinary and it is in the mundane that He calls us to be lavish. We are to love Him and thus others with all our heart, soul and mind. Everything else we get to do is an added benefit.

Day 10

Renewing Activity: Yoga

The world will know that men stood against a tyrant, that few stood against many, and before this battle was over, even a god-king can bleed. (King Leonidas)

I recently watched the movie '300'. If you have not seen it the movie is based on 300 Spartans standing against a vast Persian army. Then I asked, okay Lord what spiritual truth can I glean from this movie? In the movie, 300 Spartans fight off thousands of Persians for one reason; they stood as one. Their minds and bodies were fighting as

WINTER

one, they used their shields as one and they used their swords and spears as one. They were in one accord and because of this they accomplished much! Is this how you and I stand or do we tear one another down?

Day 11

Renewing Activity: Yoga

I have made my vow, there is no turning around.
I have burned the bridges, they can no longer be found.

I thought about these words and how often I make a promise but then seem to forget it. How my words and actions do not line up. Then I thought about my relationship to Christ; I have made a vow to love, honor and serve Him – do I take that seriously – is there no turning around? Or do I turn around or to the side much too often. Have I burned those bridges that hold me to past hurts, past offenses, past strongholds that want to drag me down? Or can I truly say, they can no longer be found. Taking this closer to home, I have made a vow to my wife, my children, my co-workers, etc. Do I honor that?

Day 12

Renewing Activity: Find something in your house you no longer need and give it away

What are your eyes fixed upon?

"My eyes are fixed on all your commandments. I fix my eyes on your ways. Open my eyes that I may behold wondrous things out of your law. My eyes long for your promise. My eyes long for your righteous promise. My eyes are awake before the watches of the night that I may meditate on your promise" (Psalms 119: 6, 15, 18, 82, 123, 148). What are you looking at today? Hebrews 12:2 exclaims: "Let us fix our eyes on Jesus." To fix our eyes on Jesus - we need to know what He says - this is not found on TV, in magazines, nor on Facebook but only in the Bible - that is truth. So what are your eyes fixed upon?

WINTER

Day 13

Renewing Activity: Yoga

"Men occasionally stumble over the truth but most of them pick themselves up and hurry off of it as if nothing ever happened." - Winston Churchill

When people are trained to look for counterfeit money, they are not trained by looking at the counterfeit but they are trained by looking at the real money. They study the real money so they know each detail, each line and each little piece that fits. In order to know the counterfeit they must first know the real thing. There is no other way. Along these same lines spiritually in order to know the real truth, the one truth, we must study it. We must study the Bible, each detail, each line and each little piece that fits. We must stop studying the counterfeits. We must stop reading so many books about the Bible and using them as the truth. Yes, they can be helpful but it is not the truth. The only real truth comes from the word of God. If we do not know the truth every lie that comes along will cause us to be anxious. It will cause us to be blown around like a ship gone astray. Adolf Hitler said, "The bigger the lie, the more people will believe in it." What lies do we believe in? Do we know the truth enough to counteract the multitudes of lies that we get bombarded with each day?

Day 14

Renewing Activity: Yoga

Living for the smile of the Father

Ed McGlasson writes in his book, 'A difference a Father makes', "There is a difference in living for the smile of the father versus earning the smile of the father. We should want to live for the smile of the father more than living for the trophies of the world." As I was reading this it reminded me of times I tried to earn my dad's smile versus trying to live for it. Do you know that God loves you? Do you know that He sings over your life? Do you know that He is smiling at you? From this knowledge, do you love your wife and kids in the same manner (as Christ loves)? Parents, are you more interested in the trophies that you get at work or your hobbies, than living for the smile of the one that matters? What do your kids and others see you living for?

WINTER

Day 15

Renewing Activity: Yoga

Let my love open the door to your heart.

These words played over the radio as I was waiting for a friend. It was like Christ was speaking to directly to my heart. He is and forever will be asking, 'Let my love open the door to your heart…" The question is will you open that door?

Day 16

Renewing Activity: Make a homemade meal or goodies for a neighbor

Walk in love

Ephesians 5:2 reads, 'And walk in love, as Christ loved us and gave himself up, a fragrant offering…' Walking in love is so much more than just saying you love someone. Walking in love is about action, it is about speaking love, thinking love, being love. Walking in love is about thinking beyond our own limited view and seeing life through another person's eyes and circumstances. It is about guarding our heart from offense when it is trampled upon, about loving when it hurts and it is about loving when no one sees. An anonymous quote reads, "Love is just a word until someone comes along and gives it meaning." Is love just a word to you or to those around you? Do you give it meaning?

Day 17

Renewing Activity: Yoga

Show no partiality

Do you show partiality? James gives us a picture of what we do many times. We see a person who is well dressed or wealthy and allow them to have the honored seat. But the person who is not well-dressed, we put them in a lowly seat or even outside. James, 5:2 reads, "Listen my beloved brothers, has not God chosen those who are poor in the world to be rich in faith and heirs to the kingdom." I think James is speaking more about the attitude of heart versus monetary riches. You can be a billionaire and have an attitude of meekness, kindness, etc. You can also be poor financially but still be stingy. As always, Christ is after the deeper issues, the heart!

WINTER

Day 18

Renewing Activity: **Yoga**

Authenticity is really about who you are

K. Ferrazzi writes, "Authenticity is about knowing who you are and not trying to come across as someone or something that you are not." Then Poet E.E. Cummings adds, "The hardest challenge is to be yourself in a world where everyone is trying to make you someone else." Do you know who you are? Or are you trying to be something others around you have created? Are you living up to some standard that you have created for yourself? If you stopped and looked in the mirror right now would you know the person staring back at you?

Day 19

Renewing Activity: **Think of a way to warm someone's heart**

How dare we say we know Him?

I heard these words in a song…"How dare we say we know Him, when we shut our mouth…How dare we say we know Him, when we store up for ourselves…How dare we say we love Him, when we love not our brother…How dare we say we know Him, when we sit inside these four walls feasting with ourselves while the beggar starves in the street" It is not just about giving to the poor but being authentic to all people and giving to all equally. Even "rich" people need something! It is about our heart and what flows from it. Where is your heart today?

Day 20

Renewing Activity: **Yoga**

For anyone who is looking, He is actually everywhere and ever-present.
This is our constant labor of devotion – to look for love and to let our hearts
be found by His continual reaching. From the beginning of time, from everlasting,
God's love has always been excessive, too much and extreme!

Oh the truth of that – that God's love is too much, too extreme, too excessive. That it absolutely is all consuming in its pursuit of us. A battle rages against the advancement of this love and it is our call to not let our hearts grow dull but seek the fiery place of His heart. Today, will you let your heart be found?

WINTER

Day 21

Renewing Activity: Write an email to yourself explaining what you have accomplished and then share it

Lend me your eyes I can change what you see

These are words from a song called, "Awake my Soul." As I listened to these words I thought, how true. My vision is so limited at times to what I know or think I know. If we were willing to look through someone else's eyes, it would give us a better perspective on how they view life. We may not be as quick to judge them or their situation. It would most certainly change our heart towards them. Do we really want to see the world through their eyes so we can be changed? If we are honest many times we dare not see because of what it will cost us. It will cost us time, finances, safety and security. So dare we look through another's eyes — dare we?

chapter 18

non-raw food plan

- **Beginner Version:** Follow the plan without changing anything else in your life.
- **Intermediate Version:** Follow the plan plus drink only water for the 21 days.
- **Advanced Version:** Follow the plan; drink only water and do not watch TV for 21 days.

Below you will find an outline for what meals will be included in these 21 days. The recipes and grocery lists can be found in Appendix B.

Day 1, 4, 7, 10, 13, 16, 19
Breakfast: Cherry Pineapple Celery Juice
Lunch: Carrot Ginger Apple Soup
Dinner: Honey Baked Squash

Day 2, 5, 8, 11, 14, 17, 20
Breakfast: Romaine Rolls
Lunch: Spring Garden Salad
Dinner: Asian Salad

Day 3, 6, 9, 12, 15, 18, 21
Breakfast: Mango Cereal
Lunch: Greens and Protein
Dinner: Exotic Mushroom and Millet Soup

Snacks

Fresh Grapes, Strawberries or Cherries
Dry Nuts: Almonds, Cashews or Pecans
Fruit Nut Mix
Apples and Almond Butter

S P R I N G

Day 1

Renewing Activity: Yoga

As you focus your thoughts on Me, be aware that I am fully attentive to you.

Do you ever wonder if God really listens to your prayers? He does! Do you ever wonder if He is paying attention to you? He is! We think, surely there are more important things for Him to deal with than our own problems and situations. In the grand scheme of life, while there may be more pressing matters than finding your car keys, have you ever stopped and asked Him to help? Remember, as you focus your thoughts on Him, His full attention is on you. His thoughts towards you outnumber the sand on the seashore. He longs for relationship with you. Simply, He loves you. Do you believe it?

Day 2

Renewing Activity: Yoga

Demolish and Take Captive

I have been thinking lately about my thought life. What is it I think about most? How does one thought lead to 20 more that I did not see coming? I texted a friend the other day and wrote, "Guard your thought life, it is where hopes dream and fears reside." Our thought life can either hinder or help, it can cast vision or cast fear or it can harbor anger or produce love. T. Edwards wrote, "Thoughts lead on to purposes; purposes go forth in action; actions form habits; habits decide character; and character fixes our destiny." And J. Bridges notes, "The Bible indicates that our thought lives ultimately determine our character". Solomon said, "For as a man thinks within himself, so he is" (Pro. 23:7). Here's a question to ask yourself, what is your thought life? Honestly, what do you think most about?

Day 3

Renewing Activity: Walk for 20-30 minutes

Our attitudes, words, actions and often, even our unspoken thoughts, tend to have an effect on those around us.

Today, what actions – what thoughts are you carrying that either have a positive or negative effect on those around you? Are the words on your lips or the attitude of your heart bringing life to your home and work place or is it bringing strife, grief and

SPRING

bitterness? We must be in our behavior what we are in our state of being. We must be authentic. People are looking for authenticity in a world they consider shallow and full of deception. Do they see authenticity in you?

Day 4

Renewing Activity: Paint, Draw or Journal for 15-20 minutes

Active and Living

Have you ever thought about your testimony? Testimony can be defined as 'to make a declaration of truth.' What are you declaring about the truth of God's love and light in your life? I have heard some say (I have even said it), "Man, I wish I had that person's testimony. God did an amazing work in them." Is not God doing an amazing work in you and me too? Why would we want someone else's testimony when God has a plan and purpose for each of our lives? (Read Jer. 29:11.) Could it be that our testimony is not active and living?

Day 5

Renewing Activity: Yoga

His ways are higher. His thoughts are higher.

You are God. I am man. You are sovereign. I am not. Enough said.

Day 6

Renewing Activity: Yoga

Who do you want me to love for You today?

"Is this a Christian business?," a patient asked me. I said, "Yes we are, why do you ask? She then replied, "Well, I heard the music". A few months back, a similar conversation took place but it went like this. "I've never heard this music in here before?" I said, "What do you mean?" He replied, "I have never heard Van Halen in here, normally it is Christian music." I said, "Yeah, sometimes I get tired of the same Christian song over and over again." He just nodded. As I thought about both scenarios it occurred to me that patients and people in general, are watching and apparently listening. They not only listen to what we say but they watch how we live. People are watching, what are they seeing in your life?

SPRING

Day 7

Renewing Activity: **Walk for 20-30 minutes**

Be the church, do not just attend it.

Whether you go to a church building, a house group, a coffee shop or a bar – be the church. Where and when you meet is not important. What is important is you reaching out with others in love and bringing glory to the one who deserves it, Christ. You cannot and must not think you can do it alone. While He has a specific plan for each person and each local church, that plan is part of a bigger plan which you cannot see sometimes. Listen, Christ loves the church – with all her faults, with all her man-made rules, with all her baggage, with all her gripes, complaints and inconsistencies – He loves her and died for her. And you know what – He would do it again and again and again.

Day 8

Renewing Activity: **Write an encouraging letter to a friend or family member**

I want to be the good soil

I want to be the good soil bearing 30-60-100 times more fruit. John MacArthur wrote, "Fruit-bearing is not a matter of being strong or weak, good or bad, brave or cowardly, clever or foolish, experienced or inexperienced. Whatever your gifts, accomplishments, or virtues, they cannot produce fruit if you are detached from Jesus Christ. Christians who think they are bearing fruit apart from the Vine are only tying on artificial fruit. They run around grunting and groaning to produce fruit but accomplish nothing. Fruit is borne not by trying, but by abiding." Abiding can be defined as: lasting a long time, permanence. Do you have permanence with Him that supersedes your immediate need? Are you good soil?

Day 9

Renewing Activity: **Yoga**

I want to live exegetically

After reading Francis Chan's book, Forgotten God, I learned two words: (1) Exegesis: the attempt to discover the meaning of a text objectively; starting with the text and moving out from there (2) Eisegesis: to import a subjective, preconceived meaning into the text. Chan writes, "I was taught to interpret Scriptures through exegesis

SPRING

alone… Start with God's word…then study to see what the text actually says. Eisegesis, on the other hand, is to start with an idea or conviction, then search for verses to prove your point. I want to live exegetically. How do you want to live?

Day 10

Renewing Activity: Yoga

Jesus loves me…this I know…

A great friend and mentor of mine, Grady Strop and I were talking and he mentioned the simplicity of God's love and how it is in that simplicity that we find His heart for us. However we love to over-complicate it. He then said, 'We even sing about it… Jesus loves me this I know for the Bible tells me so.' He went on to say, 'The problem with that song is that we do not know it." That led to a great discussion about faith and God's love. The question I have for you is do you know Jesus loves you? Your head may say yes because you have heard it from the pulpit or read it in the Bible but do you know it experientially? Do you know it so you can really sing, "Jesus loves me this I KNOW?"

Day 11

Renewing Activity: Interval Walking (10 minutes forward then 2 minutes backward) – repeat 2-3 times

God is in you

Have you ever taken the time to process that statement? God, in the form of the Holy Spirit, resides in you and me. How is that even possible? Jesus promises us the gift of the Holy Spirit. He tells the disciples (and us) in John 14:15 and 26, "And I will ask the Father, and he will give you another Helper, to be with you forever, even the Spirit of truth, whom the world cannot receive, because it neither sees him nor knows him. You know him, for he dwells with you and will be in you…But the Helper, the Holy Spirit, whom the Father will send in my name, he will teach you all things and bring to your remembrance all that I have said to you." When we surrender our life to Christ, the helper and comforter, the Holy Spirit literally takes up residence in our bodies. Have you considered that you are a living temple?

SPRING

Day 12

Renewing Activity: Take a homemade meal (or a plate of homemade cookies) to a neighbor

Let my manner of living be a witness that you're alive

The other day when I was driving my boys to Kindermusik, traffic was slow and the car in front of me would not turn fast enough. I growled under my breath and said, "Dang it." Immediately, Eilam, my 5 yr old said, "Dad, you said a bad word. Why are you mad?" That stopped me in my tracks and I had to wonder what manner of living I was demonstrating to my sons. Have you ever had this experience? If so, how can you let your manner of living be different next time?

Day 13

Renewing Activity: Yoga

Pursue Christ and let others watch.

This thought came to my mind the other day as I was talking to a patient. The patient was saying how she was trying to be a light, trying to witness and just trying to be a better Christian. We chatted for a little while and I prayed with her and then she left. Afterwards I wondered why do we try so hard? Why do we think our witness has to come in words? What does it even mean to be a better Christian? What if we changed our language and intent and just pursued Christ? If He was our sole pursuit, and we stopped trying to do any of the other things; stopped trying to witness or save others, stopped trying be a light and just allowed others to watch us pursue Christ. I wonder how that would impact the people around us? I believe it would be earth-shattering for them and for us.

Day 14

Renewing Activity: Yoga

We do not know what to do but our eyes are on you

Have you ever felt like you were uncertain what to do or which way to go? The question to ask yourself is when you are uncertain what to do where do you look? Do you look to the news? Do you look to Time magazine? Do you look to the scholars? Do you look to your facebook friends? Or do you look to the one who has all the answers?

SPRING

Day 15

Renewing Activity: Yoga

The heart was courageous

2 Chronicles 16:9 and 7:6 reads, "The eyes of the Lord run to and fro throughout the whole Earth, to give strong support to those hearts that are fully committed to Him...the heart was courageous in the ways of the Lord..." Think about this verse, what do you think God sees when He looks at your heart? Is your heart courageous?

Day 16

Renewing Activity: Go to a gas station and pay to fill up someone's car

Let Me...

As I was sitting at my desk this morning working on the end of the month financials, a song was playing and I had to stop to worship. As I sat there with my eyes closed and arms opened wide, 'I saw the Lord high and lifted up, I saw the kindness in His eyes, I saw the love in His face, I saw the compassion in His hands and with His arms reaching out, He spoke these words to me but also you, "I love you; I always have and always will. Come to me all who are weary for I will give you rest. You do not have to strive anymore. Let my love set you free. Let my peace overwhelm you."

Day 17

Renewing Activity: Walk for 33 minutes

The brother who was famous

Have you stopped and thought about what type of legacy you want to leave? In 2 Corinthians, Paul is writing to the church and commending Titus but then in 2 Corinthians 8:18, he adds "...the brother who is famous among all the churches for his preaching of the gospel." That sentence stopped me. This brother's name was never mentioned and not known. He is mentioned again in 2 Corinthians 12:18 but again he is not named. We do not know his name or anything about him except one thing, that he was famous for preaching the gospel. And that is all we need to know. Are you striving to be famous in a career or hobby that eternally may not matter? Or are you longing to be famous for something much more purposeful and eternal even if your name never gets mentioned?

SPRING

Day 18

<u>Renewing Activity:</u> Go to a park and play – Slide down a slide – Swing on the swing (Repeat many times)

You looking at me

As I drove to work, I heard a song with these words, "Your hands nailed through… your body bruised…your name blasphemed…You looking at me…tears falling to the ground…" And I was moved deep within my spirit. What was the last thing you heard or saw that moved you?

Day 19

<u>Renewing Activity:</u> Yoga

May our heart be found and made alive

A patient sat in my office hiding behind a mask of smart remarks and laughter. She told me her "heart was hard." I kept chatting with her and towards the end of the treatment I felt God wanted me to tell her that she was 'dark yet lovely.' So I told her just that and I also explained that the darkness was because of past hurts, offenses, and she believed what others said about her. I told her that God looks past all that and sees her heart and calls it lovely. I told her He knows her by name. She just sat there. I have no idea what that word did in her that day but I do know that God wants to turn her heart of stone into a heart of flesh. He wants her heart to be made alive! He wants all of our hearts to be made alive! Are you hiding behind a mask of fear, shame or even laughter? If so, allow the mask to fall off and be who you were created to be. "Run in the joy of the Lord because he desires to make your heart alive and free; he desires to give you a heart of flesh with revelation and understanding instead of a hard heart; set your heart on all he has for you!" (Psalm 119:32, Ezekiel 36:26, Psalm 119:112).

SPRING

Day 20

Renewing Activity: Yoga

The choice you make affects more than you, it affects everyone.

It's that simple! Every day when you wake up you have a choice to be kind or to be rude, to speak life or to speak death and to serve yourself or to serve others. You can choose to love or to hate, to exercise or be sedentary, to eat healthy or unhealthy and to live by faith or to live by fear (and so you know fear and faith cannot reside together). The choices you make affect you, your day but also affect everyone else you contact that day and possibly much longer. In what ways have you seen negative effects of your choices? In what ways have you seen positive effects of your choices? What can you do today to make more positive choices for yourself and others?

Day 21

Renewing Activity: Plant a flower (a perennial) so you can be reminded of what you have accomplished

That's the only thing you can count on

Sometimes we make small talk in our office about the weather. One day I made the comment to a patient that the weather is always changing and he said, "Yep, change is the only thing you can count on." Immediately an alarm went off in my brain and I thought, "No, that's not true." My heart screamed that is not true but my mouth did not speak it out. Why didn't I speak it? I really do not know why I didn't. Since that discussion, I have thought a lot about what we can count on. I ran through a list of things and people in my mind but at some point all the names and things I listed can disappoint. And whereas change is constant in our lives it is not the only thing we can count on. You and I can count on the love of Christ that surpasses knowledge and His peace that passes understanding.

SUMMER

- **Beginner Version:** Follow the plan without changing anything else in your life.
- **Intermediate Version:** Follow the plan plus drink only water for the 21 days.
- **Advanced Version:** Follow the plan; drink only water and don't watch TV for 21 days.

Below you will find an outline for what meals will be included in these 21 days. The recipes and grocery lists can be found in Appendix B.

Day 1, 4, 7, 10, 13, 16, 19

Breakfast: Watermelon
Lunch: Lamb and Avocado Tomato Basil Salad
Dinner: Tomato and Okra Stew

Day 2, 5, 8, 11, 14, 17, 20

Breakfast: Cantaloupe Cubed
Lunch: Corn and Kale Salad
Dinner: Mango, Cucumber, Tomato, Avocado Salad and Honey Mustard Kabobs

Day 3, 6, 9, 12, 15, 18, 21

Breakfast: Apricot, Pineapple and Banana Smoothie
Lunch: Black Bean Stir Fry on a bed of Romaine
Dinner: Corn on the Cob with Steamed Broccoli and Bell Peppers

Snacks

Cucumber, Okra or Tomato
A piece of your favorite fruit
Honey drizzled Blueberries
Boiled Eggs

SUMMER

Day 1

Renewing Activity: Yoga

A Walk to Remember

As I thought about the title of the movie, 'A walk to remember' I wondered about my walk. Am I having a walk to remember? Am I creating eternal memories in the lives of my spouse, children, family and friends? Am I investing in what matters? Does the way I walk line up with the way I speak? Is my life, my walk, one to be remembered? And now my friends, "I exhort and encourage you to walk in a manner worthy of God; in a manner that will be remembered, because He calls you into his own kingdom and glory..." (1 Thessalonians 2:12)

Day 2

Renewing Activity: Yoga

Know who you are

Knowing who you are is powerful. You are highly valued and loved. "Royalty is your identity. Servanthood is your assignment. Intimacy with God is your life source. So, before God, you are an intimate. Before people, you are a servant. Before the powers of hell, you are a ruler, with no tolerance for their influence. And wisdom (Holy Spirit) knows which role to fulfill at the proper time." (Dreaming with God, Bill Johnson) Do you know who you are?

Day 3

Renewing Activity: Yoga

Be my center

You sing and maybe even study about God being your center, your main focus - you say "Lord all I want is you - you are enough!" But does your lifestyle reveal this to be the truth? What does it actually mean to have God at the center?

SUMMER

Day 4

Renewing Activity: Write an encouraging email or text to a friend

It is our greatest weapon and our greatest strength...With this weapon we can curse or we can bless...With this weapon we can build up or tear down...With this weapon we can proclaim freedom or box in...

What is this weapon? It is our tongue, our words or our mouth! Proverbs 18:21 declares, "Death and Life are in the power of the tongue and those who love it will eat its fruits." Proverbs 12:18 expounds, "There is one whose rash words are like sword thrusts but the tongue of the wise brings healing." Jeremiah 20:9 goes on to say that the word of the Lord, "is like a fire in my bones and I cannot contain it." Do you have this same passion for the word - is it burning inside of you so much so that it cannot be contained? But when you let it out - does it produce life or death? Does it kill and divide or does it bring healing and unity? How are you using this weapon?

Day 5

Renewing Activity: Walk for 20-30 minutes

Whatcha' looking at?

Did you know you have a choice what you set your gaze upon? I am not talking about the TV or the people around you. I am speaking of something much deeper – something much more important. Are you looking at your circumstance or Christ?

Circumstances – can be temporal and short-lived. They can cast fear, doubt and anxiety or even at times bring great happiness. Circumstances point to only things of earthly significance. They can be a reminder of past failures or lost dreams. While they may give great insight into a problem they don't often lead to the solution.

Christ – is eternal and ever-lasting. He gives hope, peace and love and brings joy forevermore. Christ points to things of earthly and heavenly significance. He is a reminder of reconciliation and restoration and He gives wisdom and understanding.

SUMMER

Day 6

Renewing Activity: Yoga

> *The more we pray, the more we sense our need to pray.*
> *And the more we sense a need to pray, the more we want to pray*

My friend, prayer is the life-source of the Christian! Do not say I ought to pray - let God drive you to pray. Let Him fill you so much with his Heart that prayers just overflow. Let your life be filled with prayer, with the fragrance of Christ, His constant burning and the deep aching for deepness with Him. Let nothing else satisfy. The question begs, how is your prayer life? If we are not praying, what are we doing? There is nothing simpler than praying and reading God's word yet it is so profound and deep that it takes a life-time to pursue it.

Day 7

Renewing Activity: Yoga

> *The world will know that men stood against a tyrant, that few stood against many,*
> *and before this battle was over, even a god-king can bleed. (King Leonidas)*

I recently watched the movie '300'. If you have not seen it the movie is based on 300 Spartans standing against a vast Persian army. Then I asked, okay Lord what spiritual truth can I glean from this movie? In the movie, 300 Spartans fight off thousands of Persians as they stood as one. Their minds and bodies were fighting for the same reason, they used their shields as one and they used their swords and spears as one. They were in one accord and because of this they accomplished much! Is this how you and I stand or do we tear one another down?

Day 8

Renewing Activity: Yoga

> *Our attitudes, words, actions and often, even our unspoken thoughts,*
> *tend to have an effect on those around us*

We must be in our behavior what we are in our state of being. We must be authentic. People are looking for authenticity in a world they consider shallow and full of deception. Today what actions or thoughts are you carrying that either have a positive or negative effect on those around you? Are the words on your lips or the attitude of your heart bringing life to your home or workplace or is it bringing strife, grief and bitterness?

SUMMER

Day 9

Renewing Activity: Go for a slow walk and enjoy the outdoors

Before Jesus called the disciples to ministry, He called them to intimacy

Before Jesus ever had the disciples "go out" and "do ministry" he called them unto himself. He said, "follow Me" not follow my ministry or miracles. What are you following?

Day 10

Renewing Activity: Yoga

Extravagant Time

Life sometimes dictates how we spend our time. Not everyone has the luxury of multiple free hours in a row to spend alone with God. Parents of small children barely have time to breathe, let alone contemplate the heavens in two hours of stillness. Jesus understands where you are and loves you for it. I am sure the Lord is not offended by multi-tasking. Pray when you wash the dishes, worship on your morning jog, pray with your spouse while walking the dog in the park or sing in the spirit whenever you drive. We strive for extended periods alone with Jesus but sometimes the stage of life we are in demands time be offered in multiple little chunks while we stand, run, walk, drive or rock a baby to sleep.

Day 11

Renewing Activity: Yoga

The pull of religion can be far stronger than the freedom of relationship

Jacobsen calls it "daisy-petal Christianity" referring to the childhood game, "He loves me, He loves me not." The adult version goes something like this, I got the promotion at work –*He loves me*…I did not get a raise – *He loves me not*…I gave money to someone in need – *He loves me*…My child is seriously ill – *He loves me not*…I got a note of encouragement – *He loves me*…My car's transmission went out – *He loves me not*… and on and on. This game wears us out by keeping us stressed out, trying to discern constantly if God loves us or not. Jacobsen writes, "So it is time to toss the daisies and discover that it is not the fear of losing God's love that will keep you on His path but the simple joy of living in it every day." So are you willing to toss the daisy?

SUMMER

Day 12

Renewing Activity: Go to a local pool or splash park – smile & have fun

I wonder if they'll say that when I'm dead?

I read a story where a man was told that he was spending too much time serving and giving too much away. His gentle but honest response was, "I wonder if they'll say that about me when I'm dead?" The point being this: our life is short, a vapor, and most of the time we live selfishly, thinking only of ourselves and what we need or want. So, right now – what are you focused upon? Is it eternal or temporal? In the words of 2 Corinthians. 4:18, "So we fix our eyes on not what is seen but what is unseen. For the things that are seen are transient but the unseen is eternal."

Day 13

Renewing Activity: Yoga

The aim of our charge is love

An anonymous quote reads, "Laugh as often as you breathe and love as long as you live." I think of a small child and how much laughter they have, how the simplest thing brings them enormous pleasure. Small children love so well with their hugs and their smiles can warm our hearts. Their whole existence is wrapped in laughter and love and that is all they know (or hopefully it is). Why do we lose the simplicity of laughter and love as we grow? Is it that we have learned too much, have we become too educated? Is it that we have been wounded and never want to let that happen again? What is it about adulthood that causes us to forget that our charge is to love?

Day 14

Renewing Activity: Yoga

I'm after your heart

These are words from a song I heard and they linger in my mind. To think that God is after our heart but at the same time we are after His. What is it about the heart that is so intense and so alive? An anonymous quote reads, "The greatest treasures are those invisible to the eye but found by the heart." Do you see it? A great treasure lies within our heart. It is the pearl of great price!

SUMMER

Day 15

Renewing Activity: Yoga

Be blessed

Are you wondering what it means to be blessed? It means recognizing from where your provision, strength and hope come. Being blessed means you know who your peace and comfort come from in any storm. It means you know what matters most and you know where to invest your time and resources. Being blessed means you look at yourself first so you can truly see others. It means you build a bridge instead of burning it. It means you speak truth in love no matter the cost. Being blessed means many things but most of all it means knowing you are loved by Christ. That truth alone is enough to sustain us all our days. His gifts are a good blessing but His love is the greatest blessing. Learn that and you learn much!

Day 16

Renewing Activity: Yoga

Preach the Gospel at all times and when necessary use words

As a patient and I were talking he referenced the above quote by St. Francis of Assisi. We were talking about being authentic in our lives and what that authenticity looks like lived out day by day. I have seen the above quote within my practice but reworded slightly, "People do not care how much you know until they know how much you care." Is that not a true statement? We may seek out wisdom from people but what we really want to know is if that person really cares about us. Can they be trusted or are they just 'preaching' at us?

Day 17

Renewing Activity: Call someone just to tell them how important they are to you

You're everything

"How can I stand here with you and not be moved by you?" A question that was brought to my mind this past Saturday as I listened to a song called 'Everything.' How can I say I know Christ and stand with Him but not be moved by His heart or by His very presence? How can I know the creator of the universe – the one that John 1:1-5 declares "was before all things and all things were made through him, the one that casts out all darkness" – and not be moved toward compassion. How can I know the

SUMMER

redemption and restoration Paul speaks of in Colossians 1 and not be moved toward love? How can I not be moved by the one I was made for? And if He does not move you, what does?

Day 18

Renewing Activity: **Walk for 27 minutes**

It's OK to be angry but...

Psalms 4:4a reads, "Be angry (agitated) and do not sin." How are we to be angry and not sin? First, you must know anger will happen and there will be days that are frustrating and sometimes people are just rude and out to harm you. Second, know you have a choice of how you respond when you do become angry. You may not have this problem, but when I get angry my mouth flies open and I speak harshly and rudely. At that time I am only trusting in my own strength and wisdom and trying to make sure everyone knows I am right and justified. When that happens, I sin. I tear others down with my words, I take matters into my own hands and I usually gossip too. So how are we to be angry and not sin? Below are four tips found in Psalms 4:4-5:

1. **Ponder what happened in your own heart.** Access the situation, concerning yourself with your own heart not the other person's heart.
2. **Be silent.** Do not open your mouth following step one helps with this.
3. **Offer right sacrifices.** This means offer your heart and vindication to God and let Him bring the justice. Pray for the one who made you angry.
4. **Trust in the Lord.** Do not trust in your own thoughts or your own strength; put your hope in the Lord.

Day 19

Renewing Activity: **Yoga**

Who do you call God?

When you pray, how do you address God? When you think of the creator, what word or name comes to mind? Your answer or lack-there-of reveals much. David writes in Psalms 9:10, "Those who know your name will trust in you." It is like David is saying; you can't trust God unless you know His name. But it is more than just knowing a name it is knowing Him. You can know my name is William (aka Bo) but if that is all you know you will not trust me. You must know me to trust me. So do you know God? What do you call Him?

SUMMER

Day 20

Renewing Activity: Yoga

Roll away your stone

Jennifer and I enjoy the band Mumford and Sons. Recently, I was stopped by the words to this song, "Roll away your stone and I'll roll away mine. Together we can see what we can find. Don't leave me alone at this time. For I'm afraid of what I will discover inside." As I listened to these words I thought, do I have a stone? I am fairly sure we all do. Am I scared to roll it away to find out what is inside? If there is a stone, am I willing to allow someone to help roll it away or do I think I can do it on my own?

Day 21

Renewing Activity: Journal or paint/draw a picture capturing the last 21 days of your life

Pursue Love

Friends, today pursue love, it is the foundation that all else is laid upon. In the words of Mumford and Sons, "Love, it will not betray you, dismay or enslave you, it will set you free. Be more like the man you were made to be. There is a design, an alignment to the cry of my heart to see the beauty of love as it was made to be." Is that not what we all want, to see the beauty of love as it was made to be?

FALL

- **Beginner Version:** Follow the plan without changing anything else in your life.
- **Intermediate Version:** Follow the plan plus drink only water for the 21 days.
- **Advanced Version:** Follow the plan; drink only water and don't watch TV for 21 days.

Below you will find an outline for what meals will be included in these 21 days. The recipes and grocery lists can be found in Appendix B.

Day 1, 4, 7, 10, 13, 16, 19

Breakfast: Apple, Beet, Ginger, Lemon Juice
Lunch: Hummus and Zucchini
Dinner: Chick Pea Stew

Day 2, 5, 8, 11, 14, 17, 20

Breakfast: Pears or Asian Pears
Lunch: White Fish with Rosemary Broccoli Salad
Dinner: Kitchari (see recipe for description)

Day 3, 6, 9, 12, 15, 18, 21

Breakfast: Poached Eggs on Lettuce
Lunch: Kale Salad
Dinner: Lentil Stir Fry

Snacks

Apple with Almond Butter
Ants on a log
Bananas with Honey
Sliced Carrots

FALL

Day 1

Renewing Activity: Yoga

Think Vertical...Live Horizontal

You may be asking yourself, what does that mean? Think vertical...Live horizontal. It is simple really. We are to think more about one reality yet at the same time be effective and alive in another reality. Huh? Let me put it this way, our thoughts are to set on something higher than what we see in front of our eyes yet we have to live with what is in front of our eyes. Our mindset and what we think about, thinking vertically in our thoughts and intentions, helps us live the day to day, living horizontally in our habits and actions!

Day 2

Renewing Activity: Yoga

You came along and told me why I exist

Think back to your childhood or maybe even to last week, what words were spoken over you? What word or words to you remember the most? Does it cause you to lift your head up or turn away in shame? Also have you recognized the words you speak over yourself, your spouse, your children and your friends? A song states, "I was aimless, wandering without purpose, I was shipwrecked, I was abandoned and then You came along and told me why I exist." Christ has come alongside me to tell me who I am and why I exist. I no longer have to wander aimlessly. I am not abandoned. He tells us why we exist and He does it through the talents He gives us. He does it through our intimate times with Him and He does it through our school, work or home life. He tells us through our successes and failures and He tells us through our friends and family. The question: do you receive the truth when He tells you?

Day 3

Renewing Activity: Yoga

"My life has been revolutionized by the understanding I do not have to wait for a future day to be fully yielded to God. I can love Him with my all even today. Equally, I do not have to wait for heightened spiritual events to abandon myself unto God. Rather, I can love Him fervently through the ordinary and mundane parts of life. Love amidst the common is actually exactly what He asks of me." Dana Chandler

How this resonated in my heart. We do not have to wait – His kingdom can come upon the earth – it can manifest right now. To love God with all that we are we do not need

FALL

an event, a concert or any great super-spiritual experience. We can love God fully in the midst of cleaning the house, taking care of the children, treating patients, working at the computer, going to one more meeting, etc. It is the ordinary that calls us to be extraordinary and it is the mundane that calls us to be lavish. We are to love Him and thus others with all our heart, soul and mind. Everything else we get to do is an added benefit.

Day 4

Renewing Activity: Go to your favorite local store and buy something for a total stranger

What do you want to see God do in your life in the next year?

What is your answer to that question? Ever thought about it? I was talking to a pastor last week who has started asking his congregation and others he meets these three questions, (1) What do you want to see God do in your life in the next year? (2) What are you doing to pursue that? (2) How can I help or come alongside to make it a reality? He was telling me that when he asks, most people do not have an answer or if they do, they are doing nothing about it. Then they are shocked that someone wants to help. The answer to those questions shows the reality of your testimony in Christ. So, what are you asking God for?

Day 5

Renewing Activity: Walk for 20-30 minutes

Looking down the road

As we were driving home from Georgia this past week we found ourselves in the outer swirls of the Tropical Storm Beryl. We drove about 2 to 3 hours in wind and rain and as I drove in the midst of the storm I was gripping the steering wheel tightly. Most cars were only going 45-55 mph on the interstate and many were pulled over. As I drove in the midst of the storm I wondered if it would ever end. But as I continued driving I looked down the road and saw clear skies. At that moment I realized the rain would stop and soon I would be driving on dry ground. As I approached the clear skies, the rain slowed down, the traffic around me sped up and my hands lessened their grip. As I got into clear skies, I breathed easier and relaxed. Then as I continued to drive, I looked in my rearview mirror and saw the storm I just came through with its big black rolling clouds spread across the sky. I thanked God for getting me through that storm and then looked down the road and I saw it – another storm rolling in from the southwest. But my next thought was, that's OK, I just made it through one storm, I can make it through this one.

FALL

Day 6

Renewing Activity: Yoga

Where do you go to church?

Ever had someone ask you this question? I'm sure you have and you have probably asked it yourself hundreds of times. What do we mean with that question? People are not fully defined by where they go to church nor do we know what they believe by what church they attend. Maybe the better question is, what has Christ done in your life in the last week, month or year?

Day 7

Renewing Activity: Yoga

Be the two, not the ten

You look at your day and it seems overwhelming – the piles of emails, the stacks of papers - the bills are due – the kids are screaming – the day you had planned takes a dramatic turn and does not work out the way you think it should. What do we do in these circumstances? Do we panic and forget all that "we are about?" Do we boil over in anger at those around us? Do we only have good days (joyful days) when our circumstances dictate that outcome? RW Emerson noted, "The first thing a great person does is make us realize the insignificance of circumstance." Numbers 13-14 paints a picture of circumstance and twelve people's responses to it. God's people are heading to the Promised Land and Moses sends out twelve men (one for each tribe) to look over the land. Ten report back, "We cannot take the land." But two men report, "Let us go up and occupy the land." Ten looked in fear but two looked at a promise. As you look at your day are you the ten or the two?

Day 8

Renewing Activity: Rake leaves into a big pile – Jump in them and throw them into the air (or create another fun outdoor activity)

Let my love open the door to your heart

These words played over the radio as I was waiting for a friend. It was like Christ was speaking to me but beyond just me to all who would listen. He is and forever will be saying, 'Let my love open the door to your heart…" The question is will you open that door?

FALL

Day 9

Renewing Activity: Yoga

Jesus, I love you. What's in it for you?

These words were written on a chalkboard. Notice it does not say what's in it for me? His love, that is my reward and that is what is in it for me! So what is it in for Jesus? What is in it for the Lamb of God – the King of all Kings – the One uncreated – the One who was before all things yet is in all things – what is in it for Him? Ever wondered that or are you too busy thinking of yourself?

Day 10

Renewing Activity: Yoga

The way you invest your love, you invest your life

An investment is defined first as the act of investing effort or resources and second as a commitment, as of support or time. Thus to invest your love is to put forth a commitment, an effort, to give time and support to that one thing. So what is that one thing? What are you investing in today? And is what you are investing in worth what you are investing? If you are investing hundreds of hours at a job you love at the expense of your family, is that the life you want? If you are investing your love toward a hobby, is that what you want your life to be remembered for? If you were to ask your family, friends or even coworkers where you invest your love (thus your life) – what do you think they would say?

Day 11

Renewing Activity: Yoga

The pull of religion can be far stronger than the freedom of relationship

Jacobsen calls it "daisy-petal Christianity" referring to the childhood game, "He loves me, He loves me not." The adult version goes something like this, I got the promotion at work –*He loves me*...I did not get a raise – *He loves me not*...I gave money to someone in need – *He loves me*...My child is seriously ill – *He loves me not*...I got a note of encouragement – *He loves me*...My car's transmission went out – *He loves me not*... and on and on. This game wears us out by keeping us stressed out, trying to discern constantly if God loves us or not. Jacobsen writes, "So it is time to toss the daisies and discover that it is not the fear of losing God's love that will keep you on His path but the simple joy of living in it every day." So are you willing to toss the daisy?

FALL

Day 12

Renewing Activity: **Find something in your house you no longer need and give it away.**

This I know?

What is it that you know? Think about it – what do you know? As I was reading this morning, that question came into my mind. But why does it matter what I know? It matters for multitudes of reasons. It matters because knowing a specific skill may help with a specific task. It matters because knowing how to add and subtract will help with daily tasks. It matters because knowing helps in making better decisions - knowing just for the sake of knowing does little. For instance, if I know I should drink water but never do or if I know I should be kind but choose not to, what is the point of knowing without application of that knowledge?

Day 13

Renewing Activity: **Yoga**

Sticks and stones will break my bones but words will never hurt me

R. Kipling writes, "Words are the most powerful drug used by mankind." As a friend and I were playing golf recently he mentioned that he did not like getting made fun of if he hit the ball poorly. Who does? But I had to admit to him when he hit the tree – I could not help but laugh. As we discussed and continued to play the above phrase was mentioned but immediately the realization struck me: Those words are untrue! OK, sticks and stones may break bones but words do hurt and they leave lasting wounds far after our bones are healed. In Oxygen for the Soul, D. Bingham writes, "A suicide's body was found floating in a river and a note was written on her person. The note had only two words written on it: 'They said.' Do we realize what a word from our tongues can do? It can wreck a local church, mar a child for life, disrupt the harmony of a business office and destroy a marriage." What have you said? Are you 'they'?

FALL

Day 14

Renewing Activity: Yoga

Make owies feel better

Remember when you were a kid and you got a bump, bruise or scrap and all it took to make you feel better was your mommy or daddy getting on their knee to acknowledge your owie? Then with a kiss, you were off playing again. When and why does that change? Maybe it doesn't or maybe it shouldn't. It may not be our parents but maybe, just maybe, we still want people to acknowledge our owies and give us a kiss or at least a hug. The problem is that owies get more complicated as we grow. Instead of bumps and bruises, we get emotional wounds that are much deeper and longer lasting. But no matter the owie, an acknowledgement of it and a loving touch and/or a meaningful conversation will help.

Day 15

Renewing Activity: Paint, Draw or Journal for 15-20 minutes

Love _____?

On the whiteboard in my office I write a different question or thought each week to provoke conversation with patients. It is really fun to engage patients and make them think a little deeper than they may have on their own. And many times, their answers make me think deeper than I normally would. This week's question is Love____? I tell the patient to look at the board and read it. They say,"Love what?" Then I say, Love – fill in the blank. Their responses are interesting. When they do respond, I question them further about how they can love. But what is more interesting are the patients that have no response at all. When I initially wrote the question my response was, Love wins (every time, in all instances and in all circumstances.) For fun, I have included a few responses below.

Love me...Love myself...Love God...Love without it you are nothing...Love everyone...Love everything...Love family...Love friends...Love is patient...Love conquers all...Love my chiropractor...Love is hard...Love is everything.

FALL

Day 16

Renewing Activity: Yoga

The way, the truth and the liFe

Jesus states in John 14:6, *"I am the way, the truth and the life. No one comes to the Father except through Me."* Do you believe those words? Do you actually believe Jesus is the way? Jesus is the truth? And Jesus is the life? Or do you remove an 'F' and make the statement read: "Is Jesus the way and the truth or Is He a lie? You see if you remove the 'F' out the word life – you get lie. I believe people are watching you and me. They are watching how we respond to our spouse when conflict arises. They watch how we react or not react to our kid's direct disobedience. They are watching to see how we respond to the person who cuts us off in traffic. Watching to see if we will be honest and give back the extra change that was given to us at the cash register. People are looking to see if we think Jesus is life or if Jesus is a lie. Which do you portray?

Day 17

Renewing Activity: Yoga

For anyone who is looking, He is actually everywhere and ever-present. This is our constant labor of devotion – to look for love and to let our hearts be found by His continual reaching. From the beginning of time, from everlasting, God's love has always been excessive, too much and extreme!

Oh the truth of that – that God's love is too much, too extreme, too excessive. That it absolutely is all consuming in its pursuit of us. A battle rages against the advancement of this love and it is our call to not let our hearts grow dull and weary but seek the fiery place of His heart. Today, will you look for Him?

FALL

Day 18

Renewing Activity: **Walk for 27 minutes**

God is not boring...You are

I heard this statement and it has deeply impacted me. The speaker said we have become fascinated with everything else besides God himself and that we have become so satiated on the world that we have no appetite left for the things of God. He said we will stand in line for the latest movie at blockbuster at mid-night and then sit for 2.5 hours to watch it but when we open the Bible to read God's word we fall asleep. Then He said it "God is not boring; you are." We are so enthralled by being entertained from moment to moment that we have lost the fascination with the one who is the greatest entertainer. He is the wonderful creator and the everlasting one from beginning to end. Simply stated, we settle for so much less than what God has for us.

Day 19

Renewing Activity: **Yoga**

It's not that we consciously put God out of our minds.
We just ignore Him. He is seldom in our thoughts.

If we are honest, how often does God enter your mind throughout the day? Do you have a conscious awareness of the presence of God all day? Do you practice the presence of God like Brother Lawrence spoke about in his book, 'Practicing the Presence of God?' Or do you think about God only in the midst of a need, a prayer at lunch or on Sunday? Where and what is your mind set upon?

FALL

Day 20

Renewing Activity: Yoga

You're Everything

"How can I stand here with you and not be moved by you?" A question that was brought to my mind this past Saturday as I listened to a song called 'Everything.' How can I say I know Christ and stand with Him but not be moved by His heart or by His very presence? How can I know the creator of the universe – the one that John 1:1-5 declares "was before all things and all things were made through him, the one that casts out all darkness" – and not be moved toward compassion. How can I know the redemption and restoration Paul speaks of in Colossians 1 and not be moved toward love? How can I not be moved by the one I was made for? And if He does not move you, what does?

Day 21

Renewing Activity: Take a long bath and reflect on the last 21 days

The tongue is the only instrument that reveals what is in the heart

Ephesians 4:29, Luke 6:44-45 and James 3:10 states, "Watch what comes out of your mouth. Let nothing hateful come out of it. Speak only what is helpful, each word is a gift. It's who you are, not what you say and do, that counts. Your true being brims over into true words and deeds. What not ought to be is this: blessing and cursing coming out of the same mouth; with it we praise God but in the next breath we curse our brother." Each word you get to speak is a gift – once it is given it cannot be taken back. Before you ever say a word, it is harbored in your heart. Proverbs 16:23 states, "For the mouth speaks that which fills the heart. And be sure of this – something is filling your heart – what it is depends on you!

WINTER

- **Beginner Version:** Follow the plan without changing anything else in your life.
- **Intermediate Version:** Follow the plan plus drink only water for the 21 days.
- **Advanced Version:** Follow the plan; drink only water and do not watch TV for 21 days.

Below you will find an outline for what meals will be included in these 21 days. The recipes and grocery lists can be found in Appendix B.

Day 1, 4, 7, 10, 13, 16, 19

Breakfast: Orange Juice
Lunch: Salmon Caesar Salad
Dinner: Arugula Squash

Day 2, 5, 8, 11, 14, 17, 20

Breakfast: Banana Spinach Smoothie
Lunch: Orange Curry Carrots
Dinner: Bubble and Squeak (see recipe for description)

Day 3, 6, 9, 12, 15, 18, 21

Breakfast: Grapefruit Juice (optional 1-2 poached eggs)
Lunch: Three Bean Salad
Dinner: Winter Chopped Salad with Shrimp

Snacks

Date Pecan Nuggets
Nut milk or Orange Juice
Avocado
Carrot Sticks

WINTER

Day 1

Renewing Activity: Yoga

Cursed be anyone who dishonors their mother and father

I was reading Deuteronomy and I thought to myself, do I honor my mom and dad? What does it mean to dishonor them? I am sure there are many ways to dishonor someone but at the heart of dishonor is disrespect which can be defined as 'not appreciating or having a lack of regard.' Then these questions came to mind, do I seek their welfare? Do I consider them? Do I pray for them to be blessed in their latter years? Am I thankful for them even as imperfect as they are? Even if I can remember things they did not do or things they did do? Then I thought, now as a parent how much am I like or unlike my parents?

Day 2

Renewing Activity: Yoga

Selective Hearing: Christian Style

The urban dictionary defines selective hearing as: to possess the quality to hear only what you want to hear or the act of listening to only what you would like to hear. All people have selective hearing in some form and it is ever-increasing. 2 Timothy 4:3 says, "For a time is coming when people will no longer listen to sound and wholesome teaching. They will follow their own desires and will look for teachers who will tell them whatever their itching ears want to hear." My friends that time is now! You see I have selective hearing Christian style, choosing bits and pieces of God's words and purposes that make me feel better but many times neglecting the whole. God says this should not be. If you and I desire to hear the very heartbeat of heaven – the very heartbeat of Jesus two things must happen. First, we cannot be selective in hearing God meaning, we must hear His whole word. Secondly, to hear a heartbeat we have to be intimately close to the person whose heartbeat we are trying to hear. Do you desire to be that close?

Day 3

Renewing Activity: Yoga

He has called you by name. He knows every hair on your head. He is passionately in love with you! Give His passion permission. His heart is only good towards you. You are not alone for He has adopted you. You can call Him daddy! He is not going anywhere.

WINTER

He loves you too much, believes in you too much and has too much invested in you. His eyes are turned towards you and He is head-over heels for you. Don't run; His heart is good. He dreams over you as you sleep and delights over you as you awake. He's much bigger than you've ever imagined. Open your eyes to the unseen & watch Him do the impossible. Watch Him throw your mountain into the sea. He's in it for the long haul because He is in love and He just can't help Himself.

These words are found on a chalkboard wall in our kitchen. Let them minister to you as they have ministered to us.

Day 4

Renewing Activity: Go to your favorite coffee shop and buy someone a cup of warmth

I'm alive to live for you

I was listening to the words of this song and wondered to myself, "What am I alive for and what do I live for?" Now that may seem like too deep a question to answer but is it? Is not the true, simple yet profoundly complex answer – "I'm alive to live for Christ?" Each morning when I awake, His mercies are new. His joy is my salvation. His peace is imparted. His love is guaranteed. His kindness is bestowed. His favor is released. His justice is called forth. His goodness is shown. What else am I to live for besides Him?

Day 5

Renewing Activity: Walk for 33 minutes…If you live where it snows; Go snow sledding…Build a snowman or snow angel (Your choice)

His steadfast love endures forever

As I was reading Psalms, I was struck by the words that describe God and His affection towards us and I only read four chapters! Read below and be overwhelmed!

- **Psalm 115:** steadfast love and faithfulness, help, shield, remembers, blesses and increases forevermore
- **Psalm 116:** hears/gracious/righteous/merciful/preserves/saves/delivers/precious/looses bonds
- **Psalm 117:** steadfast love endures
- **Psalm 118:** steadfast love endures forever, answers, sets free, is on my side, does not have to fear, helps, is my strength, song and salvation, is valiant, exalts, rejoices, makes me glad and causes light to shine upon me

WINTER

Day 6

Renewing Activity: Yoga

Slaves to habits

I was on a conference call the other day and the speaker made reference to the fact that we are slaves to habits. He mentioned that as infants we are slaves to impulses but as we grow we create habits and we become slaves to those habits. This made me start thinking about myself and what habits (life-enhancing or life-draining) do I have and why? Or do I still act like a child being a slave to my impulses? I want to believe all my habits are building me mentally, spiritually and physically but after an honest assessment, I know they are not. What about you?

Day 7

Renewing Activity: Yoga

The next to me place

I went for a walk and just asked Jesus, 'What do you want to tell me?' I continued walking hearing nothing but then as sweet and soft as you can imagine, I heard and literally felt these words, *"You do not have to fast to prove your love to me. I love you regardless. I love you because I made you."* Jesus, in that moment came to "my next to me place." You see, I was thinking of doing a 3 day fast to "get back to Him – to show my love for Him." I honestly was not thinking of it that way but He revealed my motive to my own heart. It is not that God said do not fast but God's sweet revelation opened my heart to a greater reality of His love for me. Jesus came to 'my next to me place' and you know what, He loves it there. Have you invited Jesus into "your next to me place?"

Day 8

Renewing Activity: Call a friend or family member and tell them what they mean to you

I see Your face in every sunrise. The colors of the morning are inside Your eyes.
The world awakens in the light of the day. I look up to the sky and say,
I see Your face, You're beautiful.

Is this how you awaken each morning knowing that Christ calls you His beautiful, beloved one?

WINTER

Day 9

Renewing Activity: Yoga

What type of dinosaur are you?

Does your family need a Encouragesaurus or a Tyrannicalass? An Encouragesaurus is playful, kind, understanding and approachable. A tyrannical-ass is selfish, rude, harsh and unapproachable. I am recognizing that even if most days I am an encouragesaurus I can still be a tryrannicalass and when I am, it is imperative that I apologize. Listen friends, living a life of love is a choice. So choose, which dinosaur will you be today?

Day 10

Renewing Activity: Yoga

There has never been a man that is more alive

As I sit praying this morning, I realize I am not praying to the empty air or some God who does not listen or care. I am speaking and I am conversing with a friend. I am sharing my heart and in the same moment, He is sharing His. In these moments, I know there has never been a man that is more alive.

Day 11

Renewing Activity: Yoga

I have made my vow, there is no turning around.
I have burned the bridges, they can no longer be found.

I thought about these words and how often I make a promise but then seem to forget it. How my words and actions do not line up. Then I thought about my relationship to Christ, I have made a vow to love, honor and serve Him – do I take that seriously – is there no turning around? Or do I turn around or to the side much too often. Have I burned those bridges that hold me to past hurts, past offenses, past strongholds that want to drag me down? Can I truly say, they can no longer be found. Taking this closer to home, I have made a vow to my wife, my children, my co-workers, etc. Do I honor that?

WINTER

Day 12

Renewing Activity: **Find something in your house you no longer need and give it away**

What are your eyes fixed upon?

"My eyes are fixed on all your commandments. I fix my eyes on your ways. Open my eyes that I behold wondrous things out of your law. My eyes long for your promise. My eyes long for your righteous promise. My eyes are awake before the watches of the night that I may meditate on your promise" (Psalms 119: 6, 15, 18, 82, 123, 148) What are you looking at today? Hebrews 12:2 exclaims: "Let us fix our eyes on Jesus." To fix our eyes on Jesus - we need to know what He says - this is not found on TV, in magazines, nor on facebook but only in the Bible - that is truth. So what are your eyes fixed upon?

Day 13

Renewing Activity: Yoga

"Men occasionally stumble over the truth but most of them pick themselves up and hurry off of it as if nothing ever happened." - Winston Churchill

When people are trained to look for counterfeit money, they are not trained by looking at the counterfeit but they are trained by looking at the real money. They study the real money to know each detail. In order to know the counterfeit they must first know the real thing. There is no other way. Along these same lines spiritually in order to know the real truth, the one truth, we must study it. We must study the Bible, each detail, each line and each little piece that fits. We must stop studying the counterfeits. We must stop reading so many books about the Bible and using them as the truth. Yes, they can be helpful but it is not the truth. The only real truth comes from the word of God. If we do not know the truth every lie that comes along will cause us to be anxious. It will cause us to be blown around like a ship gone astray. Adolf Hitler said, "The bigger the lie, the more people will believe in it." What lies do we believe in? Do we know the truth enough to counteract the multitudes of lies that we get bombarded with each day?

WINTER

Day 14

Renewing Activity: Yoga

Living for the smile of the Father

Ed McGlasson writes in his book 'A difference a Father makes', "There is a difference in living for the smile of the father versus earning the smile of the father. We should want to live for the smile of the father more than living for the trophies of the world." As I was reading this it reminded me of how I tried to earn my dad's smile verses trying to live for it. Do you know that God loves you? Do you know that He sings over your life? Do you know that He is smiling at you? From this knowledge do you love your wife and kids in the same manner, as Christ loves? Parents, are you more interested in the trophies that you get at work or your hobbies, than living for the smile of the one that matters? What do your kids and others see you living for?

Day 15

Renewing Activity: Yoga

Out of focus

Do you ever feel 'foggy' or 'hazy' or 'unclear?' Do you feel like you wander aimlessly from day to day just existing? Do you ever wonder if you are making a positive impact on those around you? Do you ever feel like you are looking through a clouded window and that you are not able to see fully what is on the other side? If we are honest we could all say yes. We have all had days that seem out of focus, days that it seemed nothing went right and days that our heart was just not into the process of life. So then where does our focus come from?

WINTER

Day 16

Renewing Activity: **Make a homemade meal or goodies for a neighbor**

Walk in love

Ephesians 5:2 reads, 'And walk in love, as Christ loved us and gave himself up, a fragrant offering…' Walking in love is so much more than just saying you love someone. Walking in love is about action, it is about speaking love, thinking love, being love. Walking in love is about thinking beyond our own limited view and seeing life through another person's eyes and circumstances. It is about guarding our heart from offense when it is trampled upon, about loving when it hurts and it is about loving when no one sees. An anonymous quote reads, "Love is just a word until someone comes along and gives it meaning." Is love just a word to you or to those around you? Do you give it meaning? Do you walk in it?

Day 17

Renewing Activity: **Yoga**

Show no partiality

Do you show partiality? James gives us a picture of what we do many times. We see a person who is well dressed or wealthy and allow them to have the honored seat. But the person who is not well-dressed, we put them in a lowly seat or even outside. James, 5:2 reads, "Listen my beloved brothers, has not God chosen those who are poor in the world to be rich in faith and heirs to the kingdom." I think James is speaking more about the attitude of heart verse monetary riches. You can be a billionaire and have an attitude of meekness, kindness, etc. You can also be poor financially but still be stingy. As always, Christ is after the deeper issues, the heart!

Day 18

Renewing Activity: **Yoga**

Authenticity is really about who you are

K. Ferrazzi writes, "Authenticity is about knowing who you are and not trying to come across as someone or something that you are not." Poet E.E. Cummings adds, "The hardest challenge is to be yourself in a world where everyone is trying to make you someone else." Do you know who you are? Or are you trying to be something others around you have created? Are you living up to some standard that you have created for yourself? If you stopped and looked in the mirror right now would you know the person staring back at you?

WINTER

Day 19

Renewing Activity: Think of a way to warm someone's heart

How dare we say we know Him?

I heard the following words in a song…"How dare we say we know Him, when we shut our mouth…How dare we say we know Him, when we store up for ourselves… How dare we say we love Him, when we love not our brother…How dare we say we know Him, when we sit inside these four walls feasting with ourselves while the beggar starves in the street" It is not just about giving to the poor but being authentic to all people and giving to all equally. Even "rich" people need something! It is about our heart and what flows from it. Where is your heart today?

Day 20

Renewing Activity: Yoga

Life is not about waiting for the storm to pass, it is learning to dance in the rain.

An anonymous quote reads, "Sometimes the Lord calms the storm; Sometimes He lets the storm rage and calms His child." Many storms may come throughout your life and you can run from them. You can hide from them or you can pray they never happen but more than likely a storm will come. What will our attitude be when it comes?

Day 21

Renewing Activity: Write an email to yourself explaining what you have accomplished, then share it

Lend me your eyes I can change what you see

These are words from a song called, "Awake my Soul." As I listened to these words I thought, how true. My vision is so limited at times to what I know or think I know. If we were willing to look through someone else's eyes, it would give us a better perspective on how they view life. We may not be as quick to judge them or their situation. It would most certainly change our heart towards them. Do we really want to see the world through their eyes so we can be changed? If we are honest many times we dare not see because of what it will cost us. It will cost us time, finances, safety and security. So dare we look through another's eyes – dare we?

chapter

seasonal fast

- **Beginner Version:** Follow the plan without changing anything else in your life.
- **Intermediate Version:** Follow the plan plus drink only water for the 21 days.
- **Advanced Version:** Follow the plan; drink only water and do not watch TV for 21 days.

For this specific fast, you will be fasting from food and there are two choices. You can fast 4 meals per week for the 21 days or fast an entire day once each week. While you are able to choose what days or meals you fast, I would suggest that you spread out the days. So for example if you wanted to fast 4 meals a week, I would suggest that you fast lunch Monday, Tuesday, Friday and Saturday. If you wanted to fast an entire day, I would suggest a day that is less vigorous. But you may choose whatever days and times you would like. Keep in mind that the point of a fast is not just physical health but also mental, spiritual and emotional health. Thus, on the meals or day of your fast, be purposeful with your time. Read, pray, meditate and encourage someone else. For each day, there will be a word of encouragement to read and a renewing activity. I suggest reading it first thing in the morning to help start your day on a positive note, with hope and purpose.

Note: Fasting may not be recommended for some medical conditions or in conjunction with certain medications. Please consult your healthcare provider before fasting a meal or an entire day.

Day 1

<u>Renewing Activity</u>: Yoga

> *"In everyone's life at some time our inner fire goes out. It is then burst into flame by an encounter with another human being. We should all be thankful for those people who rekindle the inner spirit." - Albert Schweitzer*

SPRING

Day 2

Renewing Activity: Yoga

"The hair on his head was white like wool, as white as snow and His eyes were like blazing fire. His feet were like bronze glowing in a furnace and His voice was like the sound of rushing waters." - Revelation 1:14-15

Jesus you're beautiful

Day 3

Renewing Activity: Walk for 20-30 minutes

"Guard your thoughts and there will be little fear of your actions." - JC Ryle

Day 4

Renewing Activity: Paint, Draw or Journal for 15-20 minutes

"Above all, we [as parents] must make sure that the open book of our lives – our example – demonstrates the reality of our instruction, for in watching us they (our children and others) will learn the most." - R. Kent Hughes

Day 5

Renewing Activity: Yoga

"I do not understand why so many Christians read a Bible abounding in promises to make them something beyond themselves and yet settle for a spiritual vitality so mediocre as to seem virtually non-existent." - Stanley Tam

Day 6

Renewing Activity: Yoga

"Laugh as often as you breathe and love as long as you live." - Unknown

SPRING

Day 7

Renewing Activity: Walk for 20-30 minutes

> *"The first thing a great person does is make us realize the insignificance of circumstance." - Ralph Waldo Emerson*

Day 8

Renewing Activity: Write an encouraging email or text to a friend

> *"Words are, of course, the most powerful drug used by mankind." - Rudyard Kipling*

Day 9

Renewing Activity: Yoga

> *"My eyes are fixed on all your commandments. I fix my eyes on your ways. Open my eyes that I may behold wondrous things out of your law. My eyes long for your promise. My eyes long for your righteous promise. My eyes are awake before the watches of the night that I may meditate on your promise" - Psalms 119: 6, 15, 18, 82, 123, 148*

Day 10

Renewing Activity: Yoga

> *"There is a difference in living for the smile of the father versus earning the smile of the father. We should want to live for the smile of the father more than living for the trophies of the world." - Ed McGlasson*

Day 11

Renewing Activity: Interval Walking
(10 minutes forward then 2 minutes backward) – repeat 2-3 times

> *"The hardest challenge is to be yourself in a world where everyone is trying to make you someone else." - EE Cummings*

SPRING

Day 12

Renewing Activity: Take a homemade meal (or a plate of homemade cookies) to a neighbor

"I resolve to ask is it for good or is it for God? If it is both then ask for the grace for more, if it is only for the former then one is compelled to ponder if it is really good." - Unknown

Day 13

Renewing Activity: Yoga

"The void God created in our lives for himself will demand attention. We look desperately for something to satisfy us and fill the empty places. Our craving to be filled is so strong that the moment something or someone seems to meet our need, we feel an overwhelming temptation to worship it." - Beth Moore

Day 14

Renewing Activity: Yoga

"What other great nation has gods that are intimate with them the way God, our God, is with us, always ready to listen to us?" - Deuteronomy 4:7 (The Message)

Day 15

Renewing Activity: Yoga

"The promise of "arrival" and "rest" is still there for God's people. God himself is at rest. And at the end of the journey we'll surely rest with God." - Hebrews 4:9-10 (The Message)

Day 16

Renewing Activity: Go to a gas station and pay to fill up someone's car

"Perception: It's not what you say, but what is heard. It's not what you show, but what is seen. It's not what you mean, but what is understood. Perception is reality." - Unknown

SPRING

Day 17

<u>Renewing Activity:</u> Walk for 33 minutes

> *"The world is a dangerous place, not because of those who do evil,*
> *but because of those who do nothing." - Albert Einstein*

Day 18

<u>Renewing Activity:</u> Go to a park and play – Slide down a slide – Swing on the swing (Repeat many times)

> *"Taste and see that the LORD is good; blessed is the one who takes refuge in him."*
> *- Psalm 34:8*

Day 19

<u>Renewing Activity</u>: Yoga

> *"Take delight in the LORD, and he will give you the desires of your heart."*
> *- Psalm 37:4*

Day 20

<u>Renewing Activity</u>: Yoga

> *"May the favor of the Lord our God rest on us; establish the work of our hands."*
> *- Psalm 90:17 (NIV)*

Day 21

<u>Renewing Activity:</u> Plant a flower (a perennial) so you can be reminded of what you have accomplished.

> *"Your word is a lamp for my feet, a light on my path."*
> *- Psalm 119:105*

SUMMER

- **Beginner Version:** Follow the plan without changing anything else in your life.

- **Intermediate Version:** Follow the plan plus drink only water for the 21 days.

- **Advanced Version:** Follow the plan; drink only water and do not watch TV for 21 days.

For this specific fast, you will not be fasting from food. You will be fasting from something else and this fast may be more difficult for many. You will be fasting from media – in all its forms (internet, email, text, facebook, news, etc.). Please note: if you choose the advanced version of this fast, you should not be watching TV anyway. Now consider what additional form(s) – (yes, ideally pick more than one) of media you will fast from the entire 21 days. Here is the plan: Choose one or two forms of media and fast it for the entire 21 days. Please be reasonable when you choose. If you have a job that requires email communications then do not choose this form of media. Maybe you could choose facebook, internet (web surfing) or texting instead. But remember the point of a fast is not just physical health but also mental, spiritual and emotional health. Regardless of what type of media you choose each day you will have an encouragement to read and a renewing activity. My suggestion is to read the encouragement first thing in the morning. This will help start your day off with positivity, hope and purpose.

Day 1

Renewing Activity: Yoga

"I lift up my eyes to the mountains—where does my help come from? My help comes from the LORD, the Maker of heaven and earth." - Psalm 121:1-2

Day 2

Renewing Activity: Yoga

"Too often we underestimate the power of a touch, a smile, a kind word, a listening ear, an honest compliment or the smallest act of caring, all of which have the potential to turn a life around." - Leo Buscaglia

Day 3

Renewing Activity: Yoga

"Trust in the LORD with all your heart and lean not on your own understanding; in all your ways submit to him, and he will make your paths straight." - Proverbs 3:5-6

SUMMER

Day 4

Renewing Activity: Write an encouraging letter to a friend or family member

"Commit to the LORD whatever you do, and he will establish your plans."
- Proverbs 16:3

Day 5

Renewing Activity: Walk for 20-30 minutes

"...those who hope in the LORD will renew their strength. They will soar on wings like eagles; they will run and not grow weary, they will walk and not be faint."
- Isaiah 40:31

Day 6

Renewing Activity: Yoga

"Humbly confess your faults; be detached from the world and abandoned to God. Love Him more than yourself and His glory more than your life. The least you can do is to desire and ask for such a love." - Francois Fenelon

Day 7

Renewing Activity: Yoga

"Watch your thoughts they become words. Watch your words they become actions. Watch your actions they become habits. Watch your habits they become character. Watch your character it becomes your destiny." - Unknown

Day 8

Renewing Activity: Yoga

"For I know the plans I have for you," declares the LORD, "plans to prosper you and not to harm you, plans to give you hope and a future." - Jeremiah 29:11

Day 9

Renewing Activity: Go outside…take a deep breath and enjoy a slow walk and the nature around you

"Your God is present among you, a strong Warrior there to save you. Happy to have you back, he'll calm you with his love and delight you with his songs."
- Zephaniah 3:17

SUMMER

Day 10

Renewing Activity: Yoga

"Resolve to be tender with the young, compassionate with the aged, sympathetic with the striving, and tolerant with the weak and the wrong. Sometime in life you have been all of these." - Lloyd Shearer

Day 11

Renewing Activity: Yoga

"Hard work spotlights the character of people: some turn up their sleeves, some turn up their noses, and some don't turn up at all." - Sam Ewing

Day 12

Renewing Activity: Write five things you like about yourself and read them aloud

"A Mediocre teacher tells. A Good teacher explains. A Superior teacher demonstrates. A Great teacher inspires." - William Arthur Ward

Day 13

Renewing Activity: Yoga

"The name of the LORD is a fortified tower; the righteous run to it and are safe." - Proverbs 18:10

Day 14

Renewing Activity: Yoga

"Come to me, all you who are weary and burdened, and I will give you rest." - Matthew 11:28

Day 15

Renewing Activity: Yoga

"Do not be anxious about anything, but in every situation, by prayer and petition, with thanksgiving, present your requests to God. And the peace of God, which transcends all understanding, will guard your hearts and your minds in Christ Jesus." - Philippians 4:6-7

SUMMER

Day 16

Renewing Activity: Yoga

> *"Cast all your anxiety on him because he cares for you."* - 1 Peter 5:7

Day 17

Renewing Activity: Call someone just to tell them how important they are to you

> *"I long to accomplish a great and noble task, but it is my chief duty to accomplish small tasks as if they were great and noble."*
> *- Helen Keller*

Day 18

Renewing Activity: Walk for 27 minutes

> *"The righteous person may have many troubles, but the LORD delivers him from them all..."* - Psalm 34:19

Day 19

Renewing Activity: Yoga

> *"Know therefore that the LORD your God is God; he is the faithful God, keeping his covenant..."* - Deuteronomy 7:9

Day 20

Renewing Activity: Yoga

> *"God is not looking for those who are clever, but for those in whom He can be wise; He is not looking for those who are talented, but for those to whom He can be all sufficient; He is not looking for those who are powerful, but for those through whom He can be almighty."* - Unknown

Day 21

Renewing Activity: Journal or paint/draw a picture capturing the last 21 days of your life

> *"I believe in Christianity as I believe that the sun has risen: not only because I see it, but because by it, I see everything. "* - C.S. Lewis

FALL

- **Beginner Version:** Follow the plan without changing anything else in your life.
- **Intermediate Version:** Follow the plan plus drink only water for the 21 days.
- **Advanced Version:** Follow the plan; drink only water and do not watch TV for 21 days.

For this specific fast, you will fast a certain type of "food". Here is the plan: No sugar for 21 days. I can already hear your excuses and doubts but you can do it and you can live without sugar. It is possible! What type of sugar am I speaking of? To keep it simple, I am not talking about fruit and I am not talking about carbohydrates (yes they do turn into sugar so please try to limit them as mentioned previously). What I am speaking of is "sweets" (organic or not) – cookies, candy, sugary cereal, donuts, packaged and processed sugary foods, pop, flavored lattes, frappucinnos, mochas, cakes, ice cream and the list could go on but I think you get the picture. Get off the sugar and let your body heal! Each day you will have an encouragement to read and a renewing activity. My suggestion is to read the encouragement first thing in the morning. This will help start your day off with positivity, hope and purpose.

Day 1

Renewing Activity: Yoga

"Our problem is not so much that God doesn't give us what we hope for as it is that we don't know the right thing for which to hope. Hope is not what you expect; it is what you would never dream." - Max Lucado

Day 2

Renewing Activity: Yoga

"Be strong and courageous. Do not be afraid or terrified because of them, for the LORD your God goes with you; he will never leave you nor forsake you." - Deuteronomy 31:6

Day 3

Renewing Activity: Yoga

"The LORD himself goes before you and will be with you; he will never leave you nor forsake you. Do not be afraid; do not be discouraged." - Deuteronomy 31:8

FALL

Day 4

<u>Renewing Activity:</u> Go to your favorite local store and buy something for a total stranger

"Courage to start and willingness to keep everlasting at it are the requirements for success."
- Alonzo Benn

Day 5

<u>Renewing Activity</u>: Walk for 20-30 minutes

"I believe in the sun even if it isn't shining. I believe in love even when I am alone.
I believe in God even when He is silent." - Jew in Cologne Concentration Camp

Day 6

<u>Renewing Activity</u>: Yoga

"Sometimes the Lord calms the storm; Sometimes
He lets the storm rage and calms His child." - Unknown

Day 7

<u>Renewing Activity:</u> Yoga

"Imagination is more important than knowledge. For knowledge is limited to
all we now know and understand while imagination embraces the entire world
and all there ever will be to know and understand." - Albert Einstein

Day 8

<u>Renewing Activity:</u> Rake leaves into a big pile – Jump in them and throw them into the air (or create another fun outdoor activity)

"The LORD is a refuge for the oppressed, a stronghold in times of trouble." - Psalm 9:9

Day 9

<u>Renewing Activity</u>: Yoga

"What lies behind us and what lies before us are tiny matters
compared to what lies within us." - Ralph Waldo Emerson

FALL

Day 10

Renewing Activity: Yoga

"An error doesn't become a mistake until you refuse to correct it." - Orlando Battista

Day 11

Renewing Activity: Yoga

"I keep my eyes always on the LORD. With him at my right hand, I will not be shaken."
- Psalm 16:8

Day 12

Renewing Activity: Find something in your house you no longer need and give it away.

"One thing I ask from the LORD, this only do I seek: that I may dwell in the house of the LORD all the days of my life, to gaze on the beauty of the LORD and to seek Him in his temple." - Psalm 27:4

Day 13

Renewing Activity: Yoga

"Wait for the LORD; be strong and take heart and wait for the LORD." - Psalm 27:14

Day 14

Renewing Activity: Yoga

"Do not follow where the path may lead. Go instead where there is no path and leave a trail." - Ralph Waldo Emerson

Day 15

Renewing Activity: Paint, Draw or Journal for 15-20 minutes

"Since you are my rock and my fortress, for the sake of your name lead and guide me."
- Psalm 31:3

FALL

Day 16

Renewing Activity: Yoga

"You can complain because roses have thorns, or you can rejoice because thorns have roses."
- Ziggy

Day 17

Renewing Activity: Yoga

"Health is not a gift but something each person is responsible
for through his or her own daily effort." - Hildeo Nakayma

Day 18

Renewing Activity: Walk for 27 minutes

"I call on the LORD in my distress and he answers me." - Psalm 120:1

Day 19

Renewing Activity: Yoga

"Your living is determined not so much by what your life brings to you as
by the attitude you bring to life; not so much by what happens to you as by
the way your mind looks at what happens." - John Miller

Day 20

Renewing Activity: Yoga

"The LORD will keep you from all harm— he will watch over your life; the LORD will
watch over your coming and going both now and forevermore." - Psalm 121:7-8

Day 21

Renewing Activity: Take a long bath/shower and reflect on the last 21 days

"Any fact facing us is not as important as our attitude toward it, for that determines
our success or failure." - Vincent Peale

WINTER

- **Beginner Version:** Follow the plan without changing anything else in your life.
- **Intermediate Version:** Follow the plan plus drink only water for the 21 days.
- **Advanced Version:** Follow the plan; drink only water and do not watch TV for 21 days.

For this specific fast, you will be fasting from food and you have two choices. You can either fast 6 meals per week or fast an entire day twice per week. While you are able to choose what days or meals you fast I would suggest that you spread out the days. So for example if you wanted to fast 6 meals a week, I would suggest that you fast lunch Monday, Wednesday, Friday and Saturday and dinner Tuesday and Sunday. If you wanted to fast an entire day twice a week I would suggest that you fast on Monday and Thursday (or two days that are less vigorous). But you may choose whatever days and times you would like. Keep in mind that the point of a fast is not just physical health but also mental, spiritual and emotional health. Thus, on the meals or day of your fast, be purposeful with your time. Read, pray, meditate and encourage someone else. For each day, there will be a word of encouragement to read and a renewing activity. I suggest reading it first thing in the morning to help start your day on a positive note, with hope and purpose.

Note: Fasting may not be recommended for some medical conditions or in conjunction with certain medications. Please consult your healthcare provider before fasting a meal or an entire day.

Day 1

Renewing Activity: Yoga

"The LORD is near to all who call on him, to all who call on him in truth. He fulfills the desires of those who fear him; he hears their cry and saves them."
- Psalm 145:18-19

Day 2

Renewing Activity: Yoga

"A generous person will prosper; whoever refreshes others will be refreshed."
- Proverbs 11:25

WINTER

Day 3

Renewing Activity: Yoga

> *"One man finds an obstacle a stumbling block; another finds it a stepping stone."*
> *- Unknown*

Day 4

Renewing Activity: Go to your favorite coffee shop and buy someone a cup of warmth

> *"Destiny is not a matter of chance but a matter of choice.*
> *It is not a thing to be waited for, it is a thing to be achieved." - William J. Bryan*

Day 5

Renewing Activity: Walk for 33 minutes…If there is snow where you live, go snow sledding…Build a snowman or snow angel (Your choice)

> *"I find the great thing in this world is not so much where we stand*
> *as in what direction we are moving…" - Oliver Wendell Holmes*

Day 6

Renewing Activity: Yoga

> *"I know not what the future holds but I know who holds the future." - Unknown*

Day 7

Renewing Activity: Yoga

> *"You will keep in perfect peace those whose minds are steadfast,*
> *because they trust in you." - Isaiah 26:3*

WINTER

Day 8

<u>Renewing Activity:</u> **Call a friend or family member and tell them what they mean to you**

> *"Every illness, even though it may reveal itself by means of local symptom, is nevertheless first and always a general disease and the individual part can never be recognized without seeing the whole."*
> *- Hippocrates*

Day 9

<u>Renewing Activity</u>: Yoga

> *"If man will begin with certainties, he will end in doubts, but if he will be content to begin with doubts he will end with certainties."*
> *- Sir Francis Bacon*

Day 10

<u>Renewing Activity</u>: Yoga

> *"For I am the LORD your God who takes hold of your right hand and says to you, Do not fear; I will help you."*
> *- Isaiah 41:13*

Day 11

<u>Renewing Activity</u>: Yoga

> *"We assume, incorrectly that reality is the box we are put in and it's not. The dream of today is the reality of tomorrow. Your dream; your tomorrow."*
> *- Unknown*

Day 12

<u>Renewing Activity:</u> **Find something in your house you no longer need and give it away**

> *"Fear not, for I have redeemed you; I have summoned you by name; you are mine."*
> *- Isaiah 43:1*

WINTER

Day 13

Renewing Activity: Yoga

"If I accept the sunshine and warmth, I must also accept the thunder and lightning."
- Kahlil Gibran

Day 14

Renewing Activity: Yoga

"It's a funny thing about life; if you refuse to accept
anything but the very best you will often get it."
- W. Somerset Maugham

Day 15

Renewing Activity: Yoga

"We can do only what we think we can do. We can be only what we think
we can be. We can have only what we think we can have. What we do, what
we are and what we have all depend upon what we think."
- Robert Collier

Day 16

Renewing Activity: Make a homemade meal or goodies for a neighbor

"A successful relationship requires falling in love many times,
always with the same person."
- Mignon McLaughlin

Day 17

Renewing Activity: Yoga

"The good Lord didn't create anything without a purpose, but mosquitoes come close."
- Unknown

WINTER

Day 18

Renewing Activity: Yoga

"The LORD will guide you always; he will satisfy your needs in a sun-scorched land and will strengthen your frame. You will be like a well-watered garden, like a spring whose waters never fail."
- Isaiah 58:11

Day 19

Renewing Activity: Think of a way to warm someone's heart and then do it.

"The LORD is good, a refuge in times of trouble. He cares for those who trust in Him."
- Nahum 1:7

Day 20

Renewing Activity: Yoga

"The best mathematical equation I have ever seen: 1 cross + 3 nails = 4 given."
- Unknown

Day 21

Renewing Activity: Write an email to yourself explaining what you have accomplished and then share it with others.

"He who works with his hands is a laborer. He who works with his hands and his head is a craftsman. He who works with his hands and his head and his heart is an artist."
- St. Francis of Assisi

chapter 20

"
All truly great thoughts are
conceived while walking.
- *Nietzsche*
"

walking (read-pray-walk)

- **Beginner Version:** Follow the plan without changing anything else in your life.

- **Intermediate Version:** Follow the plan plus drink only water for the 21 days.

- **Advanced Version:** Follow the plan; drink only water and do not watch TV for 21 days.

For this Read-Pray-Walk the prayer focus is on you! At first glance, this may seem selfish but so many people I encounter have an identity crisis. They do not know who they are. They have believed lies spoken over them instead of the truth of who they are and who they can become. Throughout our lifetime the words family, friends, teachers and even enemies stick with us. Those messages can become a part of what we believe about ourselves. Believing negative things about oneself can lead to a cycle of negative choices. However, believing positive things about oneself can lead to a cycle of positive choices. Thus for this 21 days, focus on praying for yourself. Jesus said, "We are to love our neighbors as ourselves." My hope is that you will learn to love you for you!

Below you will find a prayer that is to be prayed each day. My suggestion is to read this before you walk so it is fresh in your mind. You might also find it helpful to read it multiple times per day. It may seem odd at first to pray this over and about yourself but as the days pass the truth of these words will become increasingly evident in your life. After this prayer, you will find a renewing thought. My suggestion is to read this thought first thing in the morning as it will help "set the course" of your day.

Remember, the point of the Read-Pray-Walk is not only for physical health but also mental and spiritual health. With that in mind, as you walk, make sure you pray aloud or you may want to simply meditate on the prayer and/or renewing thought. Either way, let the walk engage more than your body. Let it also engage your spirit!

Note: Walking has been known to help alleviate stress, decrease headaches and improve back pain. However in rare instances, walking may not be recommended for some medical conditions. Please consult your healthcare provider if you have questions or concerns.

SPRING

<u>Prayer</u>: *Jesus, I thank you that you pursue me even when I do not see it or understand it. I thank you that you call me worthy, beloved, honored, delightful, enough, redeemed, restored, saved, loved and a friend. Thank you for your grace. My life is rich with your delights. Even on those days that are hard, I know You are good and faithful and have my best interest in Your heart. Jesus, today I say no to the lies that have been spoken over me that I am not enough, that I am unworthy or will never amount to anything. Today I shout, I am a beloved child and Your banner over me is love! Today, I have nothing to prove and I rest in the midst of your intimate embrace.*

Day 1

Renewing Activity: **Walk 20 minutes**

"Seeing the crowds...He opened his mouth and taught them saying, Blessed are the poor in spirit, for theirs is the kingdom of heaven." - Matthew 5:1-3

Day 2

Renewing Activity: **Walk 20 minutes**

"Blessed are those who mourn, for they shall be comforted." - Matthew 5:4

Day 3

Renewing Activity: **Walk 20 minutes**

"Blessed are the meek, for they shall inherit the earth." - Matthew 5:5

Day 4

Renewing Activity: **Walk 20 minutes**

"Blessed are those who hunger and thirst for righteousness, for they shall be satisfied." - Matthew 5:6

Day 5

Renewing Activity: **Yoga (no walking today)**

"Blessed are the merciful, for they shall receive mercy." - Matthew 5:7

SPRING

Day 6

Renewing Activity: Walk 25 minutes

"Blessed are the pure in heart, for they shall see God." - Matthew 5:8

Day 7

Renewing Activity: Walk for 25 minutes

"Blessed are the peacemakers, for they shall be called children of God." - Matthew 5:9

Day 8

Renewing Activity: Walk 25 minutes

"Blessed are those who are persecuted for righteousness' sake,
for theirs is the kingdom of heaven." - Matthew 5:10

Day 9

Renewing Activity: Walk 25 minutes

"Blessed are you when others revile you and persecute you and utter all kinds of evil
against you falsely on my account. Rejoice and be glad, for your reward is great in
heaven, for so they persecuted the prophets who were before you." - Matthew 5:11-12

Day 10

Renewing Activity: Yoga (no walking today)

"You are the salt of the earth, but if salt has lost its taste, how shall its saltiness be
restored? It is no longer good for anything except to be thrown
out and trampled under people's feet." - Matthew 5:13

Day 11

Renewing Activity: Walk 30 minutes

"You are the light of the world. A city set on a hill cannot be hidden." - Matthew 5:14

S P R I N G

Day 12

Renewing Activity: Walk 30 minutes

"Nor do people light a lamp and put it under a basket, but on a stand, and it gives light to all in the house. In the same way, let your light shine before others, so that they may see your good works and give glory to your Father who is in heaven."
- Matthew 5:15-16

Day 13

Renewing Activity: Walk 30 minutes

Re-read the verses from Day 1-12 and as you walk ponder what you've learned.

Day 14

Renewing Activity: Walk 30 minutes

"He who dwells in the shelter of the Most High will abide in the shadow of the Almighty. I will say to the Lord, "My refuge and my fortress, my God, in whom I trust."
- Psalm 91:1-2

Day 15

Renewing Activity: Yoga (no walking today)

"For he will deliver you from the snare of the fowler and from the deadly pestilence. He will cover you with his pinions, and under his wings you will find refuge; his faithfulness is a shield and buckler."
- Psalm 91-3-4

Day 16

Renewing Activity: Walk 35 minutes

"You will not fear the terror of the night, nor the arrow that flies by day..."
- Psalm 91:5

SPRING

Day 17

Renewing Activity: Walk 35 minutes

"For he will command his angels concerning you to guard you in all your ways. On their hands they will bear you up..." - Psalm 91:11-12

Day 18

Renewing Activity: Walk 35 minutes

"Because he holds fast to me in love, I will deliver him; I will protect him, because he knows my name." - Psalm 91:14

Day 19

Renewing Activity: Walk 35 minutes

"When he calls to me, I will answer him; I will be with him in trouble; I will rescue him and honor him." - Psalm 91:15

Day 20

Renewing Activity: Yoga (no walking today)

"With long life I will satisfy him and show him my salvation." - Psalm 91:16

Day 21

Renewing Activity: Walk 45 minutes

Re-read days 14-20 and as you walk ponder if you have learned to love yourself.

SUMMER

- **Beginner Version:** Follow the plan without changing anything else in your life.

- **Intermediate Version:** Follow the plan plus drink only water for the 21 days.

- **Advanced Version:** Follow the plan; drink only water and do not watch TV for 21 days.

For this Read-Pray-Walk the prayer focus is on your family! We all desire strong, vibrant, healthy families but many times we do not take the time to invest in what really matters. I have heard it said, "A family that prays and plays together stays together."

Below you will find three prayers that can be prayed each day or choose one per day then repeat each seven times. My suggestion is to read this before you walk so it is fresh in your mind. You may also find it helpful to read it multiple times per day. Be hopeful that as you pray over your family, the truth of your words will become increasingly evident in their lives.

Remember, the point of the Read-Pray-Walk is not only for physical health but also mental and spiritual health. With that in mind, as you walk, make sure you pray aloud or you may want to simply meditate on the prayer and/or renewing thought. Either way, let the walk engage more than your body. Let it also engage your spirit!

Note: Walking has been known to help alleviate stress, decrease headaches and improve back pain. However in rare instances, walking may not be recommended for some medical conditions. Please consult your healthcare provider if you have questions or concerns.

Prayer for your spouse: (fill your spouse's name in the blanks. If you are not married yet, fill in the blank with future spouse). *Jesus, I thank you for _____. I thank you for the gifts you have given him/her. I thank you that you see much in _____. Let me have the eyes to see what You see. I desire to be uplifting in all my thoughts, words and deeds toward _____. I pray _____ would be blessed in all he/she does. Bless the work of his/her hands. Enlighten the eyes of his/her heart. Restore and redeem those areas in his/her mind, body and spirit that have been exposed to lies and replace those lies with truth. Jesus, bless our marriage and let us learn to forgive quickly and love deeply. Please let love abound more and more. May I be the husband/wife that honors _____.*

SUMMER

Prayer for your children (fill your children's name(s) in the blank. If no children, fill in the blank with future children or pray for another child you know). *Jesus, I thank you for the gift of life. I am honored that you would entrust _____ to my care. Let me be wise and discerning in all I do. Let me realize that _____ watches me more than he/she listens. Let my time be invested in what is meaningful. Let me take my job as a parent seriously. I pray you would guard _____ in all that he/she does. Help me see what You see in him/her. Allow me to call forth his/her destiny. I desire to speak life and hope over my children. I pray that _____ is pointed straight to Your heart. Be his/her refuge and strength when I am unable. Jesus, I thank you for what my child teaches me. I thank you that You love _____. Let me love like You do!*

Prayer for extended family (includes everyone else). *Jesus, I thank you for the family you have placed me in even when I do not understand why. Even in the midst of the dysfunction and sometimes chaotic lifestyle I know you have a good plan and purpose for my family. Please encounter my family with your love, grace, redemption and salvation. Jesus, I want my family to know Your fullness. Help me see my family as you see them — beloved and honored. Let my words honor my parents — especially if I know them but even if I do not know them fully. Bless my sibling(s) with much favor; I pray that they are honored among many. For the rest of my family, please touch them with your love. And Jesus, even when times are tough; be our vessel of hope.*

Day 1

Renewing Activity: Walk 20 minutes

> *"Be imitators of God, as beloved children..." - Ephesians 5:1*

Day 2

Renewing Activity: Walk 20 minutes

> *"Walk in love, as Christ loved us and gave himself up for us, a fragrant offering and sacrifice to God." - Ephesians 5:2*

Day 3

Renewing Activity: Walk 20 minutes

> *"Let there be no filthiness nor foolish talk nor crude joking, which are out of place, but instead let there be thanksgiving." - Ephesians 5:4*

SUMMER

Day 4

Renewing Activity: Walk 20 minutes

"For at one time you were darkness, but now you are light in the Lord. Walk as children of light (for the fruit of light is found in all that is good and right and true), and try to discern what is pleasing to the Lord." - Ephesians 5:8-10

Day 5

Renewing Activity: Yoga (no walking today)

"Look carefully then how you walk, not as unwise but as wise..." - Ephesians 5:15

Day 6

Renewing Activity: Walk 25 minutes

"Making the best use of the time because the days are evil, therefore do not be foolish, but understand what the will of the Lord is." - Ephesians 5:16-17

Day 7

Renewing Activity: Walk for 25 minutes

"And do not get drunk with wine for that is debauchery but be filled with the Spirit, addressing one another in psalms and hymns and spiritual songs, singing and making melody to the Lord with your heart" - Ephesians 5:18-19

Day 8

Renewing Activity: Walk 25 minutes

"Giving thanks always and for everything to God the Father in the name of our Lord Jesus Christ." - Ephesians 5:20

Day 9

Renewing Activity: Walk 25 minutes

"Submit to one another out of reverence for Christ." - Ephesians 5:21

SUMMER

Day 10

Renewing Activity: Yoga (no walking today)

*"Wives, submit to your own husbands, as to the Lord." -
Ephesians 5:22*

Day 11

Renewing Activity: Walk 30 minutes

*"For the husband is the head of the wife even as Christ is the head of the church...
Now as the church submits to Christ, so also wives should submit in
everything to their husbands."
- Ephesians 5:23-24*

Day 12

Renewing Activity: Walk 30 minutes

*"Husbands, love your wives, as Christ loved the church and gave himself up for her..."
- Ephesians 5:25*

Day 13

Renewing Activity: Walk 30 minutes

*"...that he might sanctify her, having cleansed her by the washing of water with the
word, so that he might present the church to himself in splendor, without spot or
wrinkle or any such thing, that she might be holy and without blemish."
- Ephesians 5:26-27*

Day 14

Renewing Activity: Walk 30 minutes

*"In the same way husbands should love their wives as their own bodies.
He who loves his wife loves himself."
- Ephesians 5:28*

SUMMER

Day 15

Renewing Activity: Yoga (no walking today)

"For no one ever hated his own flesh, but nourishes and cherishes it, just as Christ does the church, because we are members of his body."
- Ephesians 5:29-30

Day 16

Renewing Activity: Walk 35 minutes

"Therefore a man shall leave his father and mother and hold fast to his wife, and the two shall become one flesh."
- Ephesians 5:31

Day 17

Renewing Activity: Walk 35 minutes

"This mystery is profound, and I am saying that it refers to Christ and the church. However, let each one of you love his wife as himself, and let the wife see that she respects her husband."
- Ephesians 5:32-33

Day 18

Renewing Activity: Walk 35 minutes

"Likewise, wives, be subject to your own husbands, so that even if some do not obey the word, they may be won without a word by the conduct of their wives, when they see your respectful and pure conduct."
- 1 Peter 3:1-2

SUMMER

Day 19

Renewing Activity: Walk 35 minutes

"Husbands, live with your wives in an understanding way, showing honor... since they are heirs with you of the grace of life, so that your prayers may not be hindered." - 1 Peter 3:7

Day 20

Renewing Activity: Yoga (no walking today)

"Fathers, do not provoke your children to anger, but bring them up in the discipline and instruction of the Lord." - Ephesians 6:4

Day 21

Renewing Activity: Walk 45 minutes

"She opens her mouth with wisdom, and the teaching of kindness is on her tongue. She looks well to the ways of her household...Her children rise up and call her blessed; her husband also, and he praises her." Proverbs 31:26-28

FALL

- **Beginner Version:** Follow the plan without changing anything else in your life.

- **Intermediate Version:** Follow the plan plus drink only water for the 21 days.

- **Advanced Version:** Follow the plan; drink only water and do not watch TV for 21 days.

For this Read-Pray-Walk the focus is on your neighborhood. Why wouldn't you pray for those who live around you? The neighborhood in which you live is an important part of the soil of your life. The goal for these 21 days is to purposely walk your neighborhood. Get outside and bless those around you!

Below you will find a prayer that is to be prayed each day. My suggestion is to read this before you walk so it is fresh in your mind. You may also find it helpful to read it multiple times per day. Be hopeful that as you pray for your neighbors, the truth of your words will become increasingly evident in their lives.

Remember, the point of the Read-Pray-Walk is not only for physical health but also mental and spiritual health. With that in mind, as you walk, make sure you pray aloud or you may want to simply meditate on the prayer and/or renewing thought. Either way, let the walk engage more than your body. Let it also engage your spirit!

Note: Walking has been known to help alleviate stress, decrease headaches and improve back pain. However in rare instances, walking may not be recommended for some medical conditions. Please consult your healthcare provider if you have questions or concerns.

Prayer: *Jesus, as I walk by each house in my neighborhood give me insight into what I should pray. Lord, you know each family's needs; direct my heart and mind so I can pray your heart over them. I pray you would bless them and cause your face to shine upon them. Let them be strengthened and encouraged today. As I walk by their house, let the arrow of your love and grace be released into their home. Today Lord, do an amazing work in their midst. When I have the opportunity, let me practically and tangibly demonstrate your love to them. Jesus, bless my neighborhood.*

FALL

Day 1

Renewing Activity: Walk 20 minutes

"Then shall your light break forth like the dawn, and your healing shall spring up speedily; your righteousness shall go before you; the glory of the Lord shall be your rear guard." - Isaiah 58:8

Day 2

Renewing Activity: Walk 20 minutes

"Then you shall call, and the Lord will answer; you shall cry, and he will say, 'Here I am...'" - Isaiah 58:9

Day 3

Renewing Activity: Walk 20 minutes

"If you pour yourself out for the hungry and satisfy the desire of the afflicted, then shall your light rise in the darkness and your gloom be as the noonday." - Isaiah 58:10

Day 4

Renewing Activity: Walk 20 minutes

"And the Lord will guide you continually and satisfy your desire in scorched places and make your bones strong..." - Isaiah 58:11a

Day 5

Renewing Activity: Yoga (no walking today)

"...you shall be like a watered garden, like a spring of water, whose waters do not fail." - Isaiah 58:11b

FALL

Day 6

Renewing Activity: Walk 25 minutes

"And your ancient ruins shall be rebuilt; you shall raise up the foundations of many generations; you shall be called the repairer of the breach, the restorer of streets to dwell in." - Isaiah 58:12

Day 7

Renewing Activity: Walk for 25 minutes

Re-read days 1-6 and know that what you are doing matters. It is making a difference in your life and the lives of those around you.

Day 8

Renewing Activity: Walk 25 minutes

"The Spirit of the Lord God is upon me, because the Lord has anointed me to bring good news to the poor..." - Isaiah 61:1(a)

Day 9

Renewing Activity: Walk 25 minutes

"...he has sent me to bind up the brokenhearted, to proclaim liberty to the captives, and the opening of the prison to those who are bound..." - Isaiah 61:1(b)

Day 10

Renewing Activity: Yoga (no walking today)

"...to proclaim the year of the Lord's favor, and the day of vengeance of our God; to comfort all who mourn..." - Isaiah 61:2

FALL

Day 11

Renewing Activity: Walk 30 minutes

> *"...to grant to those who mourn in Zion— to give them a beautiful he*
> *address instead of ashes, the oil of gladness instead of mourning,*
> *the garment of praise instead of a faint spirit..." - Isaiah 61:3(a)*

Day 12

Renewing Activity: Walk 30 minutes

> *"...that they may be called oaks of righteousness,*
> *the planting of the Lord, that he may be glorified..." - Isaiah 61:3(b)*

Day 13

Renewing Activity: Walk 30 minutes

> *"They shall build up the ancient ruins; they shall raise up the former devastations; they*
> *shall repair the ruined cities, the devastations of many generations..." - Isaiah 61:4*

Day 14

Renewing Activity: Walk 30 minutes

> *Re-read days 7-13 and know that what you are doing matters.*
> *It is making a difference in your life and the lives of those around you.*

Day 15

Renewing Activity: Yoga (no walking today)

> *"For this reason, because I have heard of your faith in the*
> *Lord Jesus and your love toward the saints..." - Ephesians 1:15*

FALL

Day 16

Renewing Activity: Walk 35 minutes

"I do not cease to give thanks for you, remembering you in my prayers." - Ephesians 1:16

Day 17

Renewing Activity: Walk 35 minutes

"That the God of our Lord Jesus Christ, the Father of glory, may give you the Spirit of wisdom and of revelation in the knowledge of him" - Ephesians 1:17

Day 18

Renewing Activity: Walk 35 minutes

"Having the eyes of your hearts enlightened" - Ephesians 1:18(a)

Day 19

Renewing Activity: Walk 35 minutes

"...that you may know what is the hope to which he has called you, what are the riches of his glorious inheritance in the saints..." - Ephesians 1:18(b)

Day 20

Renewing Activity: Yoga (no walking today)

"And what is the immeasurable greatness of his power toward us who believe." - Ephesians 1:19

Day 21

Renewing Activity: Walk 45 minutes

Re-read days 14-20 and know that what you are doing matters. It is making a difference in your life and the lives of those around you.

WINTER

- **Beginner Version:** Follow the plan without changing anything else in your life.

- **Intermediate Version:** Follow the plan plus drink only water for the 21 days.

- **Advanced Version:** Follow the plan; drink only water and do not watch TV for 21 days.

For this Read-Pray-Walk the focus will be on your city and nation. Jeremiah 29:7 reminds us, "Seek the peace and prosperity of the city…pray to the LORD for it, because if it prospers, you too will prosper." For these 21 days, get out and walk around the city. Go to a local park – go downtown – go to a local church or school – literally, walk the city! However, if weather becomes a problem (this is the Winter plan), pray while you are driving around.

Below you will find a prayer that is to be prayed each day. My suggestion is to read this before you walk so it is fresh in your mind. You may also find it helpful to read it multiple times per day. Be hopeful that as you pray for your city and nation, the truth of your words will become increasingly evident.

Remember, the point of the Read-Pray-Walk is not only for physical health but also mental and spiritual health. With that in mind, as you walk, make sure you pray aloud or you may want to simply meditate on the prayer and/or renewing thought. Either way, let the walk engage more than your body. Let it also engage your spirit!

Note: Walking has been known to help alleviate stress, decrease headaches and improve back pain. However in rare instances, walking may not be recommended for some medical conditions. Please consult your healthcare provider if you have questions or concerns.

Prayer: *Jesus, you say, I am called by your name and if I would humble myself – pray and seek your face you would hear my cry and heal my city and nation. Jesus, I cry out for my city – that she would be known as a light on a hill. Lord, bring your righteousness and justice forth. Lord, touch our elected leaders – let truth and integrity rise up in the midst of fraud and deception. Jesus, bring revelation and hope to the business community. Grant the teachers and educators wisdom and discernment. Give creativity to the arts in my city; let your passion flow from painters, song writers and dancers. Let businesses become refuges for their employees and clients – let supernatural acts of kindness spring up all over my city. Jesus, I want your name and fame to be known in my city. Please, set your gaze on _____ (fill in the blank with your city's name)*

WINTER

Day 1

Renewing Activity: Walk 20 minutes

> *"If I speak in the tongues of men and of angels, but have not love,*
> *I am a noisy gong or a clanging cymbal." - 1 Corinthians 13:1*

Day 2

Renewing Activity: Walk 20 minutes

> *"If I have prophetic powers, and understand all mysteries and all knowledge..."*
> *- 1 Corinthians 13:2(a)*

Day 3

Renewing Activity: Walk 20 minutes

> *"...and if I have all faith, so as to remove mountains, but have not love, I am nothing."*
> *- 1 Corinthians 13:2(b)*

Day 4

Renewing Activity: Walk 20 minutes

> *"If I give away all I have, and if I deliver up my body to be burned, but have not love, I*
> *gain nothing." 1 Corinthians 13:3*

Day 5

Renewing Activity: Yoga (no walking today)

> *"Love is patient and kind..." - 1 Corinthians 13:4(a)*

Day 6

Renewing Activity: Walk 25 minutes

> *"...love does not envy or boast..." - 1 Corinthians 13:4(b);*

WINTER

Day 7

Renewing Activity: Walk for 25 minutes

"...love is not arrogant or rude..." - 1 Corinthians 13:4(c)

Day 8

Renewing Activity: Walk 25 minutes

"...[love] does not insist on its own way; it is not irritable or resentful..."
- 1 Corinthians 13:5

Day 9

Renewing Activity: Walk 25 minutes

"Love does not rejoice at wrongdoing, but rejoices with the truth."
- 1 Corinthians 13:6

Day 10

Renewing Activity: Yoga (no walking today)

"Love bears all things..." - 1 Corinthians 13:7(a)

Day 11

Renewing Activity: Walk 30 minutes

"[Love] believes all things..." - 1 Corinthians 13:7(b).

Day 12

Renewing Activity: Walk 30 minutes

"[Love] hopes all things..." - 1 Corinthians 13:7(c)

WINTER

Day 13

Renewing Activity: Walk 30 minutes

"[Love] endures all things..." - 1 Corinthians 13:7(d)

Day 14

Renewing Activity: Walk 30 minutes

"Love never ends..." - 1 Corinthians 13:8

Day 15

Renewing Activity: Yoga (no walking today)

"So now faith, hope, and love abide, these three; but the greatest of these is love."
- 1 Corinthians 13:13

Day 16

Renewing Activity: Walk 35 minutes

"Pursue love..." - 1 Corinthians 14:1

Day 17

Renewing Activity: Walk 35 minutes

"Do not be children in your thinking. Be infants in evil, but in your thinking be mature."
- 1 Corinthians 14:20

Day 18

Renewing Activity: Walk 35 minutes

"God is not a God of confusion but of peace." - 1 Corinthians 14:33

WINTER

Day 19

Renewing Activity: Walk 35 minutes

> *"Thanks be to God, who gives us the victory through our Lord Jesus Christ."*
> *- 1 Corinthians 15:57*

Day 20

Renewing Activity: Yoga (no walking today)

> *"...be steadfast, immovable, always abounding in the work of the Lord,*
> *knowing that in the Lord your labor is not in vain."*
> *- 1 Corinthians 15:58*

Day 21

Renewing Activity: Walk 45 minutes

> *Re-read days 1-20 and as you walk reflect on how you*
> *are loved and how you can show that love to others.*

works cited

1. Bickle, Mike. *The Rewards of Fasting.* Kansas City: Forerunner Publications, 2005. Print.

2. Briscoe, Jill. *Spiritual Arts: Mastering the Disciplines for a Rich Spiritual Life.* Grand Rapids: Zondervan Publishing. 2007. Print.

3. Chapman, Gary. *The Five Love Languages.* Chicago: Northfield Pub., 1992. Print.

4. Cohen, Lawrence J. *Playful Parenting: a bold new way to nurture close connections, solve behavior problems, and encourage children's confidence.* New York: Ballantine Publishing Group, 2001. Print.

5. Datz, Todd. *Harvard researchers launch healthy eating plate.* Harvard School of Medicine Press Release, September 2011. Web.

6. Davis, William. *Wheat Belly: Lose the Wheat, Lose the Weight.* New York: Rodale, 2011. Print.

7. DeMoss, Nancy Leigh. "Nothing Between." Reviveourhearts. np. Web. Apr. 1997.

8. DeVries, Susan. *The Most Important Year in a Woman's Life: What Every Bride Needs to Know/ The Most Important Year in a Man's Life: What Every Groom Needs to Know.* Grand Rapids: Zondervan, 2003. Print.

9. Fallon, Sally. *Nourishing Traditions: the cookbook that challenges change politically correct nutrition and the diet dictocrats.* Washington, DC: New Trends Publishing, 2001. Print.

10. *Food and Evolution: Toward a Theory of Human Food Habits.* Ed. Marvin Harris and Eric B. Ross. Philadelphia:Temple University Press, 1987. Print

11. Gallagher, Steve. *Intoxicated with Babylon: The Seduction of God's People in the Last Days.* Dry Ridge: Pure Life Ministries, 1996. Print.

12. *The Garden Book: Gardening and More.* San Diego: Thunder Bay Press, 1997. Print.

13. Groeschel, Craig. *The Christian Atheist.* Grand Rapids: Zondervan, 2010. Print.

14. ---. *Soul Detox: clean living in a contaminated world.* Grand Rapids: Zondervan, 2012. Print.

15. Hawthorne, Steve and Graham Kendrick. *Prayer Walking: Praying on Site with Insight.* Orlando: Creation House, 2003. Print.

16. Hilman, Os. *The 9 to 5 Window.* Ventura: Regal Books, 2005. Print.

17. Horne, Ross. *Health and Survival in the 21st Century.* Sydney: HarperCollins Publishers, 1997. Print.

18. Jackson, Jim and Lynne Jackson. *Discipline that Connects with Your Child's Heart.* Chaska: Connected Families, 2012. Print.

19. Johnson, Bill. *Dreaming with God.* Shippensburg: Destiny Image Publishers, 2006. Print.

20. Kroeck, Seth. *Crop Rotation and Cover Cropping: Soil Resiliency and Health on the Organic Farm.* 2004. A Project of the Northeast Organic Farming Association.

White River Junction: Chelsea Green Publishing, 2011. Print.

21. La Leche League International. *The Womanly Art of Breastfeeding*. Ed. Judy Torgus and Gwen Gotsch. 1958. Schaumburg: La Leche League International, 2010. Print.

22. Lewis, Robert. *Raising a Modern-Day Knight*. Carol Stream: Tyndale House Publishers, 2007. Print

23. Liebenson, Craig. *Rehabilitation of the Spine: A Practitioner's Manual*. Baltimore: Lippincott, Williams & Wilkins, 1996. Print.

24. Lieberman, Joe. *The Gift of Rest: Rediscovery the Beauty of the Sabbath*. New York: Howard Books, 2011. Print.

25. Manning, Brennan. *Abba's Child: The Cry of the Heart for Intimate Belonging*. Colorado Springs: NavPress, 2002. Print.

26. Pitt-Brooke, Judith and Heather Reid. *Rehabilitation of Movement: Theoretical Basis of Clinical Practice*. Philadelphia: WB Saunders Co., 1998. Print.

27. Porter, Lauren Lindsey. "Attachment theory in everyday life." Mothering Magazine May-Jun. 2009: 44-46. Print.

28. Roth, Nancy. *An Invitation to Christian Yoga*. Cambridge: Cowley Publications, 2001. Print.

29. Rubin, Jordan. *Patient Heal Thyself: a remarkable health program combining ancient wisdom with groundbreaking clinical research*. Topanga: Freedom Press, 2003. Print.

30. --- and Joseph Brasco. *Restoring Your Digestive Health*. New York: Twin Streams, 2003. Print

31. Ryken, Phillip Graham. *When You Pray*. Wheaton Crossway Books, 2000. 142. Print.

32. Seward, Brian Luke. *Managing Stress: Principles and Strategies for Health and Well-Being*. Burlington:Jones and Barlett Learning, LLC, 2012. Print.

33. Gates, Donna and Linda Schatz. *The Body Ecology Diet: Recovering Your Health*. Atlanta: B.E.D Publications, 2011. Print.

34. Scott-Moncrieff, Christina. *DETOX: Cleanse and Recharge your Mind, Body and Soul*. London: Collins & Brown Limited, 2001. Print.

35. Seaman, David R. *Clinical Nutrition for pain, inflammation and tissue healing*. Henderson: NutrAnalysis Inc., 1998. Print.

36. Sears, William and Martha Sears. *The Baby Book Everything You Need to Know About Your Baby From Birth to Age Two*. 1992 New York: Little Brown & Company, 2003. Print.

37. Silk, Danny. *Loving Your Kids on Purpose: Making a Heart-to-Heart Connection*. Shippensburg: Destiny Image Publishers, 2008. Print.

38. Selye, Hans. *The Stress of Life*. McGraw-Hill Publishers. New York, NY. 1985. Print.

39. Tilgner, Linda. *Tips for the Lazy Gardener*. Pownal: Storey Communications, 1998. Print.

40. Zavasta, Tonya. "Nature Always Right, Cooks Never: Why Eat Raw?" Beautiful on Raw. np. nd. Web. Jan 2012.

appendix A

raw food recipe & grocery list

Spring Snacks

1. **Dry Nuts:** Almonds, Cashews or Pecans. Eat plentiful and hardy amounts of nuts throughout the day. This will be filling and good for you.
2. **Bananas:** Eat 2-3 bananas per day
3. **Sliced Cucumber:** Peel and slice cucumber into a bowl. Add salt and pepper to taste.

Spring Recipes: Day 1, 4, 7, 10, 13, 16, 19

Cherry Pineapple Celery Juice

Breakfast

Ingredients:

½-1 whole pineapple

1-5 ribs celery

As many fresh or thawed frozen cherries as you like.

Directions:

Juicer: Add cherries to juicer, then celery, then pineapple. *Blender:* First add cherries to juicer, then poor cherry juice into the blender. You can also buy cherry juice or may substitute Pomegranate Juice. Add cored, chopped pineapple and chopped celery. Blend and enjoy.

Foccacia and Arugula Pea Salad

Lunch

Foccacia Ingredients:

2 cups ground flax seeds

1 cup almonds (soaked 8 hours)

1 cup apple

1 large tomato

2 T olive oil

2 T chopped fresh basil

Salt to taste

Salad Ingredients:

4-10 ounces arugula

Sugar snap or snow peas

Salt to taste

1 tsp balsamic vinegar

Directions:

Grind almonds in a blender and mix with ground flax seed. Set aside. Blend tomato, oil and apple in blender until "creamy." Combine all ingredients into a bowl and mix very well. Form into 2 loaves and dehydrate at 115 degrees for about 5-7 hours or until desired consistency. If you don't have a dehydrator, put in your oven at the lowest setting and leave the door open a bit. Stick your hand in every so often to know it's not too hot. Slice and serve with the following arugula salad.

Salad Directions:

Toss all ingredients and serve on plate. Add foccacia to side to fill out the meal.

SPRING

Tabouli

Dinner

Ingredients:

1-2 bunches parsley

2-3 bunches cilantro

1-2 bunches green onion

½-1 cup almonds
(ground up in blender)

1-2 tomatoes

1 avocado

½ cup *(or more)* of lemon juice

Salt to taste

Directions:

Chop parsley, cilantro, and onion finely and place in a bowl. Chop tomatoes and mix into greens with almonds. Once everything is mixed add lemon juice and salt and mix thoroughly. Chop and add avocado last and mix in lightly so as to avoid crushing the avocado. This is better if it sits for a day. All the amounts can vary to your taste. With the lemon juice and greens this is extraordinarily detoxifying and alkalinizing.

Spring Recipes: Day 2, 5, 8, 11, 14, 17, 20

Blueberries and Honey

Breakfast

Ingredients:

Blueberries

Honey

Directions:

Place as many frozen blueberries as you would like in a bowl and drizzle with honey. It is a great quick snack as well or use as an ice cream replacement.

Banana Raspberry Celery Smoothie

Lunch

Ingredients:

2-8 bananas

½-1 ½ cups raspberries

1-2 ribs celery

Directions:

Blend the amount you want and enjoy. The Celery will add a saltyness that will bring out sweetness and raspberry flavor.

SPRING

Asparagus Salad

Dinner

Ingredients:

1 lb asparagus w/ends broken off

1 head of shredded lettuce

5 ribs of celery

1 beet

¼ cup flax or olive oil

2 T lemon juice

2 T fresh parsley

2 tsp nama shoyu or soy sauce

1 tsp paprika

½ tsp dry mustard

¼ tsp cayenne

Directions:

Chop asparagus into bite size pieces. Grate beets and mince celery. Mix all veggies in a bowl. Combine all other ingredients and lightly mix together in a bowl to dress the salad.

Spring Recipes: Day 3, 6, 9, 12, 15, 18, 21

Pomegranate or Cherry Cereal

Breakfast

Ingredients:

1-4 cups pomegranate seeds or cherries *(cherries can be fresh or frozen)*

1-3 bananas

Directions:

Place desired amount of pomegranate seeds or cherries into a bowl. Set aside. Blend banana with a very small amount of water or nut milk into a thick creamy texture. Pour over fruit in bowl like milk and enjoy.

SPRING

Spring Garden Salad with Sunshine Dressing

Lunch

Ingredients:

8-32 ounces fresh salad greens or mesclun mix

Sprigs of fresh dill and cilantro

2-6 radishes

½ - 2 bunches green onion

Sugar snap peas

Beet, leaves and root (optional)

Dandelion greens (optional)

½ cup flax oil

¼ cup lemon juice

½ -1 cup finely chopped/grated apple

Dollop of water

1-2 dates

2/3 cup fresh cilantro or ¼ cup fresh basil

1 clove garlic

salt to taste

Directions:

Chop or tear greens into a bowl. Chop the rest of veggies and toss in. Blend oil, juice, water, herb, garlic and salt into a creamy dressing and pour as much as you'd like over the top. Serve immediately. Add nuts or seeds to salad if you want it heavier.

Celery Soup

Dinner

Ingredients:

1 bunch celery, or more

¼- ½ cup miso

¼ - ½ cup lemon juice

¼- ½ oil

Salt to taste

Optional avocado

Directions:

Blend everything together except avocado. Adjust flavors as you need. Chop and add avocado at end if desired.

SUMMER

Summer Snacks

1. **A simple vegetable like a cucumber, okra, or tomato.** Slice or eat whole.
2. **A piece of your favorite fruit.** Eat as much as you like.

Summer Recipes: Day 1, 4, 7, 10, 13, 16, 19

Watermelon

Breakfast

Ingredients:

Watermelon

Directions:

Juice it, blend it, or eat it whole. Watermelon is the perfect summer food.

Grapes and Avocado Tomato Basil Salad

Lunch

Ingredients:

As many grapes as desired; eat some while making the salad

1-3 tomatoes

1 avocado

½ to 1 ½ cup broccoli

½ - 1 ½ cup cauliflower

Lemon juice

Olive oil

Salt to taste

¼ - ½ cup fresh basil, chopped

Directions:

Take first four ingredients and chop into bite sized pieces and toss together. Use equal parts lemon and oil, whisk together adding salt to taste and the chopped basil. This can be served alone or on a bed of lettuce.

SUMMER

Squash soup

Dinner

Ingredients:

2-5 summer squash

1-2 cups or 1 pint of sprouts

½ - 1 cup tomato, carrot, celery juice *(or other blending liquid)*

1 tablespoon flax or olive oil

3-16 green onions

Directions:

Blend all ingredients, except onions, together until smooth and creamy. Chop green onion and add to top. Avocado can be chopped and added at the end as an option.

Summer Recipes: Day 2, 5, 8, 11, 14, 17, 20

Cantaloupe Blend

Breakfast

Ingredients:

½ - 1 ½ cup favorite cantaloupe

Directions:

De-seed melon and blend as much as you desire. Drink immediately and enjoy. Or just slice and eat.

Apricots or Nectarines or Plums or Grapes

Lunch

Directions:

Eat as many as you like.

Mango, Cucumber, Tomato, Avocado Salad

Dinner

Ingredients:

2-4 mangoes

1-2 average cucumbers

1-2 average tomatoes

1 avocado

Directions:

Skin and seed all ingredients.
Chop to a desirable size and mix together.

SUMMER

Summer Recipes: Day 3, 6, 9, 12, 15, 18, 21

Apricot, Pineapple Banana Smoothie

Breakfast

Ingredients:

Apricots

Pineapple, cored and peeled

Banana

Directions:

Blend together and enjoy. Begin with equal parts of all three fruits, but in time you can gradually increase the apricots and pineapple or just decrease the banana. The balance of all three is key; if out of balance it can taste a little funny, but when it's just right, it is out of this world.

Romaine Avocado Tacos

Lunch

Ingredients:

1 head of romaine or more

1-2 avocados

1-2 bell peppers or cucumbers or both

salt to taste

Directions:

Cut avocados, peppers and cucumbers into long narrow strips, but not too skinny. Peel off each leaf of romaine lettuce and add a strip of avocado and pepper or cucumber. Sprinkle salt and eat like taco. This also can be done with tomatoes, zucchini, etc.

Raw Corn on the Cob with Lemon and Coconut Oil

Dinner

Ingredients:

1-5 cobs of raw corn

Lemon juice

Salt and pepper

Coconut oil

Directions:

This one should be fairly self explanatory. Add all toppings to the raw corn...a new rendition to an old favorite. Add lemon pepper and garlic powder for extra zest.

FALL

Fall Snacks

1. **Apple Punch:** Thinly slice one orange and one lemon, place in pitcher with 1 tsp of vanilla or more to taste, a cinnamon stick broken open. Juice or blend 8-10 apples or pears and add to the pitcher. Leave in sun or warm place and let flavors blend for at least 4 hours.
2. **Ants on a log:** old fashion and good. Add all-natural peanut butter (or almond butter) to celery. Place raisins, cranberries or craisins on top of the peanut or almond butter. Smile and enjoy!

Fall Recipes: Day 1, 4, 7, 10, 13, 16, 19

Apple, Beet, Ginger, Lemon Juice

Breakfast

Ingredients:

3 apples

1 'apple sized' beet

1 inch of ginger
(unless you're not a fan, then use less)

½ lemon

Directions:

Sweet, delicious, and beautiful! Juice ingredients and drink immediately. This one blended is extremely pulpy, but if you have no juicer, blend and then pour into a bowl lined with a cloth. Pick up the corner of the cloth to make a "bag" and squeeze out all the juice; it will be a lot. The pulp can be thrown away, composted, added to salads or freeze to bake with at another time.

FALL

Gazpacho

Lunch

Ingredients:

5 tomatoes

2 cucumbers

2 garlic cloves

¼ cup parsley

1 green bell pepper

2 green onions

Juice of two limes

Salt to taste

1/3 cup olive oil

Optional: ¼ tsp cayenne

Optional: 1 avocado

Directions:

There are so many variations on this soup, make it any way you want. Here's the basics. Blend all ingredients together and serve. If using avocado, blend it in at very end as it can be over blended and turns brown.

Tabouli

Dinner

Ingredients:

1-2 bunches parsley

2-3 bunches cilantro

1-2 bunches green onion

½-1 cup almonds, ground up in blender

1-2 tomatoes

1 avocado

½ cup (or more) of lemon juice

Salt to taste

Directions:

This is one of my favorite meals. Chop parsley, cilantro, and onion finely and place in a bowl. Chop tomatoes and mix into greens with almonds. Once everything is mixed add lemon juice and salt and mix thoroughly. Chop and add avocado last so as to avoid crushing avocado. All the amounts can vary to your taste. With the lemon juice and greens, this is an extraordinarily detoxifying and alkalinizing dish!

FALL

Fall Recipes: Day 2, 5, 8, 11, 14, 17, 20

Pears or Asian Pears

Breakfast

Directions:

Pears truly are a delicacy. Getting them and waiting for them to ripen is sometimes an art, and one you have to master. It is worth it. This is the season, don't miss them.

Rosemary Broccoli Salad

Lunch

Ingredients:

3 cups broccoli

½ cups olives or walnuts or 1 avocado

2 garlic cloves

3 T olive oil

2 ½ T lemon juice or apple cider vinegar

2-3 T fresh rosemary

Salt and pepper to taste

Directions:

Chop broccoli and olives, mix into bowl. Mince garlic and rosemary and add. Mix in the rest of the ingredients and stir thoroughly. Let sit for a couple of hours or warm in a sunny window. Serve when hungry.

Corn Salad

Dinner

Ingredients:

2-4 ears of corn with corn removed

½ - 1 red bell pepper

¼ - ½ red onion

2 T lime juice

Oil to taste

2 cloves garlic

Salt to taste

Directions:

Chop pepper and onion and place in bowl with corn. Mince garlic and add to bowl. Add rest of ingredients, mix thoroughly and enjoy. As an option cilantro can also be added to this dish and is delightful.

FALL

Fall Recipes: Day 3, 6, 9, 12, 15, 18, 21

Mulled Apple Sauce

Breakfast

Ingredients:

2-8 apples

Cinnamon

Clove

Nutmeg

Directions:

Blend the apples into a sauce and add a pinch of all spices, enjoy.

Kale Salad

Lunch

Ingredients:

1-2 bunches kale

1-2 tomatoes

1-4 cloves garlic

1 colored bell pepper

1-2 avocados

½-1 onion

2 T apple cider vinegar

2 T soy sauce

2 T olive oil

Directions:

Cut kale into bite sized pieces and place in a sealable container. Chop garlic and onion, add it to container. Add oil, vinegar and soy sauce to container and seal. Shake and let sit for 4 hours. Shake occasionally. When ready add chopped pepper, tomato, and avocado. This dish is perfect for the season.

Peaches

Dinner

Directions:

Eat as many as you like and be amazed at the lightness and fullness of simple peaches.

WINTER

Winter Snacks

1. **Date Pecan Nuggets:** One date to one pecan - stuff and eat like chocolate.
2. **Glass of Nut Milk or Orange Juice:** Fruit juice satiates and nut milk fills a void. Nut milk is made by soaking 1 cup of nuts or seeds for eight hours. Rinse nuts and then blend with 2 quarts of water (in two batches). Line a bowl with a cloth and pour in mixture. Pull up corners of cloth into a "bag" and strain out the milk (do twice). The pulp can be put in other recipes or thrown out.
3. **Sliced Avocado with Balsamic Vinegar:** Half an avocado, de-seed and slice within the skin. Add salt and balsamic vinegar, spoon out and enjoy.

Winter Recipes: Day 1, 4, 7, 10, 13, 16, 19

Orange Juice

Breakfast

Directions:

Oranges can be juiced, pressed or even blended. Drink as much as desired.

Crunchy Walnut Cabbage

Lunch

Ingredients:

½-1 cup parsley

½ - 1 cup walnuts

½ head red cabbage

½ head green cabbage

½ -1 red onion

½-1 cup almonds

¼ cup lemon juice

1 T soy sauce

1 T flax, walnut or olive oil

½ inch of ginger

2 tsp cumin

1 slice of onion

1-2 cloves garlic

Directions:

Chop and mix parsley, walnuts, cabbage and onion and place in bowl. Combine rest of ingredients in a blender and liquefy. Pour over salad, mix and let stand for 30 minutes.

WINTER

Cauliflower Paella

Dinner

Ingredients:

½ -1 head of Cauliflower

5-25 olives

½ -1 colored bell pepper

Oil, salt, lemon juice

Directions:

Take a head of Cauliflower and either grate it or food process it and place in a bowl. Pit the olives and mince, add to cauliflower and let sit for a few hours. Chop bell pepper and add just before eating. Add oil, salt or lemon juice to taste and enjoy. Cauliflower is a high protein vegetable and abundant in the winter.

Winter Recipes: Day 2, 5, 8, 11, 14, 17, 20

Banana Spinach Smoothie

Breakfast

Ingredients:

2-8 bananas

1 handful or more of spinach

water or raw nut milk

Directions:

Peel desired amount of bananas (bananas can be frozen as well) and place in blender. Add desired amount of spinach. Spinach has a light flavor and is not too detectable. This is a great way to eat a lot of greens. Add raw milk, juice (freshly squeezed) or water and blend. More liquid will of course make it thinner and less will make it thicker. "Chew" each bite and drink slowly.

Citrus of Your Choosing

Lunch

Directions:

Satsuma, Tangelo, Mandarin, Ugli, Orange, Cuties, etc...Eat as much as you like.

WINTER

Yam Apple Soup

Dinner

Ingredients:

2 small yams or 4 big carrots

1 apple

2 cup or 1 pint of sprouts

1 cup apple juice

1 cup celery juice

1 bunch green onion

1 T olive oil

Soy sauce to taste

Optional: cardamom or nutmeg
to taste

Directions:

Blend yams and liquid in blender first to get it broken down. Add all the rest of the ingredients to the blender and blend until smooth. Enjoy!

Winter Recipes: Day 3, 6, 9, 12, 15, 18, 21

Grapefruit Juice

Breakfast

Ingredients:

3-10 grapefruits

Directions:

Just like the orange, juice or blend and drink till your heart's content. Grapefruit has many redeeming qualities. Look for sweet or ruby red and buy extra. Grapefruit is low in calories so eat lots.

WINTER

Apple Pie with Pecan Date Crust

Lunch

Ingredients:

1 handful of pecans

1 handful of medjool dates or deglet dates soaked in water 4 hours

1-3 apples

1-2 bananas

Vanilla and/or cinnamon

Directions:

This is a winter favorite, heavy and satisfying. Using a food processor or just mashing with your hands, mash together equal parts of pecans and dates and then press into a pie pan or a personal sized shallow bowl or small plate. Thinly slice the apples and place in pie crust. Thickly blend bananas and vanilla into a thick creamy texture and pour over the apples into the crust and enjoy some pie.

Winter Chopped Salad

Dinner

Ingredients:

2 carrots

½ diakon radish or 1 full watermelon radish

½ cup peas (fresh if you can, any variety, frozen if you need)

½ cup broccoli

2 ribs celery

½ cup cashews, sunflowers, or walnuts

Apple cider vinegar

Salt to taste

Curry or cayenne powder (if desired)

1 plate full of baby bok choy or shredded napa cabbage

Directions:

Chop all vegetables into pea sized pieces. Mix together. Blend the oil, salt, your choice of nut or seed, cayenne or curry and vinegar in blender. Add this as dressing to the chopped vegetables and mix thoroughly. Add a big pile to the plate of greens and be satisfied.

Grocery Checklist for Raw Food Spring Menu

- ❏ Pineapple
- ❏ Apple
- ❏ Lemon
- ❏ Blueberry
- ❏ Banana
- ❏ Raspberry
- ❏ Pomegranate
- ❏ Cherries
- ❏ Dates
- ❏ Celery
- ❏ Tomato
- ❏ Basil
- ❏ Arugula

- ❏ Sugar snap
- ❏ Snow pea
- ❏ Parsley
- ❏ Cilantro
- ❏ Green onion
- ❏ Avocado
- ❏ Asparagus
- ❏ Beet
- ❏ Lettuce
- ❏ Salad greens
- ❏ Dill
- ❏ Radish
- ❏ Dandelion

- ❏ Garlic
- ❏ Flax
- ❏ Almond
- ❏ Olive & flax oil
- ❏ Balsamic Vinegar
- ❏ Honey
- ❏ Nama Shoyu
- ❏ Paprika
- ❏ Dry mustard
- ❏ Cayenne
- ❏ Miso

Grocery Checklist for Raw Food Summer Menu

- ❏ Watermelon
- ❏ Grapes
- ❏ Cantaloupe
- ❏ Apricot
- ❏ Nectarine
- ❏ Plum
- ❏ Mango
- ❏ Pineapple

- ❏ Banana
- ❏ Lemon
- ❏ Avocado
- ❏ Tomato
- ❏ Basil
- ❏ Summer squash
- ❏ Sprouts
- ❏ Carrot

- ❏ Celery
- ❏ Green onion
- ❏ Cucumber
- ❏ Romaine
- ❏ Dulse
- ❏ Corn on cob
- ❏ Olive & flax oil
- ❏ Coconut oil

Grocery Checklist for Raw Food Fall Menu

- ❏ Apple
- ❏ Lemon
- ❏ Lime
- ❏ Pear
- ❏ Asian pear
- ❏ Peaches
- ❏ Beet
- ❏ Ginger
- ❏ Tomato
- ❏ Cucumber
- ❏ Garlic
- ❏ Parsley

- ❏ Green bell pepper
- ❏ Red bell pepper
- ❏ Onion
- ❏ Avocado
- ❏ Broccoli
- ❏ Corn
- ❏ Red onion
- ❏ Kale
- ❏ Cilantro
- ❏ Green onion
- ❏ Walnut

- ❏ Almonds
- ❏ Olive oil
- ❏ Cayenne
- ❏ Apple cider vinegar
- ❏ Rosemary
- ❏ Cinnamon
- ❏ Clove
- ❏ Nutmeg
- ❏ Nama shoyu

Grocery Checklist for Raw Food Winter Menu

- ❏ Orange
- ❏ Lemon
- ❏ Banana
- ❏ Tangelo
- ❏ Mandarin
- ❏ Satsuma
- ❏ Tangerine
- ❏ Apple
- ❏ Grapefruit
- ❏ Date
- ❏ Parsley
- ❏ Red cabbage
- ❏ Green onion
- ❏ Onion
- ❏ Ginger

- ❏ Garlic
- ❏ Cauliflower
- ❏ Olives
- ❏ Red pepper
- ❏ Spinach
- ❏ Yam
- ❏ Carrot
- ❏ Sprouts
- ❏ Celery
- ❏ Daikon radish
- ❏ Watermelon radish
- ❏ Broccoli
- ❏ Avocado
- ❏ Walnuts

- ❏ Almonds
- ❏ Pecans
- ❏ Cashew
- ❏ Sunflower
- ❏ Nama shoyu
- ❏ Flax & olive oil
- ❏ Cumin
- ❏ Cardamom
- ❏ Nutmeg
- ❏ Vanilla
- ❏ Cinnamon
- ❏ Apple cider vinegar
- ❏ Curry & cayenne

appendix B

non-raw food
recipe & grocery list

Spring Snacks

1. **Fresh Grapes, Strawberries or Cherries**
2. **Dry Nuts:** Almonds, Cashews or Pecans
3. **Fruit Nut Mix:** add your choice of dried nuts and dried fruit together
4. **Apples and Almond Butter**

Spring Recipes: Day 1, 4, 7, 10, 13, 16, 19

Cherry Pineapple Celery Juice

Breakfast

Ingredients:

½-1 whole pineapple

1-5 ribs celery

As many fresh or thawed frozen cherries as you like.

Directions:

Juicer: Add cherries to juicer, then celery, then pineapple. *Blender:* First add cherries to juicer, then poor cherry juice into the blender. You can also buy cherry juice or may substitute Pomegranate Juice. Add cored, chopped pineapple and chopped celery. Blend and enjoy.

Carrot Ginger Apple Soup

Lunch

Ingredients:

1 tsp olive oil or grape seed oil

4 cups chopped carrots

1 average sized onion chopped

2 cloves garlic chopped

1 inch ginger minced

2-3 tart apples cored and chopped

½ cup each: carrot, celery, parsley, fennel juice

½ cup oatmeal, or cooked oat

1 tsp nutmeg

1 tsp thyme

salt and pepper to taste

Directions:

In a crock pot or stock pot cook carrots, onion, garlic, ginger and apples with oil until softened. Add the rest of the ingredients and let simmer for 20 minutes. Transfer portions into a blender and blend until creamy. You may need to add water to get the consistency desired. Combine all the blended portions together and enjoy.

S P R I N G

Honey Baked Squash with a Side Salad

Dinner

Ingredients:

1-2 Acorn squash(s)

1/8 cup olive or grape seed oil

approx. ¼ cup honey

½ teaspoon cinnamon

salt to taste

Directions:

Half the acorn squash and remove seeds; leave skin on and place on a baking sheet with ½ to 1 inch water. Take a fork and stab squash all over to fill it with holes. Bake in oven for about 30 minutes or until squash begins to soften. Take out and drizzle with oil and honey, more or less as needed, and add salt and cinnamon to taste. Place back in oven and cook until the squash is soft and can be scooped with a spoon. While cooking make a side salad of fresh salad mix, a tomato, grated carrot and cucumber. Dress with lemon juice, salt, honey and oil.

Spring Recipes: Day 2, 5, 8, 11, 14, 17, 20

Romaine Rolls

Breakfast

Ingredients:

Banana

Romaine leaf

Directions:

Peel a banana completely and place in a washed romaine lettuce leaf and roll it up. Use two lettuce leaves for a double layer.

S P R I N G

Spring Garden Salad with Sunshine Dressing

Lunch

Ingredients:

8 oz-32oz fresh salad greens or
Mesclun mix

Sprigs of fresh dill and cilantro

2-6 radishes

½ - 2 bunches of green onion

½ -1 finely chopped/grated apple

Sugar snap peas
(as many as you like)

Beet, leaves and root *(optional)*

Dandelion greens *(optional)*

½ cup flax oil

¼ cup lemon juice

Dollop of water

1-2 dates

2/3 cup of fresh cilantro or
¼ cup fresh basil

1 clove garlic

salt to taste

Directions:

Chop or tear greens into a bowl. Chop the rest of veggies and toss in. Blend oil, juice, water, herb, garlic and salt into a creamy dressing and pour as much as you'd like over the top. Serve immediately. Add nuts, seeds or beans to salad if you want it heavier.

Asian Salad

Dinner

Ingredients:

¼ - ½ head of finely sliced
napa cabbage

½ cup fresh peas

½-1 cup chopped mushrooms

1 chopped red bell pepper

1 cup mung bean sprouts

Nama shoyu or Soy sauce

Rice vinegar

Olive oil

Directions:

Mix together all vegetables in a bowl. Add 2 – 4 tablespoons of the oil, vinegar, and shoyu and thoroughly mix in. Let marinate for 30 minutes or longer. Eat and enjoy.

SPRING

Spring Recipes: Day 3, 6, 9, 12, 15, 18, 21

Mango Cereal with Sunflowers

Breakfast

Ingredients:

1-3 mangos

Nut milk (optional)

Handful of sunflower seeds

Directions:

Cut mango from top to bottom along the widest portion of the mango. Curve the knife around the seed to one side and make a second cut around the other side. Remove seed and any excess fruit, placing fruit in bowl. Take the "cheeks" and cut down to skin but not through skin in a checkered pattern. Using a spoon, scoop out mango and place in a bowl, add nut milk (if desired) and sunflower kernels. Eat and be content!

Greens and Protein

Lunch

Ingredients:

1 bunch of Kale

1 bunch Collards

Bok choy (much as you like)

Your choice of fish or meat.

Directions:

Wash and chop kale, collards and bok choi. Place in a frying pan with a little water (not covered). Steam greens in pan adding oil and salt at the end to warm it into the greens. Transfer onto a big plate. Bake or grill your choice of fish or meat and add to the top of the greens. Add more oil and salt if you'd like or a squeeze of lemon juice. Simple and outrageous!

SPRING

Exotic Mushroom and Millet Soup

Dinner

Ingredients:

1 cup millet

1 tsp olive or grape seed oil

1 onion chopped

4 chopped celery ribs

2 garlic cloves chopped

2 cups sliced shiitake mushroom

2 cups sliced oyster mushrooms

3 cups portabella mushrooms

2 tsp thyme

1 bay leaf

7 cups vegetable stock, bought or homemade

salt and pepper to taste

Directions:

Toast millet in large pan until slightly darker and set aside, 3-5 minutes. In stock pot cook onion, celery, garlic, and half of each mushroom with oil. Cook until onion softens and then add rest of mushrooms and cook a couple more minutes. Add millets and herbs and stir into stock until millet has softened, 20 minutes. Transfer portions to blender and blend until creamy. Add salt and pepper to taste. (Millet is the only non-acid forming grain which makes it superior to others.)

SUMMER

Summer Snacks

1. **A simple vegetable like a cucumber, okra, or tomato**
2. **A piece of your favorite fruit**
3. **Honey drizzled blueberries:** Place fresh (or frozen) blueberries in a bowl. Drizzle honey (preferably local) on top.
4. **Hard-boiled egg**

Summer Recipes: Day 1, 4, 7, 10, 13, 16, 19

Watermelon

(Breakfast)

Directions:

Eat as much as you like. Blend if desired.

Lamb and Avocado Tomato Basil Salad

(Lunch)

Ingredients:

1-3 tomatoes

1 avocado

½ to 1 ½ cups broccoli

½ - 1 ½ cups cauliflower

Lemon juice

Olive oil

Salt

¼ - ½ cups fresh basil, chopped

Appropriate sized piece of lamb

Directions:

Chop tomatoes, avocado, broccoli and cauliflower into bite sized pieces and toss together. Use equal parts lemon and oil, whisk together adding salt to taste and the chopped basil. This can be served alone or on a bed of lettuce. Grill or bake lamb until desired, season with salt and pepper. Either add it to the side of the salad or slice it up adding it right into the salad.

SUMMER

Tomato and Okra Stew

Dinner

Ingredients:

1 onion chopped

1 red bell pepper chopped small

3 chopped tomatoes

10 oz okra, halfed or quartered

1 small handful minced parsley

salt and pepper to taste

Directions:

Sauté onion and red bell pepper in oil until softened. Add tomatoes and cook down into a sauce. Add okra, salt and pepper and bring "stew" to a boil, reduce to medium heat for 10-15 minutes or until soft. When ready, add parsley and serve!

Summer Recipes: Day 2, 5, 8, 11, 14, 17, 20

Cantaloupe Cubed

Breakfast

Directions:

Find the most fragrant cantaloupe, cut it in half and remove seeds. Cut off skin and dice into cubes.

Corn and Kale Salad

Lunch

Ingredients:

2 quarts water

4 ears of sweet corn (cut off cob)

1 bunch kale, chopped

2 teaspoons salt, or to taste

1 red bell pepper, diced

1 green bell pepper, diced

1 small onion, diced

1 clove garlic, diced

¾ cup olive oil or grape seed oil

2 tablespoons lemon juice

1 ½ teaspoon Cajun seasoning

Directions:

In wide pan cook corn and kale in water until corn is soft and kale is bright green. Add some salt if desired. Transfer corn and kale to larger salad bowl and mix in rest of ingredients until combined well.

SUMMER

Mango, Cucumber, Tomato, Avocado Salad & Honey Mustard Kabobs

Dinner

Ingredients:

2-4 mangos

1-2 average cucumbers

1-2 average tomatoes

1 avocado

1 yellow bell pepper

1 medium zucchini

cherry tomatoes

White mushrooms

1 teaspoon mustard powder

1 tablespoon honey

1 tablespoon olive oil

Salt and pepper to taste

Directions:

Skin mangos, cucumbers, tomatoes and avocado (de-seed if desired). Chop to a desirable/bitable size and mix together. Set aside, this is your salad. Cut yellow bell pepper and zucchini into a size that would fit on a skewer. Place these veggies and cherry tomatoes and white mushrooms on skewers alternating color and shape in an appealing pattern. Place skewers on a baking sheet. Whisk honey, olive oil and salt and pepper to taste and brush onto skewers. Broil in oven for 8 minutes, turning once or twice as needed. This can also be eaten raw if you'd like!

Summer Recipes: Day 3, 6, 9, 12, 15, 18, 21

Apricot, Pineapple, Banana Smoothie

Breakfast

Ingredients:

Apricots

Pineapple, cored and peeled

Banana

Directions:

Blend together and enjoy. Begin with equal parts of all three fruits, but in time you can gradually increase the apricots and pineapple or just decrease the banana. The balance of all three is key; if out of balance it can taste a little funny, but when it's just right, it is out of this world.

SUMMER

Black Bean Stir Fry on a Bed of Romaine

Lunch

Ingredients:

½ or 1 can of black beans

2 carrots, slivered

1 bunch green onion, slivered

2 cups mushrooms, sliced

3 garlic cloves, crushed

2 bell peppers of your choice, chopped

1 cup bean sprouts

½ to 1 head romaine lettuce, shredded

Olive oil

Directions:

Sauté garlic and green onion in a frying pan with a bit of oil for 30 seconds. Add other veggies (except bean sprouts) and cook on high until softening. Add bean sprouts and mix thoroughly for 3-4 minutes. Serve on a heap of shredded lettuce.

Corn on the Cob with Lemon and Coconut Oil with Steamed Broccoli and Bell Peppers

Dinner

Ingredients:

1-5 cobs of raw or cooked corn

lemon juice

salt

pepper

coconut oil

½ bunch broccoli

1 bell pepper

Directions:

This one should be fairly self explanatory. Add all toppings to the corn for new rendition to an old favorite. Add lemon pepper and garlic powder for extra zest. Then cut broccoli and bell pepper to desired size, steam and add salt and oil when done. This completes the meal!

FALL

Fall Snacks

1. **Apples with almond butter.**
2. **Ants on a log:** old fashion and good. Add all-natural peanut butter (or almond butter) to celery. Place raisins, cranberries or craisins on top of the peanut or almond butter. Smile and enjoy!
3. **Bananas with honey.** Sprinkle local honey on a banana and enjoy sweet freshness.
4. **Thinly sliced carrots.**

Fall Recipes: Day 1, 4, 7, 10, 13, 16, 19

Apple, Beet, Ginger, Lemon Juice

Breakfast

Ingredients:

3 apples

1 'apple sized' beet

1 inch of ginger
(unless you're not a fan, then use less)

½ lemon

Directions:

Juice and drink immediately; sweet, delicious, and beautiful. This one blended is extremely pulpy, but if you have no juicer, blend and then pour into a bowl lined with a cloth. Pick up the corner of the cloth to make a "bag" and squeeze out all the juice, it will be a lot. The pulp can be thrown, composted, added to salads, used as dog food or frozen and saved to bake with at another time.

FALL

Hummus and Zucchini

Lunch

Ingredients:

3 medium sized zucchinis

Olive Oil

Hummus

Directions:

This can be a snack or a meal depending on the amount you eat. Cut zucchinis into sticks. The zucchini can be braised in a pan with a bit of oil as well. Do eat at least half the zucchini raw. Use a premade hummus that has all ingredients that you can pronounce as this is easier than making it yourself. If you want to make your own from scratch you can find recipes readily available. Dip zucchini sticks in hummus and eat, repeat.

Chick Pea Stew

Dinner

Ingredients:

2 T olive or grape seed oil

1 small onion chopped

2 large carrots halved and thinly sliced into rounds

½ tsp ground cumin

1 tsp ground coriander

½ pound zucchini, sliced

3 ears of corn on cob, with corn cut off

1 can of chick peas, drained

1 T agar agar
(optionally used to thicken)

2 T tomato paste or 1 fresh tomato

1 cup veggie stock

salt and pepper to taste

Directions:

Toss carrots and onion in pan with oil and cook for 4 minutes. Add cumin, coriander and agar agar and stir well for 1 minute. Add all other ingredients stirring well for about 10 minutes. Add salt and pepper to taste and it is ready.

FALL

Fall Recipes: Day 2, 5, 8, 11, 14, 17, 20

Pears or Asian Pears

Breakfast

Directions:

Just as simple as it sounds, eat many pears as you want as they are very hydrating yet low in calories. Also prepare ahead to have enough ripe ones to eat. The Asian variety will be better for ripeness as they should be eaten crunchy.

White Fish with Steamed Rosemary Broccoli Salad

Lunch

Ingredients:

3 cups broccoli

½ cup olives or walnuts
or 1 avocado

2 garlic cloves

3 tablespoons oil

2 ½ tablespoons lemon juice or
apple cider vinegar

2-3 tablespoons fresh rosemary

salt and pepper to taste

Optional: Italian seasoning

1 White fish fillet,
cooked to your liking

Directions:

Chop broccoli and olives and mix in bowl. Mince garlic and rosemary and add to bowl. Mix in rest of ingredients and stir thoroughly. Let sit for a couple of hours or warm in a sunny window. This can also be prepared warm with steamed broccoli if you prefer. Add white fish of your choice to the top of the salad or slice it into the salad!

FALL

Kitchari

Dinner

Ingredients:

1 cup barley

½ cup whole mung beans or lentils

1 tsp cumin

1 tsp masala seasoning

1 T olive oil or grape seed oil

2 cloves chopped garlic

1 carrot chopped

½ cup chopped daikon radish or winter radish

2 ribs celery chopped

3 heads baby bok choy chopped

1 zucchini chopped

½ -1 chopped pumpkin or winter squash *(optional)*

Salt and pepper to taste

Directions:

Bring barley and mung beans (or lentils) and 3 ½ cups of water to boil. Then add everything else. Cook on low for 45-60 minutes or until soft. You may need to add more water and oil depending on heat level. Add salt and pepper to taste.

Fall Recipes: Day 3, 6, 9, 12, 15, 18, 21

Poached Eggs on Lettuce

Breakfast

Ingredients:

1-3 eggs

½ pound or more lettuce

Olive or grape seed oil

Directions:

Chop lettuce and fill up a bowl. Poach eggs** and add to the top of the salad. Add salt to taste and as much olive or grape seed oil as you want.

**To poach an egg use an egg poacher or cook in a sauce pan of boiling water and add a splash of vinegar. Gently crack egg into the water and let cook until desired firmness; the vinegar will help to keep egg together. If egg falls apart add more vinegar, if the egg tastes like vinegar, use less. Take out of water with a slotted spoon and add salt to taste.

FALL

Kale Salad

Ingredients:

1-2 bunches kale

1-2 tomatoes

1-4 cloves garlic

1 colored bell pepper

1-2 avocados

½-1 onion

Apple cider vinegar

Soy sauce or nama shoyu

Olive oil

Directions:

Cut kale into bite sized pieces and place in a sealable container. Chop garlic and onion, add it to container. Add equal amounts (2 T) of oil, vinegar and nama shoyu (or soy sauce) to container and seal. Shake and let sit for 4 hours. Shake occasionally. When ready add chopped pepper, tomato, and avocado.

Lentil Stir Fry

Dinner

Ingredients:

½ lb sugar snaps

Olive or grapeseed oil

1 small onion chopped

1 cup mushrooms, sliced

1 can artichoke hearts
(drained and halfed)

1 can lentils or
1 lb fresh cooked lentils

¼ cup shaved almonds

Salt and pepper to taste

Directions:

Stir fry onion in oil until soft and add mushrooms and sugar snaps. Cook for 2-3 minutes and add artichoke hearts and lentils and cook for an additional couple of minutes. Add almonds and season with salt and pepper to taste. This can be eaten alone or atop rice.

WINTER

Winter Snacks

1. **Date Pecan Nuggets:** One date to one pecan - stuff and eat like chocolate.
2. **Glass of Nut Milk or Orange Juice:** Fruit juice satiates and nut milk fills a void. Note: To make nut milk – soak 1 cup of nuts or seeds in water for eight hours. Rinse and then blend with 2 quarts of water (in two batches). Line a bowl with a cloth and pour in mixture. Pull up corners of cloth into a "bag" and strain out the milk (do twice). The pulp can be put in other recipes or thrown out.
3. **Sliced Avocado with Balsamic Vinegar:** Half an avocado, de-seed and slice within the skin. Add salt and balsamic vinegar, spoon out and enjoy.
4. **Carrot Sticks.** Wash, peel and slice as many carrots as you desire. For added flavor, buy hummus and have fun using the carrot sticks as a spoon.

Winter Recipes: Day 1, 4, 7, 10, 13, 16, 19

Orange Juice

Breakfast

Directions:

Oranges can be juiced, pressed or even blended. Drink as much as desired.

Salmon Caesar Salad

Lunch

Ingredients:

2 T Dijon mustard

3 T raw almonds

3 cloves garlic

¼ cup water (more if needed)

½ T Nama Shoyu

2 T lemon juice

1 T olive or grapeseed oil

¼ teaspoon pepper

Directions:

Bake in oven an appropriately sized piece of salmon. Blend ingredients to the left together and adjust taste or add water if needed. Take approximately ½ to 1 head of romaine lettuce and tear into bite sized pieces and arrange on a plate. Serve salmon on romaine and add dressing.

WINTER

Arugula Squash

Dinner

Ingredients:

½ - ¼ lb arugula

½ - ¼ lb mixed greens

1 butternut squash

Salt

Olive or grape seed oil

Lemon juice

Directions:

Arrange greens on a big plate and leave plain. Half and seed the squash and bake in oven with small amount of water at 450 for approximately one hour or until soft. Remove from oven and let cool a bit. Scoop out squash onto the greens and directly add salt, oil, and lemon juice to taste.

Winter Recipes: Day 2, 5, 8, 11, 14, 17, 20

Banana Spinach Smoothie

Breakfast

Ingredients:

2-8 bananas

1 handful or more of spinach

Water, Raw Milk or Nut milk or Juice (must be 100%)

Directions:

Peel desired amount of bananas and place in blender. Add desired amount of spinach. Spinach has a light flavor and is not too detectable. This is a great way to eat a lot of greens. Add desired amount of raw/nut milk, juice or water. You may also add ice if desired. More liquid will of course make it thinner and less will make it thicker.

WINTER

Orange Curry Carrots

Lunch

Ingredients:

1 cup fresh orange juice

1 cup water

4 cups medium thin sliced carrots

½ cup raisins

2 T coconut oil or grape seed oil

2 tsp curry powder

½ tsp turmeric

1/8 tsp ground cardamom *(optional)*

1 T agar agar

1 mashed very ripe banana

Salt and pepper to taste

Directions:

In stock or crock pot bring water and orange juice to a boil, add carrots and simmer until soft. Add raisins and remove from heat. In frying pan add oil, curry, turmeric and cardamom stirring constantly. Add agar agar until it becomes a paste, then remove from heat. Drain liquid from carrots and raisins making sure to save it. Add half that liquid to curry paste and stir slowly to thick sauce (adding more agar agar if desired) then add other half of liquid. Mash in the banana and add carrots and raisins, salt and pepper to taste.

Bubble and Squeak

Dinner

Ingredients:

½ savoy cabbage, cored and chopped

¼ cup olive oil, coconut oil or grape seed oil

1 onion chopped

1/2 pound mashed potatoes

1 T chopped parsley

1 scrambled egg *(optional)*

1 tomato

Directions:

Add onion to large frying pan and cook in oil for 2-3 minutes at high. Reduce heat and add cabbage and cook for about 5 minutes. Add mashed potato and stir well. Cook until it starts to brown. Stir in parsley, salt and pepper to taste. Serve with scrambled egg on side if you want and with a halved fresh tomato.

WINTER

Winter Recipes: Day 3, 6, 9, 12, 15, 18, 21

Grapefruit Juice

Breakfast

Ingredients:

3-10 grapefruits

1-2 eggs *(if desired)*

Apple cider vinegar

Directions:

Just like the orange juice, drink to your heart's content. Grapefruit has many redeeming qualities. Look for sweet or ruby red and buy extra. Grapefruit is low in calories so eat lots. If you decided to add the eggs, scramble or hard boil.

Three Bean Salad

Lunch

Ingredients:

6 oz black beans cooked and drained

6 oz chick peas cooked and drained

6 oz cannellini beans cooked and drained

1 medium beet

½ package of mushrooms

1 bell pepper, your choice

2 tomatoes, chopped

3 ounces of pitted olives diced

2 teaspoons ground mustard

2 teaspoons chopped fresh oregano

Lemon juice

Salt pepper to taste

Directions:

Bake beets in a 450 degree oven for 45 minutes or until soft. Dice into pieces and add to bowl (they can be used hot or cold). Dice mushroom and lightly sauté or use raw if preferred and add to bowl. Add the rest of the ingredients into the bowl and mix well. Adjust seasonings to your taste and you are ready to go.

WINTER

Steamed Winter Whopped Salad with Shrimp

Dinner

Ingredients:

2 carrots

½ diakon radish or 1 full watermelon radish

½ cup peas *(fresh if you can, any variety, frozen if you need)*

½ cup broccoli

2 ribs celery

Appropriate amount of shrimp *(you decide)*

½ cup cashew, sunflower, or walnut

Apple cider vinegar *(or other)*

Salt to taste

Curry powder if desired

1 plate full of baby bok choy, or shredded napa cabbage

Directions:

Chop all vegetables into pea sized pieces. Mix together in frying pan and cook in small amount of oil and water. At same time add shrimp and cook briefly until they turn pink. Place veggies and shrimp on the plate of bok choy or cabbage. Blend the oil, salt, your choice of nut or seed, curry and vinegar in blender. Dress the veggies and mix thoroughly.

Grocery Checklist for Non-Raw Food Spring Menu

- ❑ Pineapple
- ❑ Cherry
- ❑ Apple
- ❑ Banana
- ❑ Lemon
- ❑ Dates
- ❑ Mango
- ❑ Celery
- ❑ Carrot
- ❑ Onion
- ❑ Garlic
- ❑ Ginger
- ❑ Parsley
- ❑ Fennel
- ❑ Romaine and salad greens
- ❑ Dill
- ❑ Cilantro
- ❑ Bok choy
- ❑ Radish
- ❑ Green onion
- ❑ Sugar snap
- ❑ Beet
- ❑ Dandelion
- ❑ Basil
- ❑ Kale
- ❑ Collards
- ❑ Chard
- ❑ Shiitake, Oyster, Portabella mushrooms
- ❑ Veggie stock
- ❑ Olive & grapeseed oil
- ❑ Nutmeg
- ❑ Thyme
- ❑ Honey
- ❑ Cinnamon
- ❑ Flax
- ❑ Bay leaf
- ❑ Oat groats/ oat meal
- ❑ Acorn squash
- ❑ Millet
- ❑ Almond
- ❑ Sunflower
- ❑ Sesame
- ❑ Your choice of white fish or meat

Grocery Checklist for Non-Raw Food Summer Menu

- ❑ Watermelon
- ❑ Lemon
- ❑ Cantaloupe
- ❑ Mango
- ❑ Apricot
- ❑ Pineapple
- ❑ Banana
- ❑ Stonefruit
- ❑ Blueberries
- ❑ Avocado
- ❑ Tomato
- ❑ Basil
- ❑ Broccoli
- ❑ Cauliflower
- ❑ Onion
- ❑ Red bell pepper
- ❑ Green bell pepper
- ❑ Yellow bell pepper
- ❑ Okra
- ❑ Parsley
- ❑ Corn
- ❑ Kale
- ❑ Zucchini
- ❑ Garlic
- ❑ Cucumber
- ❑ Cherry tomato
- ❑ Mushrooms
- ❑ Carrot
- ❑ Green onion
- ❑ Bean sprouts
- ❑ Romaine
- ❑ Olive oil
- ❑ Cajun seasoning
- ❑ Mustard powder
- ❑ Honey
- ❑ Coconut oil
- ❑ Lamb
- ❑ Black beans
- ❑ Egg

Grocery Checklist for Non-Raw Food Fall Menu

- ❑ Apple
- ❑ Lemon
- ❑ Pear
- ❑ Asian pear
- ❑ Banana
- ❑ Beet
- ❑ Ginger
- ❑ Zucchini
- ❑ Onion
- ❑ Carrot
- ❑ Corn
- ❑ Tomato (or paste)
- ❑ Veggie stock
- ❑ Broccoli
- ❑ Avocado
- ❑ Barley
- ❑ Lentils
- ❑ Mung beans
- ❑ Daikon radish
- ❑ Celery
- ❑ Bok Choy
- ❑ Pumpkin
- ❑ Winter squash
- ❑ Arugula
- ❑ Lettuce
- ❑ Kale
- ❑ Bell pepper (your choice)
- ❑ Sugar snap
- ❑ Mushroom
- ❑ Artichoke heart
- ❑ Yam
- ❑ Hummus
- ❑ Chick peas
- ❑ Walnut
- ❑ Egg
- ❑ Almond butter
- ❑ Shaved almonds
- ❑ White fish
- ❑ Olive & grapeseed oil
- ❑ Cumin
- ❑ Coriander
- ❑ Agar agar
- ❑ Apple cider vinegar
- ❑ Rosemary
- ❑ Italian seasoning
- ❑ Masala
- ❑ Nama shoyu

Grocery Checklist for Non-Raw Food Winter Menu

- ❑ Orange
- ❑ Lemon
- ❑ Banana
- ❑ Grapefruit
- ❑ Garlic
- ❑ Onion
- ❑ Romaine
- ❑ Arugula
- ❑ Mixed greens
- ❑ Butternut squash
- ❑ Spinach
- ❑ Carrot
- ❑ Cabbage
- ❑ Potato
- ❑ Tomato
- ❑ Beet
- ❑ Mushroom
- ❑ Olives
- ❑ Bell pepper (your choice)
- ❑ Ground mustard
- ❑ Daikon radish
- ❑ Watermelon radish
- ❑ Broccoli
- ❑ Celery
- ❑ Avocado
- ❑ Balsamic vinegar
- ❑ Dijon mustard
- ❑ Nama shoyu
- ❑ Olive & grapeseed oil
- ❑ Coconut oil
- ❑ Curry
- ❑ Turmeric
- ❑ Cardamom
- ❑ Agar agar
- ❑ Apple cider vinegar
- ❑ Oregano
- ❑ Salmon
- ❑ Almond/ sunflower/sesame
- ❑ Egg
- ❑ Black beans
- ❑ Chick peas
- ❑ Cannelli bea
- ❑ Cashew
- ❑ Walnut
- ❑ Hummus

appendix C

yoga poses & instructions

M any people think yoga is about chanting ohms and relaxation. It is not! Yoga allows you to step into each part of yourself (mind, body and spirit). It brings the awareness that living externally will no longer suffice but rather living from the heart – desiring to be who you were created to be - simply, living from the inside-out. Yoga inspires more openness; it sheds the clutter of the mind; it removes obstacles in the heart to love deeply; it keeps the inner temple (our body) clean to receive. In a word, yoga is empowering!

Find a comfortable place in your home where you can take some time for yourself. Please use a yoga mat, exercise mat or towel to lie down on. If you are a musical person, play some relaxing music. If you like candles or incense; light them. The point is to make your own little sanctuary so you can relax and allow your body to lengthen and heal. The yoga you are about to experience is created to: (1) provide flexibility and (2) provoke open-ness. The key to this practice is *yielding*; disengaging the contraction of the muscles using gravity as your ally to create the flexibility and openness. Go only as far as you start to meet resistance. This will cultivate a sense of trust between your mind and your body. For all yoga poses, breathe through the nose, from beginning to end allowing the inhalation to be the same length as the exhalation. Notice the places you are holding your breath (tension) and use the exhalation to help relax. Let your breath guide you! One last thought, although this practice may be uncomfortable at first yoga should not hurt. Take your time and let the healing process begin.

Note: You will need a timer. It should take you approximately 30 minutes to complete the yoga poses. Remember to dedicate this time completely to you!

(1) Back

- Lie down on your belly and place the forearms in front of you with the elbows in front of the shoulder line. If your back feels tight move the elbows until you are comfortable.
- Place the top of the feet on the floor and relax completely letting the weight of legs relax into the ground (Figure A).

Figure A

- Have your gaze soft or your eyes closed.
- Bring all your attention into your breath. Inhaling and exhaling through the nose, long and deep and notice your belly 'dancing with the floor.'
- Using the breath; scan your entire body to see where you are experience resistance and use the exhalation to release.
- Go ONLY as far as you meet resistance - LESS is MORE!
- Hold the pose for 3 minutes. *(the reason for the timer)*
- If you find your mind wandering in other matters, please bring the awareness back into your body and breath.
- Room for growth: if you are doing this pose and feel no more resistance you can be creative with it, accentuating the lumbar curvature in your spine by bending the knees (Figure B) or straightening the elbows (Figure C).

Figure B

Figure C

② Back of Shoulders

- From the previous Back-Bending pose come back to the initial pose and thread your right arm UNDER your left arm and send the left arm as far to the right as it's comfortable so that the arms are crossed in front of your chest.
- The palms are facing down.
- Make sure the shoulders are even, if one side is lifting more bring the hands closer to each other. This will also ease the pose.
- Drop the weight of the head down. (Figure D)

Figure D

- You can use a block under the forehead for support (Figure E).
- Have your gaze soft or your eyes closed.
- Bring all your attention into your breath. Inhaling and exhaling through the nose, long and deep and notice your belly dancing with the floor.
- Using the breath scan your entire body to see where you are experience resistance and use the exhalation to release.
- Go ONLY as far as you meet resistance…LESS is MORE
- Hold the pose for 3 minutes.
- If you find your mind wandering in other matters, please bring the awareness back into your body and breath.
- Make sure you do the other side! (Thread opposite arm through)

Figure E

(3) Hips

- Come onto all fours and bring the LEFT foot forward to a 90 degree angle either in between the hands or on the outside of the left hand.
- Have the toes of your left foot point straight forward and, if able, walk the left foot to the left giving more rooms for the hips to open.
- Relax the top of the right foot (back) into the ground.
- Draw the back knee away from the hands as far as it's comfortable (Figure F).

Figure F

- You may need to use blocks or thick books under your hands to lift you up. This will ease the pose (Figure G).
- Start dropping all the weight down to the ground including the head. Make sure this is comfortable on your neck (Figure H).
- Have your gaze soft or your eyes closed.
- Bring all your attention into your breath. Inhaling and exhaling through the nose, long and deep.
- Using the breath scan your entire body to see where you are experience resistance and use the exhalation to release.
- Go ONLY as far as you meet resistance...LESS is MORE
- Hold the pose for 3 minutes.

- If you find your mind wandering in other matters, please bring the awareness back into your body and breath.
- Make sure you do the other side!

Figure G

Figure H

④ Hamstrings

- Slowly roll half way up resting your elbows on your thighs.
- Feet are hip width apart with the toes straight forward.
- Knees are bent comfortably (Figure I).

Figure I

- If you want more you can release the arms to the floor and hold the opposite elbow allowing yourself to hang down like a rag doll (Figure J).
- The head is dropping down.
- If you are comfortable you can work into straightening the knees, but not locking them, ONLY if you are absolutely comfortable everywhere (Figure K)!
- If your low back feels tight, keep the knees bent and elbows on the thighs.
- Have your gaze soft or your eyes closed.
- Bring all your attention into your breath. Inhaling and exhaling through the nose, long and deep.
- Using the breath scan your entire body to see where you are experience resistance and use the exhalation to release.

- Go ONLY as far as you meet resistance...LESS is MORE
- Hold the pose for 3 minutes.
- If you find your mind wandering in other matters, please bring the awareness back into your body and breath.

Figure J

Figure K

⑤ Front of shoulders

- Roll a towel or blanket as shown. Place underneath the bottom tip of your shoulder blades and lie down with your knees bent (Figure L).

Figure L

- Make sure you are comfortable; you might need to move the blanket up or down your back, depending on where you feel tight.
- Open your arms in 'Goal Pose' in a 90 degree angle (Figure M).
- Slowly straighten your legs (Figure N).
- If you feel very comfortable bring the arms over the head and hold the opposite elbow (Figure O).
- In this pose make sure your low back is comfortable.
- Keep the knees bent and elbows on the floor for a simpler variation.
- Have your gaze soft or your eyes closed.
- Bring all your attention into your breath. Inhaling and exhaling through the nose, long and deep.
- Using the breath scan your entire body to see where you are experience resistance and use the exhalation to release.
- Go ONLY as far as you meet resistance…LESS is MORE.
- Hold the pose for 3 minutes.
- If you find your mind wandering in other matters, please bring the awareness back into your body and breath.
- To come out of the pose, lift your hips to remove the blanket and roll to one side of your body in fetal position and breathe.

Figure M

Figure N

Figure O

⑥ Twist

- On your back, plant the feet the width of the mat (or towel). With the knees bent, clasp your hands under your head. Relax elbows to the floor.
- Take a deep breath and as you exhale drop the legs to the Right and look to the Left (figure P).

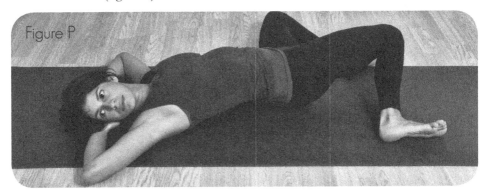

Figure P

- If you want a slightly harder variation, bring the Right ankle on top of the Left knee (Figure Q).
- In this pose make sure your low back is comfortable so bring awareness to the navel coming into the spine as you exhale.
- Have your gaze soft or your eyes closed
- Bring all your attention into your breath. Inhaling and exhaling through the nose, long and deep.
- Using the breath scan your entire body to see where you are experience resistance and use the exhalation to release.
- Go ONLY as far as you meet resistance…LESS is MORE.
- Hold the pose for 3 minutes.
- If you find your mind wandering in other matters, please bring the awareness back into your body and breath.
- Make sure you do the other side!

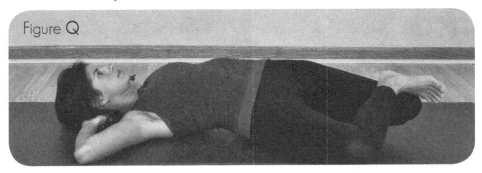

Figure Q

⑦ Relax

- On your back with the knees bent or straight, take a moment to feel. Feel your breath, feel each part of your body. Bring your hands to the belly and start breathing into the hands. Allow the belly to expand like a balloon as you inhale, relaxing completely on the exhale, repeat 10 times (Figure R).

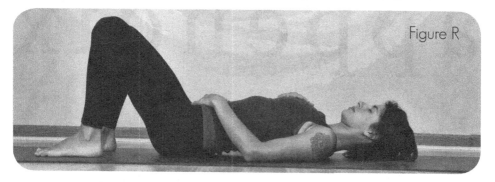

Figure R

- When ready release the hands to the side and if your knees where bent, straighten the legs into the mat allowing the feet and toes to relax.
- Let go of the need to control the breath and scan your entire body, from the feet to top of the head.
- A nice variation is placing a rolled blanket under the line of the spine starting at the sacrum (the lowest part of the spine) or just below the waist and allowing the arms and shoulders to rest down. This will open up the front of the chest allowing open-ness to occur (Figure S).
- Hold the pose for 3 minutes or as long as 10 breaths.
- To get out of the pose roll to one side in fetal position and pause. Use the hands to support the weight of your body and roll up keeping the chin close to the chest. The last part that comes up is the head.
- Keep your eyes closed for a moment in your sitting position. Feel what you have accomplished. A small prayer of gratitude is much welcomed here!

Figure S

appendix D

Christian yoga

"Yoga emphasizes body-awareness and relaxation that contributes to health; it also becomes a means of growing in the centeredness that contributes to Holy Living, as we unite our prayer with our bodies and our bodies with our prayers" (Roth 7). I have been asked many times, "Can I do yoga if I am a Christian? The simple answer I give is, "Yes of course you can." However, the bigger issue that needs to be addressed is why a Christian would think they could not participate in yoga. Some people believe yoga is based on Hinduism/Buddhism? Others have been told that yoga will pull them away from Christ? Still others are afraid of the meditation and chants that heard about in yoga. The reality, Christians run, do cross fit, Zumba and a thousand other things to improve health, so why not yoga?

Let me explain something, Colossians 1:15-20 reveals a truth that I think we often overlook.

> He (Christ) is the image of the invisible God, the firstborn of all creation. For by him all things were created, in heaven and on earth, visible and invisible, whether thrones or dominions or rulers or authorities—all things were created through him and for him. And he is before all things, and in him all things hold together. And he is the head of the body, the church. He is the beginning, the firstborn from the dead, that in everything he might be pre-eminent. For in him all the fullness of God was pleased to dwell, and through him to reconcile to himself all things, whether on earth or in heaven, making peace by the blood of his cross.

Did you catch that? Everything – that even means the practice of yoga – was created by and for him! This doesn't mean that man hasn't distorted it and made it something that can be worshipped. Fortunately for us Christ is in the redemption/restoration business and he is able to redeem yoga for His purpose and glory! I had a yoga teacher tell me this stunning realization he had while teaching one day. "I was having my students quiet themselves and it was like a moment of truth struck my spirit. Yoga did not influence Christ; Christ influenced yoga and everything else!" That simple, yet profoundly deep-life-changing, realization is the essence of why Christians can do yoga!

In our mechanical world – where pieces and parts can be replaced so easily – we have lost the idea of the unity of mind, body and spirit. We have lost the idea that each part matters to the whole. If we lose unity we have lost too much. Yoga (root word: *yug*) means "yoke" or "join together." We are to understand that our mind, body and spirit are joined together intricately and purposely. "The body is meant for the

Lord and the Lord for the body. The spirit does not free us from the body but helps us to use our bodies in responsible living through our worship, through our work, through all that we do before God" (Roth 5-6).

As you begin to Create a Trinity Lifestyle embrace yoga and embrace the beauty and simplicity of what God desires to do in your mind, body and spirit!

appendix

thoughts on Christ

As I explained in the first part of this book, I was raised in the church and had an invitation to accept Christ each week. That, in many ways, may have watered down the impact of that acceptance but I am thankful for it. However, many people – maybe including you – have never had an invitation to look at Christ in all His fullness. I am not going to try to convince you Christ is "real" or scare you with the threat of hell. I am not going to present a religion that "fixes" everything. I am not going to tell you I am right and you are wrong. I am; however, going to tell you that I have forever been changed by Christ. I also realize that every person is on a personal journey. I have heard it said, "There is only one way to God; that is Christ. However, there are a thousand ways to Christ." My job is not to save you but rather encourage you – where you are at (not where I think you should be) – along that journey.

I will present seven questions I most often hear and then give a brief answer. In no way am I pretending to be a theologian or that I have all the answers. But what I offer is Christ, simple and true.

1. *What is the gospel?* Gospel literally means "good news" and most commonly encompasses the New Testament books of the Bible: Matthew, Mark, Luke and John. What is the good news? It is that we can have a relationship with God through Christ. Because of His finished work on the cross, we do not have to make it in this life alone, trying harder and harder. Through Christ, we have already made it. We are loved and valued and that is the good news!

2. *Is Christ real?* Any historical book records Christ to be a real person. Was He the son of God, the Messiah? You decide, either He was who He said He was or He was insane.

3. *Is the Bible true?* I believe it to be. Do I understand everything in it? No. Am I supposed to understand everything in it? Probably not. You know I also believe quantum physics to be true but I don't understand much of it either. Does my understanding of it make it any less valid? No. And you may be asking yourself that if it is true, why are there different translations of the Bible? Who knows, but I think it is because people relate to the written word in different ways and God in His infinite creativity and wisdom allows it. Would it be easier if there was only one? Maybe? Would that make it more believable? Doubtful.

4. *Do I have to say a specific prayer to become a Christian?* No. While what has become known as the "sinner's prayer" is not found in the Bible, it is a confession of trust and faith in Christ. I think the greater question is if Christ hears my weak words when I have no idea what to say? The answer to that is a resounding yes!

5. *Is it really that simple?* The major argument I hear over and over about believing Christ is that it cannot be that simple. The fact of the matter is that, yes, it is that simple. All you have to do is believe and accept His free gift. He has created you in His image. You are a beautiful-complex-magnificent creation made to love and be loved. This simplicity of the gospel is a stumbling block to our complicated human minds but what better way to get to our hearts!

6. *What do Christians really believe?* There are 5 major tenets of the Christian faith: (1) The Bible is the inspired word of God (2) Virgin Birth (3) Deity of Christ (4) Death and Resurrection of Christ (5) Second Coming of Christ. Some theologians add a sixth: The Father, Son and Holy Spirit are one (the Trinity). Do I understand how all that works? No. Do I have to understand how all of it works? No. Do I believe it? Yes.

7. *Why do Christians disagree so much?* Well, Christians are humans and we love to be right. If you look at that question a little deeper it is not that Christians disagree per say, it is that denominations disagree. Huh? Most Christians will not disagree or argue over the five tenets I referenced above but church denominations will argue over whether healings occur today or whether prophecy is real or if speaking in tongues are valid or whether or not a woman can preach and on and on. We argue over the practices not the doctrine. Is Christ the son of God sent to the world to save the lost? Yes! Are you to eat meat, worship on Saturday or Sunday, have a beer, etc? I don't know, maybe. I wish we would stop arguing over what matters least, our own thoughts, and unite over what matters most, Christ's love for people.

At this point, I hope you are at least thinking of Christ. I wish to share a verse with you. John 3:16-17, "For God so loved the world, that he gave his only Son, that whoever believes in him should not perish but have eternal life. For God did not send his Son into the world to condemn the world, but in order that the world might be saved through him" A different translation offers this: "This is how much God loved the world: He gave his Son, his one and only Son. And this is why: so that no one need be destroyed; by believing in him, anyone can have a whole and lasting life. God didn't go to all the trouble of sending his Son merely to point an accusing finger, telling the world how bad it was. He came to help, to put the world right again" (The Message). I love that! You may have heard and/or read this verse a thousand times but have you ever let the reality of the verse sink deep into your consciousness? Let's try this:

For God *(the perfect un-created creator)* so loved *(He actually loves us; that alone should blow our minds)* the world *(yep that is everyone)*, that he gave *(not expecting anything in return)* His only son *(basically all He had)* that whosoever *(everyone again)* believes *(not necessarily a specific prayer but a heart cry that is verbalized)* in Him *(that is Christ and Christ alone)* should not perish *(not taste the eternal separation from God)* but have eternal life *(assurance and hope of an everlasting love relationship)*. For God did not send His Son into the world *(it was not some haphazard plan but an intentional pursuit of you and I)* to condemn the world *(God is not a tyrant in the sky waiting to smite His people; His heart longs for restoration of relationship)* but in order that the world might be saved through Him *(Christ is the way, the truth and the life. He died so you and I could live)*. (John 3:16-17) *(emphasis added)*

As I mentioned before my role is not to convince you. It is your decision and that is the beauty of what Christ allows. I pray you will consider the immediate and eternal impact of your decision. If you are a believer reading this, I have two parting thoughts for you: (1) John 13:35 reads, "By this all people will know that you are my disciples, if you have love for one another." Do people know you because of the love of Christ? (2) Colossians 1:26-27 reads, "[Christ is] the mystery hidden for the ages… God chose to make known how great among the Gentiles are the riches of the glory of this mystery, which is Christ in you, the hope of glory." Do people know you carry this glorious mystery of hope inside of you?

appendix

a word on forgiveness

> ❝ There is no love without forgiveness, and there is no forgiveness without love.
>
> - Bryan H. McGill ❞

The below words are from my wife, Jennifer. I can only hope that they will impact you as much as they have impacted me and countless others.

When Bo asked me to write about "how and why I forgave him," I needed to go back into my journals to see the outpouring of emotions that went along with the forgiving process. As I read what I wrote, what seems like an eternity ago now, I noticed my writing pointed to a heart full of pain and resentment. I saw a woman, no, really a little girl crying out from the depths of the untouchable and begging for relief. As I continued to read and think about the last few years of our life, I am reminded of the miraculous power that the act of forgiving possesses and the amazing redemptive power of love.

When I picked up the note Bo left on the kitchen table and began to read, I was devastated, yet at the same time so angry. My heart was broken and I immediately started asking myself what did I do wrong? How I can I make this better? How can I make him come home? I just wanted my husband back, even if he did not want to be there. As my mind raced and my eyes poured tears; emotions that I had never known began to surface: separation, divorce, revenge and self pity, With so many emotions, I needed to control my environment; it was the one thing I thought would bring me solace. I changed the locks to the house, changed bank accounts and cleared the house of all Bo's clothes. Then, the emotional pain of being left would sink deeper and I would bring his clothes back inside in hopes that he would be home soon. Even as the days passed and my emotions ran wild, a single word seemed to resonate within the deepest part of me. That word was forgiveness. I asked myself, where was this word coming from? I had no clue but one thing I knew for sure, I DID NOT want to forgive. No one, especially Bo, deserved forgiveness for something as hurtful as abandonment and adultery. As the days continued to pass and I had no idea where my husband was, I asked myself, how do I forgive? Why should I forgive? Why should I pardon one for their inexplicable actions of pure hatred and disrespect? Then these words seem to explode in my mind: "Because I forgave you!"

Let me try to explain what occurred in my spirit as I meditated on those four words. You see, I too was a harlot, an adulterer. I had never cheated on my husband but what was done to me; I had done multiple, even a thousand times to Jesus, my bridegroom. In scripture I am described as the bride of Christ and as a bride I had numerous affairs. I cheated on Jesus and caused Him inexplicable pain. I broke His heart, ran His name through the mud, caused Him much tribulation, made Him cry and stripped Him of everything that He is. But what did Jesus do? He cried for me to return. He yearned for me to come back. He longed for me to recognize the depths of His love. He gently and sweetly said, "I love you and I forgive you." I finally began to understand the depth and power of forgiveness. If Jesus can forgive me of everything I had done to Him, then how could I not forgive the one who had hurt me? How could I not tell Bo, "I love you and forgive you?" Did those words come easy? No. Did my forgiving Bo mean what he did was not wrong and hurtful? No. Did it take time and counseling for Bo and me to restore our marriage? Yes.

People that know mine and Bo's story ask me, "How did you forgive so easily." It was not easy. It was a process but as hurt and broken as I was, I realized that I was made to love and be loved. I, Jennifer, was loved, valued and forgiven. How could I not extend that same love and forgiveness? Forgiveness is not easy; it is a choice. It is a choice that has the power to change lives. I can only hope that you will allow it to change your life as it has changed mine and Bo's.

appendix G

additional resources

- **24-7 Worship:** www.ihopkc.org/prayerroom
- **Anti-inflammatory nutrition:** www.deflame.com
- **Beautiful Outlaw:** www.beautifuloutlaw.net
- **Bible References:** www.biblegateway.com
- **Blendtec:** www.blendtec.com
- **circle ME:** www.circleme.me
- **Create a Trinity Lifestyle:** www.trinitylifestyle.com
- **Daniel Fast:** www.daniel-fast.com
- **Effects of Stress:** www.stress.org
- **Healthy Living:** www.healthylivinghowto.com
- **Leaders who Last:** www.davekraft.squarespace.com
- **Motion Palpation (chiropractic):** www.motionpalpation.org
- **Proper Sleep:** www.better-sleep-better-life.com
- **Quotes:** www.thegracetabernacle.org/quotes/gracequotes.html
- **Standard Process:** www.standardprocess.com
- **Trinity Chiropractic:** www.trinitychiro.com
- **WestBow Press:** www.westbowpress.com
- **Weston Price Foundation:** www.westonaprice.org
- **Yoga Body & Balance:** www.yogabodyandbalance.com